AF895830

Setting the Table for Tier 2 Small Group Social and Emotional Learning and Academic Interventions for K-12 Students

PEG DONOHUE, PH.D.

Central Connecticut State University

cognella

SAN DIEGO

Bassim Hamadeh, CEO and Publisher
Amy Smith, Associate Editorial Manager
Abbey Hastings, Senior Production Editor
Jess Estrella, Senior Graphic Designer
Kylie Bartolome, Licensing Specialist
Natalie Piccotti, Director of Marketing
Kassie Graves, Senior Vice President, Editorial
Alia Bales, Director, Project Editorial and Production

Printed in the United States of America.

cognella® ACADEMIC PUBLISHING
320 South Cedros Ave., Ste. 400, Solana Beach, CA 92075

Brief Contents

Detailed Contents

Foreword

It is with great enthusiasm that I introduce this practical and insightful new book, *Setting the Table for Tier 2 Small Group Social and Emotional Learning and Academic Interventions for K-12 Students*. As educators and counselors, we are constantly faced with the challenge of meeting the diverse needs of our students, ensuring their academic success, and nurturing their holistic development. Based on a growing body of research and my personal experience in the field, I believe the multitiered systems of support (MTSS) framework is a promising approach to help us achieve these goals. Within the MTSS framework, effective and efficient Tier 2 systems and practices are critical to supporting students who have elevated needs or who have been impacted by the schoolwide climate and practices. This is especially the case for school-based mental health professionals who have the unique and specialized training, knowledge, and skills to develop, implement, and evaluate Tier 2 supports, including group counseling and skill-based groups.

As a former school counselor and school site MTSS coordinator, I was integrally involved in collecting and analyzing data, using data to identify student needs, developing and implementing Tier 2 supports, and monitoring student progress to determine if the supports were having the intended impact. Depending on the availability of resources, I was often put in the position of needing to pull together curriculum for small groups. The challenge was always the amount of time it took, but also the need to provide activities, skills instruction, and counseling that was effective, efficient, and practical. A resource I really needed was this book! Dr. Donohue integrates her extensive experience and expertise as a school counselor and counselor educator into a comprehensive approach to providing Tier 2 supports. This book is a roadmap to identify and implement a variety of Tier 2 supports and monitor the supports using data.

One of the greatest strengths of this book is its practicality. School-based mental health professionals need well-planned Tier 2 group supports ready to go so that students can get the supports they need efficiently and have spaces to process their experiences. The Tier 2 kits that are central to this book illustrate how school -based mental health professionals can use data to identify student needs, hit the ground running with a group plan aligned with standards, and provide impactful and measurable support for students.

As someone who spends the bulk of my counselor educator professional life thinking about, researching, and writing about the Tier 2 process, I think this book advances school-based mental health professionals' role in schools and in MTSS implementation. We need to continue to collect and analyze a variety of data to understand what students need. This includes centering students' voices and experiences. We also need to continue to develop and implement Tier 2 supports that are contextually relevant and culturally sustaining for the students we are serving. This includes engaging students in Tier 2 supports and learning from their experience to improve not only Tier 2 supports, but also the school environment. I am thankful that school-based mental health professionals now have this book as a resource to carry out this critical work.

Jake Olsen, PhD
Associate Professor
School Counseling
California State University Long Beach
Cofounder, School Counselors for MTSS

Preface

When hosting guests for a dinner party, my mother always did things with intention. She selected a menu that she thought most guests would find interesting and satisfying. She often chose dishes that would challenge my children to try new things but included many of their favorites. After moving many times, she knew how to bring together people who begin the evening as strangers but who might enjoy getting to know one another and form lasting friendships. Indeed, many good friends have been started around my parents' dining table. Before guests arrived, the table was set. Plates, napkins, flatware, drinking glasses were put out. A bread bowl was filled. A water pitcher was at the ready. The scene was set, with care, for gathering a group who would enjoy good food, lively conversation, and a night of fun.

Planning for small group counseling requires the same level of care. We select our participants based on common areas of strength and needs. Prior to the first group meeting, we screen members and plan activities. Good group leaders "begin with the end in mind" by asking questions like these:

- What do I want my group members to know about themselves by the end of the group?
- What skills do I want my group members to acquire through this process?
- How will I know my group members have learned the strategies I have focused on in the group?

Thus, my intention is to create a comprehensive resource dedicated to planning and implementing K–12 small group/Tier 2 interventions focused on social and emotional learning (SEL) competencies and academic skills (AS). My most challenging but most rewarding work as a school counselor for 16 years was spent developing and running groups. At first these groups were largely unplanned, usually chaotic, and unfocused. I was unsure if I was helping my students become more confident or more adept at reading social cues. It seemed more the exception than the rule that students generalized what they learned in groups to their classroom or their social worlds. When I began learning more about multitiered systems of support (MTSS), the benefits of a structured and systemic Tier 2 approach came into focus. I started identifying students for the groups using data and teacher referrals. I sought out evidence-based interventions (EBIs) that included norm-referenced pre- and posttests. If I could not find an EBI that suited the needs I was attempting to address, I created a research-informed (RI) intervention by scanning the group intervention literature emerging from the related fields of school counseling, school psychology, and school social work. My guiding question was "What works with kids struggling with (social interaction, time management, academic engagement, decision-making, etc.)?" At the midpoint of the group intervention, I surveyed teachers to find out if students were using the strategies they were learning in groups. I made changes each time I conducted the groups to increase effectiveness. When students were identified as needing intervention, I had to be prepared to act fast—within 72 hours of a referral, optimally.

I started housing all of the materials for each group in a three-ring binder (parent letters, permission slips, lesson plans, handouts, pre- and posttests, teacher surveys, etc.). When group interventions called for art supplies or game pieces, I purchased plastic bins to keep all of my materials together so that I could simply grab the kit and meet with the students wherever a space was available in the building.

When I became a counselor educator, I started assigning the development of Tier 2 kits my first semester. My graduate students in school counseling take a course entitled Collaborative Consultation in Schools. One of their key assignments is to develop an RI and culturally affirming Tier 2 unit/kit focused on SEL competencies and AS. I have collected over 25 excellent examples of Tier 2 kits that could be used in K–12 schools to address concerns such as emotional regulation, time management, decision-making, test-taking anxiety, and preparing for life on a college campus. These small group interventions were thoughtfully developed by aligning activities with recent research on best practices in these and other common barriers to academic, college/career, and social success. My students have developed excellent resources over the years, some of which are shared here. Most importantly, my students have utilized their Tier 2 kits during their fieldwork semesters and as they have started their careers as school counselors who align their work with MTSS.

As a school counselor educator, I have also focused on developing my students' understanding of the MTSS framework. This orientation to the work helps my students become creative, effective, and efficient practitioners. Meeting the needs of students with similar concerns through small group intervention makes the work of a school counselor more intentional and impactful. When consulting with school-based mental health teams, I often find that they struggle most with planning and implementing Tier 2 groups. At a recent national school counseling conference, over 500 participants flocked to a 20-minute session on Tier 2 interventions. My hope is that this resource will help practicing school-based mental health providers to overcome the logistical hurdles to running groups.

How to Use This Book

The first section of this book gives school-based mental health professionals the key knowledge necessary to develop or refine their Tier 2 small groups. This section could be read and discussed as part of a professional learning community (PLC) to get all interventionists on "the same page" about the scope, focus and mechanics of developing a repertoire of four to five effective and developmentally appropriate Tier 2 interventions. We don't need to have an extensive menu of interventions—just key interventions that meet the needs of students in our school community. Of course, those needs are dynamic. This book can be useful to school-based teams who are committed to building and refining systems to ensure that they are prepared to meet their students' needs.

The second section of this book provides ready-to-use Tier 2 kits arranged by topic. The pillars of SEL are a central organizing factor for the kits:

1. Self-awareness
2. Self-management
3. Social awareness
4. Relationship skills
5. Decision-making skills
6. Academic success skills

In addition, academic success skill kits have been included to support elementary, middle, and high school students. Each kit has everything interventionists need to begin planning and running successful small groups.

Like any resource, elements can be amended to meet the specific student needs. We will also address the critical goal of developing small group interventions that are culturally affirming, inclusive, and relevant to all group members.

Lastly, when possible, practitioners who have implemented the Tier 2 kits will share their experiences by discussing their students' progress and how they overcame hurdles to implement the intervention with fidelity.

Acknowledgments

First and foremost, I would like to thank my Central Connecticut State University students who graciously shared their Tier 2 kits and reviewed drafts amid their day-to-day work as graduate students or school counselors. They had no idea that their assignments for their Collaborative Consultation class would end up in print! It's their hard work and creativity that make up the heart of this book. I am enormously grateful for their daily dedication to guiding and supporting students in their care while collaborating with their colleagues to provide safe, inclusive, and nurturing environments in their schools. As a professor, it is immensely gratifying to see them flourish amidst the challenges all educators face.

Breanna Soto
Curtis Darraugh
Erica Mastronardi Cumpstone
Emma Bee Schwarz
Gabrielle Granitto
Jennifer Estrella Vanterpool
Jenna Angello
Jacki Pierce Jaclyn
Katie Molinari Ashley Moutinho
Karina Ngyuen
Kayla Snyder
Lucia Greene
Nicole Ferreria
Stephanie Barbagallo
Stephanie Williams
Vareesha Rahman

I could not have completed this task without my former students who agreed to review the final manuscript. Ashley Moutinho and Stephanie Williams, I could not be more grateful to you and prouder of the work you are doing each day to help your students navigate the challenges of growing up in the world today.

I would also like to thank my good friend and favorite school psychologist, Karyn Hester, for sharing her experience of implementing effective small groups in a high school setting. Fellow educators, Karen Evans and Lisa Sherman, have given me the priceless gifts of their friendship, support, and guidance as we have raised our families together. I thank my lucky stars for their presence in my life.

I want to thank my smart, talented, and kind sisters, Ann Dowley and Ellen Stewart, for giving me quiet places to write during my sabbatical and a steady supply of good humor and encouragement. I am indebted to my parents, Mike and Sandy Dowley, for checking in on my progress and being models of the adage "hard work pays off." I could not have completed this book without the help of my very talented and compassionate daughter, Isabella Donohue, who checked several of my Spanish translations. I am so proud of her drive to help others. My wonderful son, Joey, deserves recognition for his patience and many kindnesses while I worked away at my computer. I am one of the lucky ones to have a supportive husband who recognized how important it was for me to see this project to completion. I am immensely proud of the way he has dedicated his life to teaching fifth and sixth graders while nurturing our family; his love sustains me always. In short, my family and friends are everything to me.

My work as a school counselor educator and researcher has been enormously enriched by my colleagues in the Department of Counselor Education and Family Therapy at Central Connecticut State University, especially my school counseling partner Sarah Evans-Zalewski, and my mentors, Kathleen Laundy and Cherie King. I am also grateful to Dr. Michael Alfano who opened the door to my career as a School Counselor Educator at CCSU. My other "work family," also known as School Counselors for MTSS collaborative, includes Jennifer Betters-Bubon, Emily Goodman-Scott, Jake Olsen, and our inspiring partners Natalie Edirmanasinghe, Rebecca Pianta, Stephanie Smith-Durkin, Alexandra Frank, and Damien Sweeney. We have traveled together for the better part of a decade and have engaged in an ongoing and productive conversation about the role school counselors can play in designing and implementing MTSS to ensure schools prioritize becoming more equitable, nurturing, and compassionate communities where both students and educators thrive. I have no doubt that these colleagues have made me a better counselor educator, presenter, researcher, writer, and human. Thank you from the bottom of my heart.

Finally, I would like to thank my patient and talented editors, Kassie Graves and Amy Smith, and their team at Cognella, for believing in the first kernel of an idea for this project and putting in the hard work to help make it a reality.

Introduction

LEARNING OBJECTIVES

1. Understand the importance of supporting K–12 students with similar needs through small group intervention.
2. Understand the basic components of effective small group psychoeducational groups.
3. Distinguish the difference between psychoeducational groups and counseling groups.
4. Recognize the need for small group interventions to address specific SEL competencies.
5. Highlight how to address academic skills through effective small groups.

Small Groups Interventions

Whenever I begin teaching my group counseling course, I invite my graduate students into the learning by letting them in on an important fact about this mode of counseling: Magic happens in groups! We are social creatures by nature. We look to others for clues and cues about how and when to act. There is subtle learning happening all the time in a group. Most importantly, as a species, we heal in community. Isolation is often associated with sadness and a worsening of symptoms, so we set up small group counseling sessions with a goal in mind. Perhaps the group is designed to help third graders manage their emotions during recess and when they return to class, or provide opportunities for sixth graders to build their social awareness by reading others' facial expressions, or to develop a group for high school juniors to explore how they go about making decisions, large and small, about their postsecondary plan. Self-awareness, self-management, social awareness, relationship skills, and decision-making make up the five key components of social and emotional learning. They can be taught and practiced in small groups. Most importantly, a group helps us to feel less alone. "I am not the only one. If this person can manage the same obstacles I am facing, then maybe I can too," a group member may think to themselves.

Gearing Up for Small Groups

Most graduate programs in school counseling and school social work include one introductory group counseling course. Some school psychology programs offer a group dynamics course as either an elective or a requirement. Regardless of your profession, you'll need to know the basics about running a group before you begin. A course focused on group counseling theory and best practices would be a sufficient beginning. Knowing the ethical guidelines about group counseling is a must. If you aren't in a graduate program in a helping profession, make sure to colead groups with someone who has master's-level training. As we will mention numerous times in this book, coleadership of groups helps us in a myriad of ways. As novice school-based mental health practitioners, we hone our facilitation skills and knowledge of group dynamics over time and through ongoing continuing education.

If you are using an evidence-based Tier 2 intervention, make sure you are trained to use the materials by the individual(s) who developed the group curriculum or a close colleague to ensure you are implementing the Tier 2 intervention with fidelity. If you are using one of the research informed Tier 2 kits in this book, make sure to keep a record of what is working well with the group process and where there is room for improvement. Collecting data is the best way to see if the group is helping students in the ways that we had hoped.

The Difference Between Counseling Groups and Psychoeducational Groups

In a word, the difference is the focus on skill building in psychoeducational groups. When planning psychoeducational groups we hope that our members leave their group experience with new skills and strategies to address their initial concern. In a best-case scenario, they may also end up learning a great deal about themselves and about the other group members.

There are no magic wands in education! Wouldn't you like to be the person handing them out to your colleagues? The effectiveness of small group interventions gives us reason to be optimistic that initiating and/or maintaining groups in schools is worthwhile for students and teachers and families.

Small Groups Focused on Specific Social-Emotional Learning Competencies

The five social-emotional learning (SEL) competencies we all hear so much about are essential building blocks for our lifelong learning. Aristotle famously said, "Knowing yourself is the beginning of all wisdom." Helping our students to identify their emotions, to manage their responses in highly stressful situations, to be aware of others, to build healthy productive relationships, and to make decisions that give them that all-important "yes" feeling inside can begin as young as preschool. They will encounter emotions, stress, challenging relationships, loneliness, and the pull to follow what everyone else is doing as they navigate the minefield of growing up in today's world.

Component 1: Self Awareness

Our friends at Collaborative for Social and Emotional Learning (CASEL, 2020) define self-awareness as "the abilit[y] to understand one's own emotions, thoughts, and values and how they influence behavior across contexts. This includes capacities to recognize one's strengths and limitations with a well-grounded sense of confidence and purpose" (para. 3).

What does this look like?

- being able to name my emotions when I am having them
- developing an accurate perception of who I am
- being able to name my strengths and weaknesses
- growing in my self-confidence
- believing I can take care of my responsibilities and make changes when necessary

What questions do I ask myself to become more self-aware?

- How am I feeling? Why?
- Am I at my best today? Why or why not?
- How do I want to show up (for school, with my friends, at home) today?
- Am I experiencing stress today? Why or why not?
- Do I feel like I belong in my community?

Component 2: Self-Management

Self-management is defined as "the abilit[y] to manage one's emotions, thoughts, and behaviors effectively in different situations and to achieve goals and aspirations. This includes the capacity to delay gratification, manage stress, and feel motivated and a sense of agency to accomplish personal and collective goals" (CASEL, 2020, para. 4).

What does this look like?

- counting to 10 before responding
- controlling an impulse (to run, to hit, or to yell)
- self-discipline and delaying gratification
- setting realistic and attainable goals
- getting and staying organized

What questions do I ask myself to manage my emotions better?

- Do I need a break right now?
- Who can I ask for help?
- How does this challenge impact me reaching my goal?
- How do I want to respond?

Component 3: Social Awareness

I am socially aware when I "understand the perspectives of and empathize with others, including those from diverse backgrounds, cultures, and contexts" (CASEL, 2020, para. 5).

What does being socially aware look like?

- taking on the perspective of a peer or colleague
- demonstrating empathy
- appreciating the richness of diversity
- showing respect for self and others
- taking a stance of curiosity when confronted with someone who's experiences are different from my own

What does social awareness sound like?

- I wonder how that made the other person feel?
- How would I feel in a similar situation?
- My friend seems sad right now. Perhaps I should see if they want to talk or some company.
- Trying out a new custom from another country

Social Awareness From Preschool Through High School			
The Child Understands...			
Preschool	Elementary School	Middle School	High School
Expressions and situations of "basic" emotions–e.g., happy, sad, angry, scared	That one can • Use thinking to regulate emotions • Purposely hide or express emotions	That one can feel simultaneous, "mixed" emotions	That emotions experienced may depend on one's experiences and personality traits

FIGURE 0.1 Social Awareness from Preschool through High School.

Component 4: Relationship Skills

Relationship skills are "the abilit[y] to establish and maintain healthy and supportive relationships with both individuals and groups" (CASEL, 2020, para. 6).

What do relationship skills look like?

- two people communicating what they are feeling in the moment
- engaging with others who are new to me as well as those who are familiar to me
- developing a friendship that withstands the test of time
- being a productive member of a team

What do relationship skills sound like?

- I statements: When you ____________, I feel ____________
- asking for clarification from others
- stating a difference of opinion calmly

Component 5: Decision-Making Skills

Decision-making is "the ability to make constructive choices about personal behavior and social interactions based on ethical standards, safety, and social norms" (CASEL, 2020, para. 7). The older we become, the more important and impactful our decisions become. Helping young people learn to make sound decisions at an early age sets the stage for them to make decisions about peer groups, school activities, drugs/alcohol, and their postsecondary plan.

What do decision-making skills look like?

- identifying problems that are creating barriers for me right now
- analyzing possible solutions
- solving problems that arise in social situations
- reflecting on how I feel about a decision I made
- considering the ethical implications of a decision

What does good decision-making sound like?

- How will my decision impact those I love?
- What are the potential outcomes of my choice?
- What is the best choice for me?
- Will taking this course of action help me reach my goals?

The SEL and Academic Skills Connection

Researchers continue to debate the impact of SEL skills on academic performance. A well-known meta-analysis (Durlak et al., 2011) reported an 11-percentile average gain in achievement for students who participated in a regular Tier 1 SEL program/curriculum. Students who have strong SEL competencies exhibit more prosocial behavior, work well in collaboration with others, and are better able to manage the stress that is inherent in the learning process. Thus, these skill sets (self-awareness, self-management, social awareness, relationship skills, and decision-making) are largely beneficial to setting and reaching academic goals. There are many ways to define academic success: good grades, engagement in the learning process, student satisfaction, acquired knowledge, skills, and competencies—all leading to career success. We know that some students stumble academically. Learning to be a positive problem solver who can manage emotions (big and small) can help a student achieve more in their career journey than they ever expected. A significant portion of learning is social; small task groups are commonplace in learning environments in preK–12 and certainly in higher education. In short, we wanted to develop lessons that call on students to use their SEL skills to engage in their academic journey with awareness, joy, and persistence. Hopefully the lessons in this section will make it possible for students who struggle to feel good about themselves as students will take on a new perspective of themselves as a person who is striving today to be a little bit better than they were yesterday.

Considering Developmental Stages When Planning Small Group Interventions

It's important for school-based interventionists to consider **students' developmental needs**, **cultural experiences**, **reading level**, and **interests** when developing interventions. For this reason, we have developed Tier 2 kits centered around the five SEL competencies and academic success for elementary, middle, and high school students separately. Some middle school resources could be amended to be suitable for high school students and vice versa. What are the developmental tasks of each grade level?

Preschoolers

- Begin peer interaction while managing shifts in emotion.
- Initiate prosocial behaviors and interactions, along with friendships.
- Stay connected with key adults.
- Understand basic emotional expressions, situations, and experiences—and ways to manage them (often with adult assistance)—along with early efforts to solve interpersonal problems.
- Begin to follow social rules, such as taking turns and sharing resources.

Elementary-aged children

- Form dyadic friendships and stable peer connections.
- Control aggressive impulses, especially when angry or disappointed.
- Demonstrate emotional regulation within the peer group.
- Show emotions in appropriate contexts.
- Resolve more complex social difficulties with a flexible variety of solutions.

Middle school students

- Build social awareness to comprehend more complex emotional situations in self and others.
- Form a largely group-based identity with increasing independence from adults.
- Improve ability to resolve conflicts within dyadic and group situations.

High school students

- Achieve more mature relationships with others.
- Increase emotional independence from parents and other adults (while maintaining these relationships).
- Understand unique emotional perspectives.
- Form an individuated personal identity (first group based, then individuated).
- Improve ability to articulate set of values and an ethical system to guide behavior.

For more information on this, please see CASEL (2018, p. 2).

Summary

School counselors and school-based mental health team members are uniquely qualified to develop and implement small group or Tier 2 interventions to address discrete skills necessary as students progress through their K–12 journey. The skills we focus on in this resource are social and emotional skills (namely self-awareness, self-management, social awareness, relationship skills, and decision-making) and academic skills. Research suggests that equipping students with these key competencies increases the likelihood they will graduate high school and complete their postsecondary plan successfully. Preparing to run small groups takes practice and collaboration, and the results benefit not only the students in the group, but the entire school community. Students who get the support that they need, especially in their early school years, are better able to cope with the inevitable challenges that accompany growing up. This chapter helps us consider how we foster these skills through small groups aimed at specific developmental stages.

References

CASEL. (2020). *CASEL's Framework: What are the Core Competence Areas and Where are They Promoted?* CASEL Framework Briefs. https://casel.org/casel-sel-framework-11-2020/?view=true

CASEL. (2018, November). *Keeping SEL developmental: The importance of a developmental lens for fostering and assessing SEL competencies*. CASEL Framework Briefs. https://casel.s3.us-east-2.amazonaws.com/CASEL-Resources-Keeping-SEL-Developmental.pdf

Durlak, J. A., Weissberg, R. P., Dymnicki, A. B., Taylor, R. D., & Schellinger, K. B. (2011). The impact of enhancing students' social and emotional learning: A meta analysis of school based universal interventions. *Child development*, *82*(1), 405–432.

Credits

Fig. 0.1: Susanne A. Denham/CASEL, Selection from "Keeping SEL Developmental: The Importance of a Developmental Lens for Fostering and Assessing SEL Competencies," https://casel.org/casel-resources-keeping-sel-developmental/. Copyright © 2018 by CASEL.

CHAPTER 1

Tier 2 Explained

LEARNING OBJECTIVES

1. Define multitiered systems of support.
2. Understand the importance of building efficient systems in schools, which includes identifying students in need and serving them through necessary universal, targeted, and intensive interventions.
3. Understand the significance of a collaborative approach to designing, implementing, and refining systems through data-based decision-making.
4. Define Tier 2 intervention components.
5. Understand the role of a Tier 2 team.
6. Learn the methods for identifying students for Tier 2 teams.
7. Learn culturally affirming approaches to Tier 2 groups
8. Prepare for effective small group interventions.

In schools we build systems to ensure things run smoothly and so that students and staff have a positive environment to learn and work in. For example, we have a system for onboarding a new student who arrives after the school year begins. They meet with a specific staff member, learn about the school and expectations, share any helpful information about their learning needs, and are assigned a teacher. Similarly, we build systems to support the academic, social and emotional, and college and career development needs of our students. We know all students are different and need different things at different times.

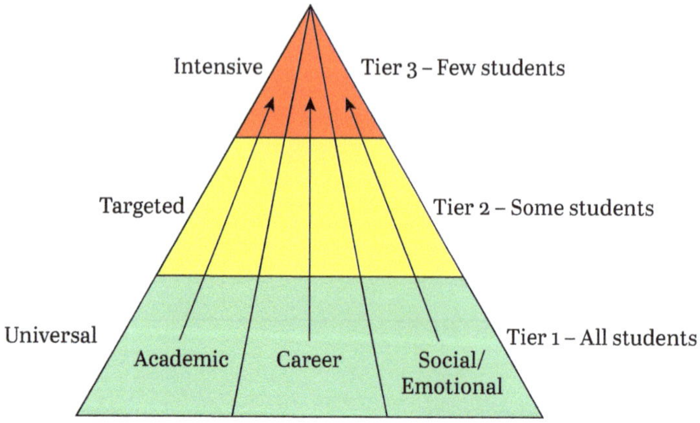

FIGURE 1.1 MTSS triangle of interventions.

Multitiered Systems of Support

The multitiered systems of support (MTSS) is a framework for supporting students by developing and implementing whole-school interventions (Tier 1), targeted interventions for some students served in small groups (Tier 2), and intensive support in one-on-one arrangements (Tier 3); (Fallon et al., 2023). This proactive and preventative system is built with the specific needs of the students in the school in mind. When 20% or more of students demonstrate a need through a screener or attendance or behavior data, the intervention would be best included in Tier 1 for all students. For example, if an SEL assessment shows that 30% of fourth-grade students have difficulty reading peers' facial expressions, all of the students are instructed in this area.

There are many core features of MTSS: First, a multidisciplinary team is in place to bring a rich perspective on what is happening in the school to plan their unique MTSS (Cholewa et al., 2023). Second, all decisions are based on data. Student data is regularly collected and analyzed to ensure that interventions make a difference and to identify students who need additional support. Key evidence-based practices are used by all staff members in the environment. For example, all staff teach students the three core school expectations (be safe, be responsible, and be respectful). When students are doing the right thing, staff will often say, "Thank you for being responsible when the substitute had to leave the room unexpectedly." Developing systems is at the heart of MTSS. This means that the MTSS team and school leadership are working toward a continuous cycle of improvement. They are examining data to make sure that the systems and practices used by the staff are meeting students' academic, social and emotional, and college and career needs. When school staff focus on creating systems, collecting data, and using evidence-based practices, they can achieve greater equity for the students by meeting them where they are with greater accuracy. As you can see, the Center for Positive Behavior Interventions and Supports depicts this relationship (Figure 1.2).

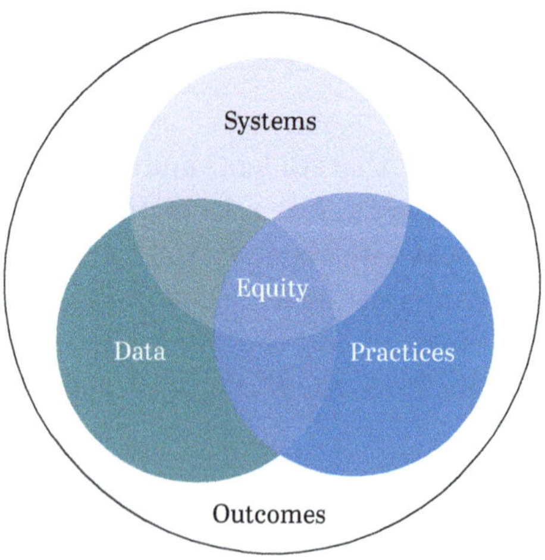

FIGURE 1.2 Components of positive behavioral interventions and supports (PBIS).

Tier 2 Interventions

A Tier 2 intervention is a small group designed to support students' growth in an identified area. For example, an eighth-grade teacher might identify eight to 10 students who are struggling to stay organized and meet assignment deadlines during the month of September. After meeting with the school counselor, who is part of the MTSS team, they decide to initiate a group focused on executive functioning for these students. The school counselor utilizes their Tier 2 executive functioning kit (see Chapter 13) as they meet with the students in this group for 8 weeks. A key feature of Tier 2 groups is to utilize a preassessment to clearly identify areas of growth needed, to monitor progress during the group (see Chapter 4 for examples), and to conduct a post assessment to ensure students got what they needed. If students make progress, they no longer need to take part in interventions, but their progress is monitored 6–8 weeks after the intervention to ensure they are utilizing their new strategies. If students don't make progress, they either repeat the Tier 2 intervention or are referred to a Tier 3 intervention. In this case, they may meet one-on-one weekly with a student support team member to set goals about the specific executive functioning skills that they are having difficulty mastering.

Tier 2 (or advance Tiers) teams meet to discuss both the progress of the students currently getting Tier 2 interventions and the systems the team has developed for referring students, monitoring progress, and exiting students from intervention. These teams can be led by teachers, administrators, or student support team members. They should be meeting regularly and documenting their work. Ideally school/district teams will develop a written MTSS plan to standardize practices across the school/district. The team members should have clearly defined roles and adequate training to ensure the success of the Tier 2 team.

Successful Tier 2 interventions are planned well in advance and utilize evidence-based interventions, implemented with fidelity over a 6–8 week time period and co-led by two individuals. Implementing an intervention with fidelity means that all elements of the design program are utilized as instructed by the designers. Thus, if a group follows a sequence of six 1-hour sessions over a 6-week period, the intervention is implemented with fidelity. However, if a group creates their own sequence and completes only four of six 1-hour sessions over a 2-week period, the intervention is not being implemented with fidelity. Coleadership ensures that interventionists can work closely to observe student growth and keep the intervention moving forward if one staff member has to step away. This model is also helpful to give newer staff members greater confidence in running effective Tier 2 groups.

Evidence-Based Interventions

Everyone working in a school is busy. We pivot from a classroom lesson to a parent meeting, to a faculty meeting, to bus duty, all within a short period of time. We address student concerns, parent emails, new initiatives, and required paperwork. Finding the time to plan and conduct small group intervention is difficult. Fortunately, educational researchers have been busy developing small group interventions and piloting them with diverse groups of students to ensure the intervention can be deemed evidence based. This means that two or more studies have been conducted using rigorous research methods to ensure that this curriculum will yield the desired effect if done with fidelity (or as designed). Some interventions have not undergone a rigorous study but have been developed with key research in mind. These interventions are research informed. Most of the interventions in this book are either evidence-based or research informed. That means our intervention developers and I did our homework before assembling our Tier 2 kits by selecting activities and approaches that are backed by current literature.

An example of an evidence-based intervention that can be used in either Tier 1 or Tier 2 is *Student Success Skills*, which was developed by counselor educators Drs. Greg Bringham and Linda Webb. They were asked to create a curriculum that would help Florida students feel a sense of community at school and improve academically. After developing the curriculum Bringham and Webb assembled research teams to make sure that they were achieving the desired results with small pilot groups and later with larger populations. It was important to them to listen closely to the feedback that they were given and to ensure their curriculum was inclusive of all learners.

Research-Informed Interventions

FIGURE 1.3 Young girl practicing yoga.

As stated, a research-informed intervention is developed by drawing elements from successful studies to incorporate into the intervention. For example, a Tier 2 kit developed for middle schoolers in this book includes the use of specific mindfulness activities to help students build capacity in regulating their strong emotions. The interventionists who designed this intervention read multiple studies about specific mindfulness strategies to use with students ages 12 to 14, which help students to create more space between stimulus and response. They paired them together and gave their Tier 2 kit a test run. Once students utilized it during three to four pilot runs, they made changes to increase effectiveness, increase student engagement, and include culturally affirming practices when using the intervention.

MINDFULNESS IS:

Pay attention
On purpose
In the present moment
Without judgment

—Jon Kabat-Zinn

Integrating mindfulness into small group sessions can open students up to learning as they take a break from their busy school day. One small group facilitator shared their experience:

Students in my third-grade emotional regulation group we call "ZenKids" like to put out our yoga mats in a circle and sit or lay down quietly until all of the students have arrived. They take turns ringing our chime to signal it is time for our guided mindfulness meditation we also call a "brain break." We do some deep "belly breathing" and sometimes listen to quiet music. Sometimes we take turns reading a short poem that relates to our topic for our group session. I find that the students look forward to this routine and are better prepared to take part in the group than if I just start in on our weekly group session as soon as they enter the room. Several of the students have sought out quiet time in the room when they are feeling dysregulated or are having a challenging day.

Here is a list of resources for identifying evidence based and research informed interventions:

- Collaborative for Academic, Social, and Emotional Learning (CASEL)
- Intervention Central
- What Works Clearinghouse
- Center for School Counselor Outcome Research and Evaluation (CSCORE)

Use of Universal Screening to Support Tier 2 SEL Interventions

In light of increased mental health needs for students in schools in the past 5 years, many MTSS teams have opted to include a universal assessment or screener to get a sense of the effectiveness of their Tier 1 programming and to identify students who are in need of Tier 2 or Tier 3 interventions. A universal screener is simply the process of collecting valid and reliable data multiple times a year for all students or a designated group of students. The type of screener utilized reflects the data that the MTSS team deems important to collect. For example, a district who uses Second Step and Steps to Respect as their SEL curriculum might ask students in grades 3–12 to complete the Delaware Social-Emotional Competency Scale (DSECS-S). This 16-item self-report assesses students' perceptions of their SEL skills. The assessment is free and measures four out five SEL skills (it does not measure decision-making skills). Ideally screening will happen in October and February to identify students who could benefit from a Tier 2 intervention group. Furthermore, assessment data could be utilized to clarify discrete gaps in SEL skills.

Common SEL Screeners

In addition to the DSECS-S, other SEL screeners include teacher reports such as the Devereux Student Strengths Assessment (DESSA). The DESSA measures eight domains of social emotional well-being, including personal responsibility, optimistic thinking, goal-directed behavior, social awareness, decision-making, relationship skills, self-awareness, and self-management. Another SEL screener, the Social-Emotional Assets and Resilience Scales (SEARS), has both a teacher (12 items) and student self-report (35 items). The scope of this assessment is the five CASEL competencies. A third screener, the Social, Academic, and Emotional Behavior Risk Screener (SAEBRS), was developed to provide a more comprehensive picture of a student's overall functioning. (For more information on universal screening to identify students in need of Tier 2 interventions, please see Chapter 7.)

Identifying Students for Tier 2 Intervention

Students who are "flagged" by a universal screener would likely benefit from a small group intervention. It's important that their needs must match the nature of the group. Beyond universal screening, your MTSS team may select specific cut scores that qualify a student for consideration for Tier 2 interventions. The table below (1.1) might be developed by a middle school or high school team to determine which students to include.

TABLE 1.1 Example Cut Scores to Identify Students in Need of Tiered Support

Area of Concern	Tier 1	Tier 2	Tier 3
Attendance	> 3 absences by October 30	< 4 absences by October 30	< 7 absences by October 30
Behavior	> 2 office referrals by October 30	< 3 office referrals by October 30	< 6 office referrals by October 30
Homework completion	> 3 incomplete homework assignments by October 30	< 4 incomplete homework assignments by October 30	< 7 incomplete homework assignments by October 30

Teachers, parents/caregivers, and student support staff are good referral sources for Tier 2 intervention groups. It's important these adults understand the purpose and goals of the group prior to making referrals. Students themselves are an excellent source of referrals. Students who refer themselves to a small group are likely very motivated to learn new skills and are aware of shortcomings that are getting in the way of their learning. Be aware of students who want to join groups simply to get out of a less desired activity (like math class)!

Culturally Sustaining or Affirming Tier 2 Intervention Planning

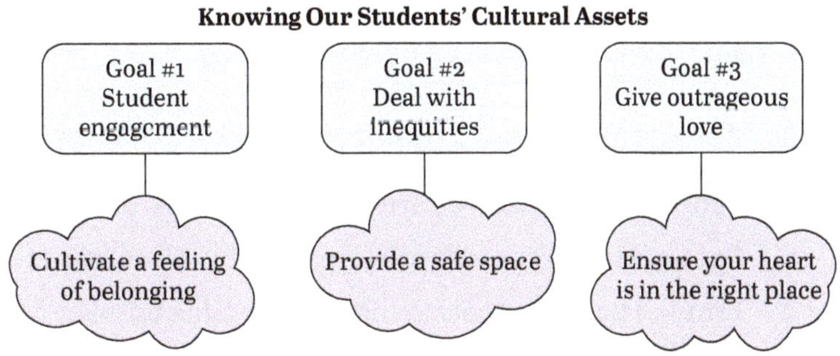

FIGURE 1.4 Knowing our students' cultural assets.

(For more information on culturally affirming Tier 2 interventions, please see Chapter 6.)

Tier 2 interventions are most effective if they are designed to meet the needs of the unique students in the group. For example, if the group includes several Spanish-speaking immigrant students from Ecuador, materials for the group members and their families should be made available in both English and Spanish. The Cognitive Behavioral Intervention for Trauma in Schools (CBITS) program, discussed later in this chapter, has been translated into at least five different languages (Spanish, Korean, Russian, Armenian, and Japanese; National Child Traumatic Stress Network [NCTSN], 2015). Culturally affirming interventions are developed and implemented by treating others' culture and experiences with respect and high regard. That means Tier 2 interventionists consistently ensure that their work matches the values, beliefs, and instructional strategies of the students who are being served. Interventions must be relevant to the students and their families in the environment. School counselors and their MTSS teams must consider what environmental elements are pathways or barriers to the success of this intervention (Betters-Bubon et al., 2016).

Case Study

Improving Time Management and Organization Skills for High School Freshmen

One of the Tier 2 kits you will find in this book focuses on time management and organization for high school students. The two school counselors who designed it piloted it during their internship and continue to use it as practicing high school counselors. Each year they identify eighth graders who have struggled academically during their articulation meetings with middle school counselors from their feeder schools. In their district they have developed detailed spreadsheets to support a smooth transition for all incoming freshmen. School counselors have "whole student" data to look at, which includes literacy proficiency, numeracy proficiency, overall academic performance, academic interventions in the past year, social/emotional interventions in the past year, attendance, discipline, and so forth. They organize the spreadsheet to look at the needs of their assigned caseload. They can identify students with similar needs, such as to improve time management and organization. Their groups begin the first week of school to support students' transitions. One school counselor works at a high school where counselors hold a weeklong "high school boot camp" for identified students on her caseload. Students complete pre- and posttests to help the counselor further "drill down" on discrete skills needed to improve time management and organization. Here is an example of a pre-/posttest they used:

Time Management and Organization Pre-/Posttest

1.	I notice that my grades are impacted by how I manage my time.	YES	NO
2.	I notice that my grades are impacted by how organized I am.	YES	NO
3.	I think I have the tools to manage my time wisely.	YES	NO
4.	When I am attending class, I can locate my materials easily.	YES	NO
5.	When I am doing my homework, I can locate my materials easily.	YES	NO
6.	I understand the role that time management and organization will play in my academic life now and in the future.	YES	NO

Through the six sessions, students learn and practice skills to improve their time management and organization. At the midpoint and end of the group, the school counselor sends a brief survey to one of the student's teachers to get feedback. Here is an example of a teacher feedback survey:

Student Time Management and Organization Teacher Survey

1. The student comes to my class on time.

   Always Usually Occasionally Never

2. The student comes to class prepared.

   Always Usually Occasionally Never

3. The student hands in assignments on time.

   Always Usually Occasionally Never

4. The assignments handed in are done to the student's best ability.

   Always Usually Occasionally Never

5. The student demonstrates pride in their work.

   Always Usually Occasionally Never

Each student charts their progress weekly and rates their level of organization for the week. Their final graphs look like Figure 1.5. It's helpful for them to see their progress.

When the school counselor attends their regular MTSS meeting to discuss students who are in need of Tier 2 support, they share a composite graph of all students assigned to the group to demonstrate that the intervention is working. Any student who is not improving will be considered for more intensive Tier 3 support to address areas of concern.

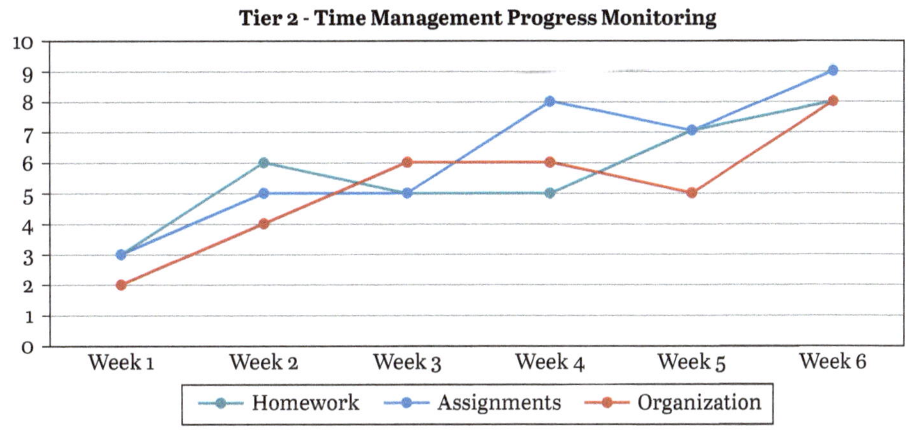

FIGURE 1.5 Tier 2 time management intervention: progress monitoring.

Students were monitored for 4 weeks postintervention and provided additional one-on-one support as needed. During a booster session of the group 6 weeks after the group concluded, students were excited to share their first term report cards with their school counselor since their grades improved between the beginning and end of the term after employing the skills they learned in the small group.

Setting the Table for Small Group Intervention

Once you have identified students who have similar needs that can be likely be met in a targeted small group, you will need to do the following before your first scheduled session:

Image 1.1

Preparing to Conduct a Tier 2 Group

Once you have identified students with similar needs for a small group, you need to do the following:

1. Identify a coleader(s) to facilitate the group with you, if possible.
2. Select a location where you can meet each week consistently.
3. Select a time (or a rotation of times) you can meet each week.

4. Send a parent/caregiver letter home informing them of the group. Some schools have a policy of asking parents for permission; if so, make sure to do that. If parents speak/read a language other than English, make sure to get the letter translated.
5. Inform an educator(s) who works most directly with students (homeroom teacher, etc.).
6. Select an evidence-based or research-informed Tier 2 Kit to utilize. Make sure all of the materials you will need for the 6–9-week group are assembled.
7. Conduct pre-intervention meetings with students so that they know what to expect in the group and how to make the most of their experience.

During the first group meeting it's helpful to conduct a pretest to gauge their skill level and self-perceptions in the area you are addressing (e.g., executive functioning skills). Select a way to monitor progress throughout the group (e.g., tracking completed assignments for students working on their executive functioning skills). The pre-/posttest and progress monitoring materials should be in your Tier 2 kit as well. This book contains six complete Tier 2 kits for each level (elementary, middle, and high school). Simply place the items needed in the Tier 2 kit and get started!

Fidelity of Implementation Through Peer Coaching

We know that evidence-based interventions are only as effective as the interventionist. It's important to follow the small group curriculum as closely as possible to get the desired effect. Students will be absent and school assemblies will be scheduled. However, make sure to do all you can to follow the sequence prescribed in the Tier 2 intervention. Having a partner or peer to keep you accountable when conducting a Tier 2 intervention is helpful, especially as you build your capacity to utilize the intervention. You and your partner should ask essential questions: How is the intervention working? What resistance are we bumping into? You and the peer might take turns observing one another implementing the intervention and give one another useful feedback. It's helpful if this peer has training and experience with the intervention and has seen the intervention yield the desired results. For example, if you have a peer who has successfully helped groups of students measurably improve their executive functioning skills using the research-informed or evidence-based intervention you are learning to use, they will make an excellent peer mentor and/or coleader as you become more familiar with the intervention.

A school psychologist shared her experience in providing Cognitive Behavioral Interventions for Trauma in Schools (CBITS). Her experience implementing with the assistance of peer coaching and check-ins with CBITS trainers is a helpful model to consider as you are building capacity in a specific Tier 2 Intervention.

MY EXPERIENCE IMPLEMENTING CBITS GROUPS FOR HIGH SCHOOL STUDENTS

Karyn L. Hester

Cognitive Behavioral Interventions for Trauma in Schools (CBITS) is an evidence-based program designed to support middle school– and high school–age students who have experienced a traumatic event (Jaycox, 2003). Bounce Back was designed for elementary school–age students (Langley et al., 2015). My initial training of CBITS took place in Connecticut with the Child Health & Development Institute (CHDI) of Connecticut, Inc. (a nonprofit organization dedicated to improving behavioral health and well-being of children in the state), funded by the Connecticut State Department of Children and Families (DCF), which provided the training, materials, data monitoring system, and ongoing supervision to facilitators.

CHDI provided a 2-day training workshop (virtual or in-person) with a focus on implementation, screening and data monitoring, and skill building. The trainers shared helpful tips and suggestions for supplementing content with examples and engaging activities. At that time, I was working as a school psychologist in a large urban high school with students who were exhibiting significant problem behaviors and experiences with traumatic events. My school district agreed to support my implementation of at least one group per year and the disclosure of nontrackable student data for data tracking. After the training, the program kit was delivered to me with all the necessary worksheets, visual tools, and supplies organized for each of the 10 sessions, an easy "grab-n-go" system.

I began offering CBITS to high school students in fall 2020. The school district announced the program biannually in the monthly newsletter to parents, and information was disseminated to all counselors, social workers, school counselors, administrators, and teachers, along with the referral process. Staff were asked to briefly discuss the CBITS program with student candidates to gauge their interest prior to submitting the referral. After initial screening of the referred students, I sent letters home to obtain parent consent for participation and screening.

With parent consent, students were screened for exposure to a significant traumatic event and associated problem behaviors and symptoms using the CPSS-V (modified version of Child PTSD Symptom Scale) and Ohio Youth Problem and Functioning Scales. If the self-reported concerns met the predetermined threshold of concern, a diagnosis of posttraumatic stress disorder (PTSD) is likely and the student is eligible to participate in the group. Important to note, the in-school group precludes students who have experienced sexual violence, since they would be better supported outside of school setting in a special group with similar experiences. Ideally, the group would consist of a minimum of four participants, similar in age and gender, and would be about 45 minutes in duration across 10 sessions. I have found early engagement improves when fidgets are accessible (e.g., gel pens, sand tray), real-life examples are provided by the participants, scenarios are randomly drawn from a stack of prewritten index cards, and, of course, snacks are provided.

Collaboration with teachers and parents are a critical component to the CBITS program. Therefore, soon after the group begins, I reach out to teachers and parents of the participating students to build knowledge on trauma symptoms, cognitive behavioral concepts, and the skills that will be taught. Visual materials are sent via email (or mail) to further gain buy-in and support the generalization of skills across home and school settings. Students are also asked to share homework worksheets with parents, and parents are invited to two sessions (typically virtually) mid program to review and reinforce critical information.

CHDI offers significant supervision to support clinician's implementation of CBITS (or Bounce Back) and additional booster training sessions annually. During my first year of implementation, I was required to attend a monthly virtual consultation, whereby a group of newly trained clinicians had a chance to ask questions and share tips with an experienced clinician. Additional biannual supervision meetings with a CHDI coordinator occur each year to address any concerns and follow up with continued implementation, particularly related to data tracking. CHDI, in collaboration with DCF (in Connecticut), provides a system for clinicians to enter nontrackable information regarding student participants' demographics, community service providers, school and program attendance, general behavior ratings, and fidelity of implementation. Pre- to postscreen data is input to measure the effectiveness of the program, specifically reduction in symptoms of concern and problems behaviors, and recommendations for additional treatment, if needed. Over the past 3 years, I am pleased to report 75% of my student participants have experienced a reduction in their PTSD symptoms, and 37% improved their overall functioning.

Note: The public health authorities (Substance Abuse and Mental Health Services Administration [SAMHSA] and Connecticut DCF) have a vested interest in delivering community-based trauma-focused services to children in Connecticut.

Summary

Tier 2 interventions are designed to provide targeted support to a small group of students over a 6–8-week period of time. These small groups are most effective when they are designed with intention and employ an evidence-based or research-informed curriculum. Like many things in education, preparation is key. When addressing social and emotional growth areas, these psychoeducational groups have clear learning objectives, a scope and sequence of lessons, an avenue for collecting pre-/postdata as well as a system for progress monitoring, and are designed to be engaging for students. Small group participants are most often identified through caregiver or teacher referral, self-referral, or universal screening data, or based on regular analysis of attendance, behavioral, or competency data. To be effective, Tier 2 groups must be culturally affirming and inclusive of the students represented in the group. Materials such as children's literature or case examples should reflect the diversity of the students being served. Finally, once a small group is launched, it must be implemented with fidelity in order to yield the desired impact in order to equip students with essential strategies.

References

Betters-Bubon, J., Brunner, T., & Kansteiner, A. (2016). Success for all? The role of the school counselor in creating and sustaining culturally responsive positive behavior interventions and supports programs. *Professional Counselor, 6*(3), 263–277.

Cholewa, B., Laundy, K., & Williams, J. (2023). School counselors consulting and collaborating within MTSS. In *The school counselor's guide to multi-tiered systems of support* (pp. 94–115). Routledge.

Fallon, L. M., Everett, S., La Salle, T. P., Luh, H. J., Feinberg, A., & Sugai, G. (2023). Multi-tiered systems of support: The what, why, and how for school counselors. In *The school counselor's guide to multi-tiered systems of support* (pp. 1–27). Routledge.

Jaycox, L. (2003). *Cognitive-behavioral intervention for trauma in schools.* Sopris West Educational Services.

Langley, A., Gonzalez, A., Sugar, C., Solis, D., & Jaycox, L. (2015). Bounce back: Effectiveness of an elementary school-based intervention for multicultural children exposed to traumatic events. *Journal of Consulting and Clinical Psychology, 83*(5), 853–865. https://doi.org/10.1037/ccp0000051

National Child Traumatic Stress Network. (2015). *National child traumatic stress network position statement: Prerequisite clinical competences for implementing effective, trauma-informed interventions.* http://www.nctsn.org/sites/all/modules/pubdlcnt/pubdlcnt.php?file

Credits

Fig. 1.1: Emily Goodman-Scott, Jennifer Betters-Bubon, Jacob Olsen, and Margaret D. Donohue, *Making MTSS Work*, p. 27. Copyright © 2020 by American School Counselor Association.

Fig. 1.2: Source: https://www.pbis.org/current/returning-to-school-during-and-after-crisis.

Fig. 1.3: Copyright © Freepik/catalyststuff.

Fig. 1.4: Source: Adapted from https://www.ccsd15.net/Page/8988.

IMG 1.1: Copyright © 2018 Depositphotos/nikolae.

■ CHAPTER 2

Common Tier 2 Interventions

LEARNING OBJECTIVES

1. Identify evidence-based interventions.
2. Identify research-informed interventions.
3. Understand the importance of adopting four to five Tier 2 interventions all team members can implement with fidelity.

At most schools, small group interventions are provided to address behavior (Check In, Check Out [CICO]), social skills/making friends, SEL competencies, executive functioning, and academic success. If the MTSS intervention team has the capacity to provide four to five evidence-based or research-informed interventions with fidelity, they are in pretty good shape. MTSS teams work together to identify evidence-based or research-informed Tier 2 interventions that best meet the cluster of needs regularly identified through their referral process. As these needs change, interventions will need to be updated, modified, or replaced. Table 2.1 provides a list of commonly used evidence-based and research-informed Tier 2 supports.

TABLE 2.1 Evidence-Based and Research-Informed Tier 2 Supports

Intervention	Description	Evidence
Breaks Are Better https://www.pps.net/cms/lib/OR01913224/Centricity/Domain/5007/BrB-Implementation-Manual.pdf	Modification of Check-In Check-Out for students who escape or avoid academic activities, tasks, or assignments; expected academic behaviors defined and reinforced, opportunities for breaks in appropriate way; daily progress report (DPR); goal setting; free	CE/P/I

CICO https://www.guilford.com/books/Responding-to-Problem-Behavior-in-Schools/Hawken-Crone-Bundock-Horner/9781462539512	Daily goal check-ins with teachers and coach, DPRs, weekly/bi-weekly progress monitoring, K–12; individual adult attention, skill development; $30	EBI
Coping Cat https://www.workbookpublishing.com/coping-cat-workbook-2nd-edition-ages-7-13.html	Session outlines, activities for ages 7–13; anxiety; $24	EBI
Coping Power http://www.copingpower.com/	Lesson plans, activities, handouts for late elementary and middle school; academic skills, social skills, problem solving, conflict resolution; $60+	EBI
Incredible Years Social Skills and Problem-Solving Curriculum http://www.incredibleyears.com/	Lessons, activities for ages 0–12; challenging behaviors, social skills, emotional skills	EBI
Resilience Education Program (REP) https://smhcollaborative.org/rep/	Lessons, activities, grades 4–8; supports students with internalizing behaviors; free	EBI
Second Step http://www.secondstep.org/second-step-social-emotional-learning	Lesson plans, activities, handouts for grades preK–8; learning skills, emotion management, problem solving; $400+ per kit, $2,000+ for K–8 site license	EBI
Skills for Academic and Social Success (SASS) https://www.guilford.com/books/Helping-Students-Overcome-Social-Anxiety/Warner-Colognori-Lynch/9781462534609	Strategies, examples, handouts for grades 6–12; social anxiety; $26	EBI
Social Academic Instructional Groups (SAIG) https://mps.milwaukee.k12.wi.us/en/Families/Family-Services/Intervention---PBIS/SAIG-Curriculum.htm	Lesson plans, activities, handouts for grades preK–12; classroom skills, social/emotional skills, attendance; free	RI
Student Success Skills Group Counseling https://studentsuccessskills.com/our-evidence-based-curriculums/student-success-skills-group-manual/	Lesson plans, activities, handouts for grades 4–12; classroom strategies, social problem solving, goal setting; $85	EBI
Support for Students Exposed to Trauma (SSET; adapted from CBITS for school counseling and teachers) http://ssetprogram.org/	Series of 10 group lessons, eight to 10 students per group; ages 10–14; focus on skill building for anxiety/nervousness, withdrawal/isolation, depressed mood, acting out, impulsive/risky behavior. Includes manual and online training course; free	EBI
Trails to Wellness https://trailstowellness.org/	Cognitive-behavioral therapy and mindfulness groups, manual with materials for weekly sessions for grades 3–12; depression, anxiety, coping; free	RI
True Goals https://www.truegoals.org/	School counseling curriculum, lessons, activities, handouts, progress monitoring for grades 3–12; classroom or small group; solution-focused research-based goal setting techniques; free	CE/P/I

EBP = Evidence-based practice; EBI = Evidence-based intervention; RIP = Research-informed practice; CE/P/I = Cutting-edge/promising/initial evidence

*Olsen, J. (2021). Evidence-based and research informed tier 2 supports. California State University Long Beach.

Interventionists can utilize this list to create Tier 2 kits to augment their intervention menu. Many have training associated with their materials. This helps ensure the intervention is implemented with fidelity. You may notice that Second Step is on the list. This has been largely utilized as a Tier 1 curriculum in elementary schools. There is a middle school version. The lessons taught to whole classes can be retaught in small groups, thereby providing extra practice.

Breaks are Better (BrB) is a modification of CICO for students who engage in problem behaviors maintained by escape or avoidance from academic activities, tasks, or assignments. BrB may be especially effective for students who frequently are off-task in class. The intervention builds from CICO as students do the following:

- Carry a point card and earn points for meeting schoolwide expectations.
- Interact with students prior to and after class.
- Receive frequent feedback on in-class behavior.
- Meet with the intervention facilitator before and after school each day.
- Earn incentives for meeting schoolwide expectations.

The modifications making BrB different from CICO are what make BrB effective for escape motivated students. These modifications include

- Expected academic behaviors are defined and reinforced
- Explicit opportunities to take breaks in an appropriate way

CICO is a "go-to intervention" that can be customizable to the student. Generally students are made aware of two to three behaviors that get in the way of their learning. They set goals to use replacement behaviors and are awarded points for doing so. For example, for a student who frequently calls out in class, the replacement behavior is to "raise my hand to speak in class." This positively stated goal is included on a CICO points card. Teachers give the student feedback (0, 1, or 2: never, sometimes, often) demonstrating the behavior in their class. Points are tallied and reported to the home and school contact person. Students who score an adequate number of points are rewarded either daily or likely. While this is a common Tier 2 intervention,

How I take my breaks	1. Hold up index finger	2. Wait for thumbs up or down from teacher	3. After thumbs up, cross out your card	4. Start the timer for 2 minutes	5. Take the break using a break option	6. When the timer goes off go back to work
When I ask for a break:	✓ When I want to stop working for a few minutes ✓ When I am having a hard time keeping my eyes on the teacher ✓ When I want to get out of my seat ✓ If I get frustrated or just need a break		**What if my teacher gives a thumbs down?**	✓ Set your timer for 2 minutes but keep working! ✓ When the timer goes off you can ask for a break again		**My break choices are...**

FIGURE 2.1 BrB student directions.

School Name

Check In Check Out (or other name of program i.e. "PAWS")

Student name: ____________________ CICO mentor: ____________________ Date: ______________

	Expectation #1	Expectation #2	Expectation #3	Total points	Teacher initials
Period 1	0 1 2	0 1 2	0 1 2		
Period 2	0 1 2	0 1 2	0 1 2		
Period 3	0 1 2	0 1 2	0 1 2		
Period 4	0 1 2	0 1 2	0 1 2		
Period 5	0 1 2	0 1 2	0 1 2		
Period 6	0 1 2	0 1 2	0 1 2		
Period 7	0 1 2	0 1 2	0 1 2		
Period 8	0 1 2	0 1 2	0 1 2		

Key:

2 points	Behavior was appropriate; student managed his/her own behavior.
1 point	Behavior was somewhat appropriate; student needed one reminder.
0 points	Behavior was inappropriate; student continued problem behavior after reminder(s).

FIGURE 2.2 CICO daily progress sheet.

one shortcoming is the fact that very little time is spent teaching the child to become aware of when they are dysregulated or apt to engage in undesired behavior and how to effectively use the replacement behavior. Thus, CICO may become a feature of a more comprehensive Tier 2 intervention such as those described in this chapter and in this resource.

Coping Cat is a cognitive-behavioral treatment for children with anxiety. The program incorporates four components: recognizing and understanding emotional and physical reactions to anxiety. Clarifying thoughts and feelings in anxious situations. Developing plans for effective coping. An adolescent version for students ages 14–17 is called The C.A.T. Project.

Coping Power is a preventative intervention delivered to students in late elementary to middle school. The program uses skills-based training to increase social competence, self-regulation, and positive parental involvement. It has proven to reduce substance use and delinquency while lowering aggression for participants.

Incredible Years Social Skills and Problem-Solving Curriculum encourages elementary-aged children by utilizing dinosaur-themed materials and life-size puppets to capture their attention and improve their social-emotional skills and capabilities in various areas, such as building friendships, controlling anger, resolving problems, adhering to school rules, and other applicable skills.

FIGURE 2.3 Coping Cat logo.

FIGURE 2.4 The Incredible Years logo.

Ruling Our Experiences (ROX) Groups for Girls is a 20-week evidence-based curriculum and resource for school-based mental health providers to help female students succeed in relationships, academics, careers and life. Female licensed school counselors, social workers, and educators become program facilitators. The ROX Program for Girls is a cocurricular experience that has been validated with more than 40,000 girls since 2006 and is aligned with the American School Counselor Association's (ASCA) mind-sets and behaviors. Key topics addressed are communication, body image, leadership, relationships, social media, stress and pressure, self-defense and college and career readiness. Olivia Carter, the 2021 School Counselor of the Year, shared on her podcast Candid Counselors that "Tuesdays are my ROX days. It's my favorite day of the week!"

The Resilience Education Program is a targeted Tier 2 intervention for students at risk for internalizing concerns, such as depression and anxiety. It is comprised of the following:

- Cognitive behavioral instruction: Students are taught key coping and problem-solving skills across five lessons in a small group setting.
- CICO: Students meet with their teachers and a mentor on a regular basis to receive feedback regarding their behavior. Students also have the opportunity to receive rewards contingent on their appropriate behavior.
- Resilient families: Parents/caregivers are provided important information and resources to support their child's emotions and behavior in the home.

FIGURE 2.5 Ruling Our Experiences logo.

Second Step is both a Tier 1 SEL curriculum and a Tier 2 small group approach designed to reinforce specific SEL competencies. It is designed to reduce impulsive, high-risk, and aggressive behaviors and increase children's social competence and other protective factors. The program builds on cognitive behavioral intervention models integrated with social learning theory, empathy research, and social information-processing research. It is intended to teach children to identify and understand their own and others' emotions, choose positive goals, and successfully manage reactions when emotionally aroused.

FIGURE 2.6 Second Step social skills curriculum.

Skills for Academic and Social Success is a school-based intervention designed to help students overcome social anxiety by participating in this psychoeducational group. Students review case examples and sample scripts to demonstrate how to implement psychoeducation, cognitive strategies, social skills training, exposure, and relapse prevention with groups and individual students.

Social Academic Instructional Groups (SAIG) were developed by Milwaukee Public Schools. The group lessons are based on the circle format, revolve around restorative practices, and rely heavily on *Skillstreaming* (McGinnis & Goldstein, 2003). Each SAIG with a group of students should last 9 weeks. There are two group themes: classroom survival skills and emotional management skills.

Self-Care SAIG lessons are based on the circle format and revolve around restorative practices. Each SAIG with a group of students should last 9 weeks, with each school selecting the lessons that will fit the needs of its students.

Skillstreaming is an evidence-based prosocial skills training program that builds social-emotional competence. It employs a four-part training approach—modeling, role-playing, performance feedback, and generalization—to teach essential prosocial skills to children and adolescents.

Strong Start, Kids, and Teens is an evidence-based SEL curriculum designed to improve cognitive, affective, and social functioning. Strong Start is appropriate for K–2, Strong Kids is meant from grades 3–8, and Strong Teens is tailored to the needs of students grades 9–12. Each 10-lesson curriculum can be used as a Tier 1 whole-school SEL curriculum or in Tier 2 small group intervention.

Student Success Skills is a curriculum based on the premise that students learn best when in a supportive environment. The lessons focus on developing self-management/self-regulation, prosocial behaviors, and cognitive/learning skills.

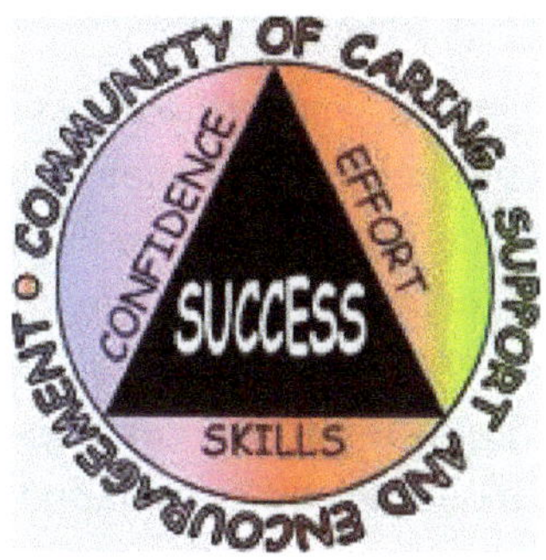

FIGURE 2.7 Skills for Success logo.

Support for Students Exposed to Trauma (SSET; adapted from CBITS for school counselors and teachers) is an evidence-based intervention focused on managing the distress that results from exposure to trauma. It is designed to be implemented by teachers or school counselors with groups of 8 to 10 students. SSET is designed for children in late elementary school through early high school (ages 10–16) who have experienced events such as witnessing or being a victim of family, school, or community violence; being in a natural or man-made disaster; being

FIGURE 2.8 TRAILS to Wellness logo.

in an accident or fire; or being physically abused or injured and who are experiencing moderate to severe levels of posttraumatic stress symptoms.

TRAILS (Transforming Research into Action to Improve the Lives of Students) to Wellness provides school-based clinicians with evidence-based Tier 2 and Tier 3 interventions. The TRAILS CBT and mindfulness sessions provide students with skills for managing common mental health concerns. Grounded in CBT and mindfulness—the gold-standard practices for which the program is named—TRAILS is designed to be delivered by school mental health professionals, such as school counselors, social workers, or psychologists.

True Goals is a small group curriculum composed of 10 principles focused on goal setting and motivation. Students met weekly for 10 weeks, covering one principle per week. Students choose their own goals and then connect this process to both their personal interests and values. The curriculum also prompts participants to learn more about their levels of motivation, self-knowledge, self-direction, and ability to create positive relationships.

Innovative Approaches

School counselors and school-based mental health professionals seek opportunities to develop groups that will be of high interest to their students, centering groups around principles of art therapy, music therapy, or ecotherapy. Specialized training is necessary in these approaches. Ecotherapy involves activities that take place in a natural setting, such as group leadership, team building, and nature walks, and are focused on building a restorative connection to nature.

Summary

There are a plethora of evidence-based and research informed Tier 2 interventions for school counselors and other school-based mental health specialists to become familiar with while selecting four to five key interventions for their site. Those interventions, which have been rigorously reviewed by qualified teams of researchers, are likely going to be most effective. This chapter provides Tier 2 interventionists with helpful starting points for exploring interventions and the corresponding training. When adopting a new Tier 2 intervention, it's best to pilot with a single small group before scaling up to routine use.

References

McGinnis E., & Goldstein, A. P. (2003). *Skillstreaming in early childhood: New strategies and perspectives for teaching prosocial skills*. Research Press.

Olsen, J. (2021). *Evidence-based and research informed tier 2 supports.* California State University Long Beach.

Credits

CHAPTER 3

Practical Considerations for Small Group Facilitators

LEARNING OBJECTIVES

1. Screen members for group interventions.
2. Engage parents/caregivers in consent and assent processes.
3. Set norms, build rapport while fostering community in group.
4. Address challenges to implementing small groups.
5. Find workarounds for implementing small groups.
6. Collaborate with administrators and teachers to create sustainable Tier 2 interventions.
7. Apply the interventions in this book.

Screening Group Members

When preparing for a new group, it is helpful to develop a list of pertinent screening questions for each candidate for the group. I often ask students if they have ever been in a group before and what the experience is like. We talk about confidentiality and the goals of the group. Before they leave our meeting they know what to expect during each group meeting. For example, they learn that we will start with a brief check-in about the previous week, followed by one to two activities focused on the skill set we are working on and a "check-out" to talk about their key takeaways and what is coming up for them in the coming week. We discuss their right to decline the invitation to the group. They also know that, if they agree to be in the group, they can pass on a question or activity at any time and they can drop out of the group at any time. For older students we might consider developing a group member contract that they sign, giving their consent to joining the group and participating to the best of their ability. Finally, we want to assure students who participate in groups that we are available to speak with them individually before or after any group meeting if they have questions or concerns. In many ways, this screening meeting is how we begin building rapport with group members, especially with students who we have not interacted with before.

Parent/Caregiver Permission and Involvement

Whenever meeting with a student over a lengthy period, it is a good idea to let parents/caregivers know prior to the beginning of the group. Many schools have a policy whereby parents/caregivers most give permission for students to participate. It's helpful to prepare a one-page synopsis of the group, including what skills their student will be learning in the group. One school-based mental health provider shared that they offer an online "information night" for parent/caregivers before each group begins. Those with questions can log on, become more familiar with the interventionist, and get clarity about what their child will be doing in group sessions. Parents/caregivers are often concerned about what academic content their child is exposed to while they are in group, so it is important to address that in the permission slip or via an informational meeting.

It's also helpful to involve parents/caregivers in your work as a small group interventionist. Regularly emailing about the specific skills the group is addressing and the "homework" students have is helpful to engage parents/caregivers in the success of the group. A school counselor who led a conflict resolution group asked their students to select someone in their family to teach the five steps of conflict resolution to. This helped reinforce the learning that they were doing in group. One group member brought the list of five steps to the dinner table, briefed the whole family, and then proceeded to post the list on their refrigerator for all to see! After the group ended, the students' parents conferenced with the school counselor at "report card night" and shared that the entire family had benefited from learning the five steps of conflict resolution and they were experiencing more harmony at home!

Group Dynamics

As I stated earlier, this book is meant to serve as a reference for school-based mental health providers and interventionists. It is not designed to be a group counseling textbook but could be a helpful accompaniment. The role of the group facilitator is the cornerstone of planning and implementing effective groups. The more consistent, caring, and compassionate a group facilitator is, the more successful they will be. These are the main tasks of a group facilitator:

- Screen members to make sure all are appropriate.
- Plan activities that will help group members build intended skills.
- Establish and maintain rapport with group members.

- Track pre- and post–progress monitoring data about group members.
- Facilitate productive communication among group members.
- Set norms of behavior with and for group members.
- Clearly define the norm of observing confidentiality regarding what is shared in the group.
- Ensure that group members feel physically and emotional safe during sessions; address any threats to group members' safety.
- Bring healthy closure to the group when it concludes.
- Be available to support group members before, during, and after the group experience.

Challenges to Implementing Small Groups

There are many challenges to implementing small groups in schools. Most schools have closely followed schedules, which may or may not include an intervention or "flex" period. Scheduling small groups can be a significant barrier to getting one off the ground. Teachers may be hesitant to let their students leave given the pressure to cover content prior to state testing. Keeping track of students who are out for illness, band lessons, sports, academic intervention, and small groups can make the complex job of teaching even more stressful. Teachers who do not understand the intent or the efficacy of the group might be especially reluctant to comply with your request to remove a student from class.

Another constraint to running small groups is the size of school-based mental health professionals' caseloads and crises that arise throughout the school day. School counselors, social workers, and psychologists are often very busy throughout the school day. While they may develop a daily schedule including small group meetings, they can be pulled to support a student or student(s) in a crisis situation. Another scarcity in schools is funding. Some group counseling curricula are costly, and many group activities require supplies, which can be compiled into Tier 2 kits.

Something I have heard often when visiting schools is "We don't do groups," which means that the staff attempts to meet all of their students' needs through Tier 1 classroom lessons or Tier 3 individual support. Often after asking more questions, many school-based mental health professionals do not feel prepared to run effective groups in schools or simply believe it will take too much time.

Some school-based staff are wary of bringing together students with disciplinary needs for fear that the students will act up and not get anything out of the group experience. This is always a possibility. Group intervention is not for every student. It is, however, a more efficient way for school-based mental health professionals to meet the needs of a greater number of students in the course of a school year.

Workarounds for Implementing Small Groups

Table 3.1 has suggestions for addressing common challenges to implementing groups in schools.

TABLE 3.1 Common Challenges and Workarounds for Running Small Groups in Schools

Challenge	Workaround(s)
Scheduling group session meeting times when there is not an intervention block in schedule	• Plan small groups before or after school or during common lunch period(s). • Rotate the time of day / class period that the group meets to avoid students missing the same class each week. • Collaborate with special teachers to take a student out of their class for a 6-week period to avoid missing academic instruction.
Teachers being reluctant to allow students to leave class to attend a small group	• Share one-page synopsis and recent student data pertinent to group with teacher(s) so that they understand the purpose and effectiveness of group intervention. • Seek administrative support to ensure group participation is given high priority since the intent is for students to be more available to learning as often as possible.
Size of school-based mental health professionals' caseloads	• Keep track of how many students on your caseload require Tier 2 interventions. • When possible, advocate for additional staff to meet needs. • Collaborate with outside mental health providers who can facilitate effective small groups.
Crises that arise throughout the school day	• Create a schedule within your student support team office so that there is someone available to meet the needs of students who walk in with concerns or when crises occur. • Colead groups so that one adult can remain with the group while the other attends to the crisis. • Track the data about the need for coverage to advocate for additional staff when possible.
Lack of funding for group supplies	• Identify low-cost and no-cost evidence-based or research-informed group curricula that are pertinent to your students' needs. • Take inventory of current supplies and identify additional needed. • Approach parent–teacher organization, administrators, and/or community organizations to fund a small grant to launch a new small group intervention.
Staff feeling unprepared to run small groups	• Organize a professional learning community (PLC)–focused on small group interventions. Use a book (like this one or others) as a basis for your PLC. Share responses to the book and share experiences to help build capacity in small group interventions. • Request specific professional development on small group intervention from your administration. • Attend state, regional, or national conferences for which group interventions are a key focus.
Concerns about student behavior in small groups	• Screen students to see if they are appropriate for the group. • Keep group sizes manageable. • Use a coleadership model. • Develop clear expectations and an understanding about what violating those expectations would mean for their future involvement. • Design high-interest activities for the students. • Stick to a predictable structure for the group.

Collaborating With Administrators and Teachers to Create Sustainable Tier 2 Interventions

After 25-plus years as a school counselor in two states, I can confidently say that "the principal makes the weather" in schools. The times that I was most effective as a school counselor and MTSS team member were instances when I had a positive and productive relationship with our administration. I made developing a strong alliance with my administrators central to my work. I know that the better we work together, the better we are for our students. It's helpful to engage administrators in your discussions and planning for small groups. You will need their support and access to resources such as supplies and training. Once you have small groups up and running, make sure to share your data with you administrators on a regular basis. You want to remind them that small groups are an effective and efficient way for you to meet the needs of more students in less time. This is not dissimilar to the use of Tier 2 groups to support students with similar needs to boost their literacy and numeracy. Thus, the precedent is set in schools to group students to meet needs.

Applying the Interventions in This Book

The interventions in this book were developed to use in elementary, middle, and high schools to support social emotional and academic development. Like any intervention, it makes sense to pilot it first with a smaller group (four to five students) and ask for ample feedback from participants and teachers and parents/caregivers. Discuss what could make the process more enjoyable or more effective. Ask students if they think other students would enjoy taking part in the group and why or why not. As one does with a new recipe, take notes about each session in the margins. What went well? What could be improved? Share your experiences with other interventionists and make improvements as you go.

CHAPTER 4

Show Me the Data!

Progress Monitoring and Data Collection

LEARNING OBJECTIVES

1. Understand the importance of utilizing data to identify students for Tier 2 intervention.
2. Understand the importance of utilizing data to monitor students' progress during Tier 2 interventions.

When we begin a small group, we have often identified students using data. It's important to look at that data through an equity lens. For example, who is being referred to groups? How often are students being referred to groups? We may rely on attendance, behavior, discipline, or academic data. We may ask for teacher referrals. Regardless, identifying students for our Tier 2 groups is the beginning of the "data story."

Screening Meetings Prior to Group

Once we screen our identified students by sharing what to expect in the group and answer their questions about the group experience, we are ready to gather some pre-intervention data. This data should be directly correlated with the theme or focus on the group. For example, if our group is designed to help students improve their homework completion and weekly test scores, we need to gather that information about each of our students who will be joining our group. Often, it is easiest to include that data in a spreadsheet. Some schools utilize data dashboards that are helpful in gathering student data. Figure 4.1 is an example of the way a Tier 2 leader might assemble pre-, mid-, and post-intervention data.

Notice that the first line is dedicated to class averages so that interventionists have a sense of how students perform compared to their peers. With older students, this can be helpful, motivating and empowering to invite them to chart their own data to witness their own growth

Pre-Intervention					Mid-Intervention				Post-Intervention			
Student ID	Current GPA	HW Completion - Language Arts	HW Completion - Math	Date	Current GPA	HW Completion - Language Arts	HW Completion - Math	Date	Current GPA	HW Completion - Language Arts	HW Completion - Math	Date
Class Avg	3.3	75%	&5%	26-Oct								
17539	1.7	50%	58%	26-Oct								
17542	2.2	49%	49%	26-Oct								
17586	2.3	44%	60%	26-Oct								
17599	2.4	39%	48%	26-Oct								
17501	2.5	51%	52%	26-Oct								
17544	1.8	48%	49%	26-Oct								
17533	2.3	38%	40%	26-Oct								
17589	1.9	57%	67%	26-Oct								
17560	2.4	60%	59%	26-Oct								
17575	2.1	45%	48%	26-Oct								
17596	2.1	38%	60%	26-Oct								
17593	2.1	29%	50%	26-Oct								

Student ID	Current GPA	HW Completion - Language Arts	HW Completion - Math	Date	Current GPA	HW Completion - Language Arts	HW Completion - Math	Date	Current GPA	HW Completion - Language Arts	HW Completion - Math	Date
Class Avg	3.3	75%	&5%	26-Oct								
17539	1.7	50%	58%	26-Oct								
17542	2.2	49%	49%	26-Oct								
17586	2.3	44%	60%	26-Oct								
17599	2.4	39%	48%	26-Oct								
17501	2.5	51%	52%	26-Oct								
17544	1.8	48%	49%	26-Oct								
17533	2.3	38%	40%	26-Oct								
17589	1.9	57%	67%	26-Oct								
17560	2.4	60%	59%	26-Oct								
17575	2.1	45%	48%	26-Oct								
17596	2.1	38%	60%	26-Oct								
17593	2.1	29%	50%	26-Oct								

FIGURE 4.1 Tier 2 pre-, mid-, and post-data.

or to see where they fall short. This helps students to set and hopefully obtain realistic goals for themselves. We want to see progress, not perfection! If students can improve to the point that they are utilizing the skill 80% of the time, we can feel successful as interventionists. Of course, they are only privy to their own data. A Tier 2 group leader may decide to share group averages to show how the group is improving overall. At mid intervention, if there are students who are not beginning to demonstrate growth or their data shows decline, it might be helpful to meet with them one-on-one and ask what they think is impacting them. Student feedback during a group can be helpful to "course correct" for students who aren't getting what they need from the group. Post-intervention data helps us to find out if the intervention yielded the desired effect. We can average each column to get a sense of average GPA, language arts (LA) homework (HW) completion, and math HW completion before and after the small group. We can then calculate both individual percentage growth and the growth of the group overall.

Thus, a report to our MTSS team might look like this:

- The average GPA of the students in the academic success group prior to the intervention was 2.2.
- After the intervention, the average GPA was a 3.2. ↑ 1.0 increase in GPA.
- The average LA HW completion rate as 41% prior to the intervention.
- After the intervention the average HW completion was 65%. ↑ 24% increase in LA HW completion.
- The average math HW completion rate was 52% prior to the intervention.
- After the intervention the average HW completion was 71%. ↑ 19% increase in math HW completion.

Other Data to Chart Growth

Student-completed pre- and posttests are helpful measures to show that students are learning and applying what group leaders are emphasizing in a group. It's helpful to find a measure that is norm referenced so that the questions have been tested rigorously. For example, you might use a student's score on the Social Skills Improvement System (SSIS) Rating Scales to initially assess students' social skills, problem behaviors, and academic competence. This tool is normed to be used as a progress monitoring tool at mid intervention and as well as a post-intervention tool. Some of the SSIS questions include the following:

- I ask for help from adults.
- I follow directions.
- I interact well with other children.
- I stay calm when I disagree with others.
- I show kindness to others when they are upset.
- I stay calm when I am teased.

Teacher reports are also helpful for gauging effectiveness of small groups. The younger the students, the better able teachers are to assess whether students are consistently employing strategies they are learning through the intervention.

Parent/caregiver reports can also shed light on how a student is progressing in specific skill areas. This practice also engages parents in the small group experience in a meaningful way. For example, you might provide the following checklist to second- or third-grade parents/caregivers to complete pre-, mid-, and post-intervention.

EXHIBIT 4.1: PARENT/CAREGIVER CHECKLIST

Social skill	Y	N
My child engages in play, which includes themes never personally experienced (e.g., going to space).	Y	N
I have observed my child negotiating during play.	Y	N
My child engages in well-organized play.	Y	N
I have observed my child playing with small groups and making up their own games with rules.	Y	N
My child plays cooperative games (getting better at coping with losing).	Y	N

(Adapted from the KidSense, Play and Social Skills Development Checklist, n.d., https://childdevelopment.com.au/resources/child-development-charts/play-and-social-skills-developmental-checklist/)

For any small group, interventionists can develop a strategy for making notes about how students are working toward mastery of skills that are being taught through psychoeducational groups. One method I used as a school counselor was to dedicate a file folder to each group. I placed a sticky note for each student in the folder. Each week, after the group, I made two to three quick observations about the student and placed it in the folder, adding to their pile of sticky notes. At the end I had six to eight observations about the student that were helpful to me when assessing how beneficial the group was for each student (Figure 4.2).

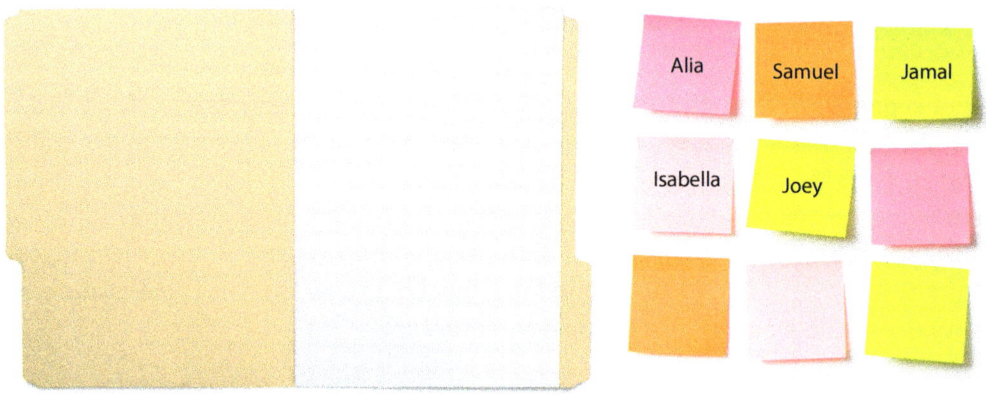

FIGURE 4.2 File folder organization idea for group leader note taking.

Self-Monitoring

Another important way for students to monitor their growth is by developing an easy-to-use self-monitoring system. For example, students in one of my executive functioning groups were encouraged to keep track of missed and completed HW assignments. Each time they came to group, the first thing they did after check-in was to update their bar graph by indicating how many classes they were caught up in. This meant they were tracking how many classes in which they were successfully on track and how many they needed to put additional focus on in order to get back in good standing.

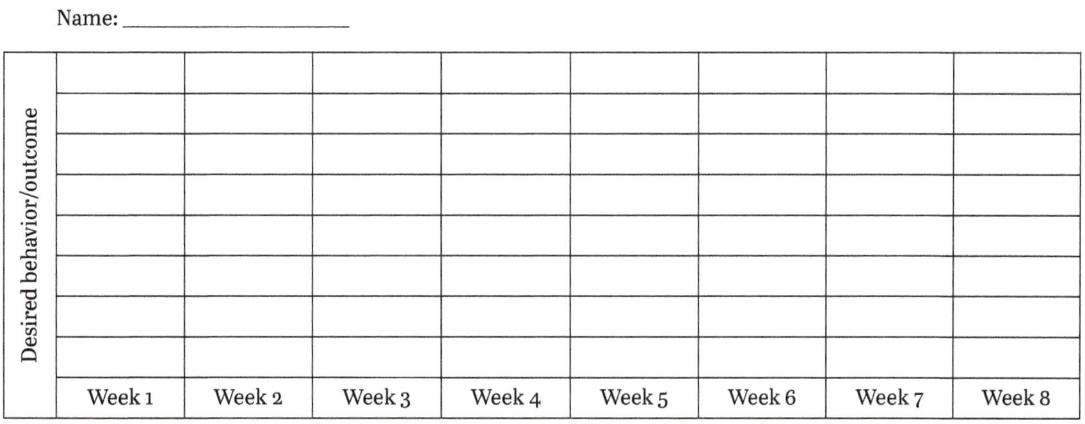

FIGURE 4.3 Student self-tracking form for Tier 2 intervention group.

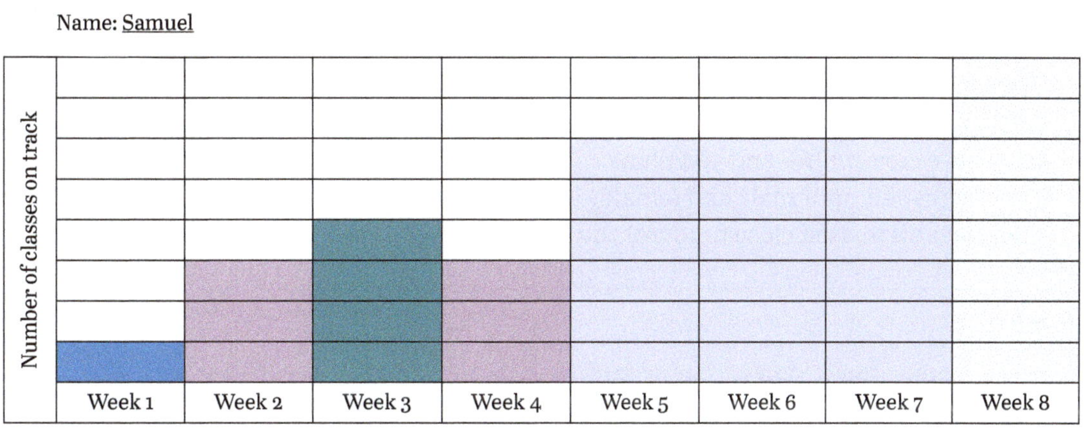

FIGURE 4.4 Sample student self-tracking form for Tier 2 intervention group.

If a Student's Data Does Not Show Growth

This happens sometimes. It's important to consider why the student did not acquire the skills and strategies provided in the group. Did they miss sessions? Were they experiencing significant stress? Were they distracted by a group member or members? Then consider one of two options: another opportunity to participate in the same group or a similar group (Tier 2) or one-on-one counseling or coaching (Tier 3). The MTSS team can support interventionists when discussing students who do not respond to interventions and make a shared decision about what course of action to take to best meet the student's needs.

For more information on data collection and Tier 2 groups please check out the following resources:

Goodman-Scott, E., Betters-Bubon, J., Donohue, P., & Olsen, J. (Eds.). (2023). *The school counselor's guide to multi-tiered systems of support*. Taylor & Francis.

Goodman-Scott, E., Betters-Bubon, J., Donohue, P., & Olsen, J. (2020). *Making MTSS work.* American School Counseling Association.

Hatch, T. (2013). *The use of data in school counseling: Hatching results for students, programs, and the profession*. Corwin Press.

Kaffenberger, C., & Young, A., (2008). *Making DATA work.* American School Counseling Association.

LEARNING ACTIVITY

What Type of Group Would You Plan for These Students?

A middle school MTSS team is looking at disciplinary data over the past semester. The majority of the office referrals happen before school, lunchtime and immediately after school. When you look at the data more closely, you notice the following about the 10 students with the most disciplinary referrals:

- They are enrolled in both before- and after-school care, making their school day last from 7:00 a.m. to 6:00 p.m. Mondays–Fridays.
- They have current IEP and 504 plans.
- They are evenly split male and female.
- They have all missed close to 10% of the school year.

One Possible Approach

The school counselor and school psychologist bring student data to the MTSS team to discuss while and explore possible interventions. As the team considers that most students have a 30-hour school week and these students have a 55-hour school week, the team might invite the directors of the before- and after-care programs to help them consider options. What are they observing before and after school? What activity options do the students have when they are in their care? The care program leaders consider the need for the students to have quiet down time instead of being "on" and interacting with others all of the time. They propose creating a quiet space for their students to read, relax, and do homework. They get four donated cots for students to nap on in case they are worn out from their day or do not get enough rest at night. The school counselor and school psychologist decide to run 6-week small groups with the girls as one group and the boys in another to talk about managing stress and their long school day. They fill out a pretest about their current levels of fatigue at the end of the week and their ability to manage stress. During the group they learn about practicing mindfulness or "brain breaks" and yoga and create calming collages as a final activity. They write a letter to their parents/caregivers about what they have learned. Students complete a posttest, which shows that they are experiencing less fatigue at the end of the week because they can reset when attending before and after care and they can use the skills they learned in their small group. After reviewing the discipline data for each of the students who participated, the team noticed a 50% decline in their discipline behavior. Parents/caregivers are encouraged to conference with the group leaders about their child's progress.

Summary

We use a myriad of student data to identify who is in need of 6–8-week Tier 2 interventions. Increasingly, schools are equipped with online student data platforms and/or dashboards to help school-based student support team members monitor student progress once intervention is underway. Engaging students in charting their own data can help them to take ownership of the changes they are trying to make to improve their academic performance and overall wellness. We need to be prepared to address situations when we do not see improved student data despite intervention. No improvement serves to inform us that we need to try another approach. School-based MTSS teams work together to develop systems for collecting, analyzing, and utilizing data to support effective Tier 2 interventions.

Credits

CHAPTER 5

Tier 2 Intervention Kit Ingredients

Image 5.1

LEARNING OBJECTIVES

1. Identify key materials to include in streamlined Tier 2 kit.
2. Clarify importance of addressing ASCA Mind-sets and Behaviors in small group interventions.
3. Highlight need for implementation fidelity when facilitating small group interventionss.

Each Tier 2 kit prepared for your students should have the same standard components. Interventionists utilizing the kits should be able to quickly scan the materials and begin effective implementation with fidelity:

- One-page description of the skill set (e.g., self-awareness) and current research
- Pre-intervention communication with families/teachers in languages represented in the school
- Permission slip (if applicable)
- Learning objectives
- CASEL standards addressed (if applicable)
- ASCA mind-sets and behaviors
- Materials needed
- Pre-/post-assessment
- Sessions 1–6
- Post-intervention communication to parent/guardian
- Plan for implementation fidelity

One-Page Description of Target Skill Set and Current Research

To develop common language, Tier 2 kits include a brief one- to two-page description of targeted skills and strategies to set the stage for effective implementation. The beginning of each section of this book includes a brief summary of the key skill set. Current research on "what works" is included. This summary might also be shared with parents as a means of informing them of the focused goals.

Pre-Intervention Communications With Parents/Guardians/Teachers

A key component of effective intervention is transparency with all of the other key adults in students' lives. This communication should include a brief description of the group, intended goals, meeting times, resources, and a way of contacting the interventionist. Whenever possible, this communication should be shared in the languages represented in the school community.

Permission Slip

Some schools require a parent/guardian permission slip for students to participate in small group intervention. This provides the parent/guardian the opportunity to opt out of the group if they deem that best for their child. Permissions slips should also be provided in home languages.

CASEL Standards Addressed

For the Tier 2 kits focused on self-awareness, self-management, social awareness, relationship skills, and decision-making skills, it's important to align the lesson plans to standards established by CASEL.

EXHIBIT 5.1: THE CASEL 5

The CASEL 5 addresses five broad, interrelated areas of competence and examples for each: *self-awareness, self-management, social awareness, relationship skills,* and *responsible decision-making*. The CASEL 5 can be taught and applied at various developmental stages from childhood to adulthood and across diverse cultural contexts to articulate what students should know and be able to do for academic success, school and civic engagement, health and wellness, and fulfilling careers.

www.casel.org/what-is-SEL

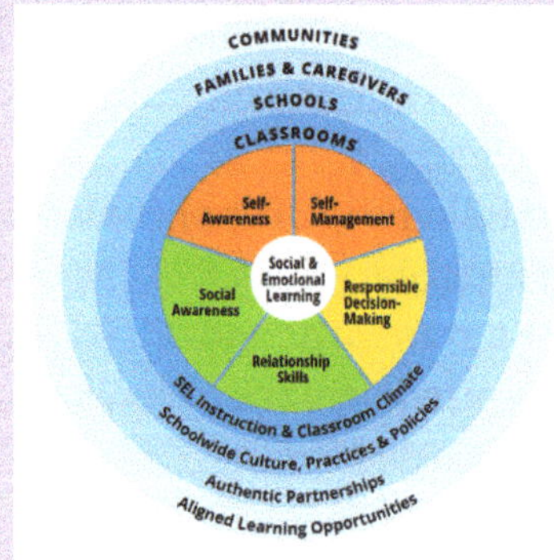

SELF-AWARENESS: **The abilities to understand one's own emotions, thoughts, and values and how they influence behavior across contexts.** This includes capacities to recognize one's strengths and limitations with a well-grounded sense of confidence and purpose. Such as:

- Integrating personal and social identities
- Identifying personal, cultural, and linguistic assets
- Identifying one's emotions
- Demonstrating honesty and integrity
- Linking feelings, values, and thoughts
- Examining prejudices and biases
- Experiencing self-efficacy
- Having a growth mind-set
- Developing interests and a sense of purpose

SOCIAL AWARENESS: **The abilities to understand the perspectives of and empathize with others, including those from diverse backgrounds, cultures, and contexts.** This includes the capacities to feel compassion for others, understand broader historical and social norms for behavior in different settings, and recognize family, school, and community resources and supports. Such as:

- Taking others' perspectives
- Recognizing strengths in others
- Demonstrating empathy and compassion
- Showing concern for the feelings of others
- Understanding and expressing gratitude
- Identifying diverse social norms, including unjust ones
- Recognizing situational demands and opportunities
- Understanding the influences of organizations/systems on behavior

SELF-MANAGEMENT: **The abilities to manage one's emotions, thoughts, and behaviors effectively in different situations and to achieve goals and aspirations.** This includes the capacities to delay gratification, manage stress, and feel motivation and agency to accomplish personal/collective goals. Such as:

- Managing one's emotions
- Identifying and using stress-management strategies
- Exhibiting self-discipline and self-motivation
- Setting personal and collective goals
- Using planning and organizational skills
- Showing the courage to take initiative
- Demonstrating personal and collective agency

RELATIONSHIP SKILLS: **The abilities to establish and maintain healthy and supportive relationships and to effectively navigate settings with diverse individuals and groups.** This includes the capacities to communicate clearly, listen actively, cooperate, work collaboratively to problem solve and negotiate conflict constructively, navigate settings with differing social and cultural demands and opportunities, provide leadership, and seek or offer help when needed. Such as:

- Communicating effectively
- Developing positive relationships
- Demonstrating cultural competency
- Practicing teamwork and collaborative problem-solving
- Resolving conflicts constructively
- Resisting negative social pressure
- Showing leadership in groups
- Seeking or offering support and help when needed
- Standing up for the rights of others

RESPONSIBLE DECISION-MAKING: **The abilities to make caring and constructive choices about personal behavior and social interactions across diverse situations.** This includes the capacities to consider ethical standards and safety concerns, and to evaluate the benefits and consequences of various actions for personal, social, and collective well-being. Such as:

- Demonstrating curiosity and open-mindedness
- Identifying solutions for personal and social problems
- Learning to make a reasoned judgment after analyzing information, data, facts
- Anticipating and evaluating the consequences of one's actions
- Recognizing how critical thinking skills are useful both inside and outside of school
- Reflecting on one's role to promote personal, family, and community well-being
- Evaluating personal, interpersonal, community, and institutional impacts

Source: CASEL, Selection from "CASEL'S SEL FRAMEWORK: What Are the Core Competence Areas and Where Are They Promoted?," p. 2.

ASCA Mind-Sets and Behaviors Addressed

The ASCA (2021) developed 36 standards aimed at supporting student academic success and college and career/life readiness for all students. These standards are based on research and identify the following mind-sets as helpful to student development:

EXHIBIT 5.2: ASCA MIND-SET STANDARDS

Category 1: Mind-set Standards

School counselors encourage the following mind-sets for all students.

M 1. Belief in development of whole self, including a healthy balance of mental, social/emotional and physical well-being
M 2. Sense of acceptance, respect, support and inclusion for self and others in the school environment
M 3. Positive attitude toward work and learning
M 4. Self-confidence in ability to succeed
M 5. Belief in using abilities to their fullest to achieve high-quality results and outcomes
M 6. Understanding that postsecondary education and lifelong learning are necessary for long-term success

Source: American School Counselor Association, "Category 1: Mindset Standards," *ASCA Student Standards: Mindsets and Behaviors for Student Success*, p. 2. Copyright © 2021 by American School Counselor Association. Reprinted with permission.

School counselors and fellow students support team members to develop and implement culturally sustaining/affirming learning opportunities, appraisal, advisement, and counseling to address the following learning strategies, self-management skills, and social skills.

Thus, when developing a small group intervention, interventionists are encouraged to identify both mind-sets and behaviors that are addressed in each session.

EXHIBIT 5.3: ASCA BEHAVIOR STANDARDS

Category 2: Behavior Standards

School counselors provide culturally sustaining instruction, appraisal and advisement, and counseling to help all students demonstrate:

Learning Strategies		Self-Management Skills		Social Skills	
B-LS 1.	Critical thinking skills to make informed decisions	**B-SMS 1.**	Responsibility for self and actions	**B-SS 1.**	Effective oral and written communication skills and listening skills
B-LS 2.	Creative approach to learning, tasks and problem solving	**B-SMS 2.**	Self-discipline and self-control	**B-SS 2.**	Positive, respectful and supportive relationships with students who are similar to and different from them
B-LS 3.	Time-management, organizational and study skills	**B-SMS 3.**	Independent work	**B-SS 3.**	Positive relationships with adults to support success
B-LS 4.	Self-motivation and self- direction for learning	**B-SMS 4.**	Delayed gratification for long-term rewards	**B-SS 4.**	Empathy
B-LS 5.	Media and technology skills to enhance learning	**B-SMS 5.**	Perseverance to achieve long- and short-term goals	**B-SS 5.**	Ethical decision-making and social responsibility
B-LS 6.	High-quality standards for tasks and activities	**B-SMS 6.**	Ability to identify and overcome barriers	**B-SS 6.**	Effective collaboration and cooperation skills
B-LS 7.	Long- and short-term academic, career and social/emotional goals	**B-SMS 7.**	Effective coping skills	**B-SS 7.**	Leadership and teamwork skills to work effectively in diverse groups
B-LS 8.	Engagement in challenging coursework	**B-SMS 8.**	Balance of school, home and community activities	**B-SS 8.**	Advocacy skills for self and others and ability to assert self, when necessary
B-LS 9.	Decision-making informed by gathering evidence, getting others' perspectives and recognizing personal bias	**B-SMS 9.**	Personal safety skills	**B-SS 9.**	Social maturity and behaviors appropriate to the situation and environment
B-LS 10.	Participation in enrichment and extracurricular activities	**B-SMS 10.**	Ability to manage transitions and adapt to change	**B-SS 10.**	Cultural awareness, sensitivity and responsiveness

Source: American School Counselor Association, "Category 2: Behavior Standards," *ASCA Student Standards: Mindsets and Behaviors for Student Success*, p. 2. Copyright © 2021 by American School Counselor Association. Reprinted with permission.

Materials

A comprehensive list of the materials needed for each group is included in each lesson plan. This likely includes handouts, art supplies, progress monitoring sheets, and written group lesson plans. Since interventionists are busy and Tier 2 interventions are meant to be administered quickly after the plan is made, it is helpful to have the Tier 2 Kit in a plastic bin ready to transport to available meeting spaces in the school. It is also helpful if the kits are regularly replenished as groups conclude in order to be at the ready for the next 6–8-week group.

Pre-/Post-Assessment

In order to demonstrate that the intervention is effective, key data must be collected. Baseline data (discipline, academic progress, attendance) should be collected prior to the intervention dependent on the intended skill set. Over time regular brief surveys of students' targeted skills should be tracked. Examples of pre-/post-assessments can be found in each section of Tier 2 kit.

Sessions 1–6

Brief plans for each session should be assembled in an easy-to-read format. These plans include learning objectives, CASEL standards address (if applicable), ASCA mindsets and behaviors addressed, materials needed, handouts, and a step-by-step plan for the session. Each Tier 2 kit has lesson cards that can be copied directly out of this resource and added to the core materials in the kit. These lesson plans can be refined as needed.

Post-Intervention Communication

Again, clear communication before, during, and after the intervention helps to support the home–school connection necessary to support students and their mastery of intended skills. This letter should include a summary of the goals addressed, pertinent common vocabulary, and where to find additional resources. Depending on the age of students enrolled in the group, specific data about their progress can be shared. For example, in a final communication about a group focused on improving homework completion should include a brief summary about the student's progress (e.g., Lionel initially completed 43% of his HW prior to taking part in the group. At the end of our sessions, he was completing 82% of his assigned classwork and HW on a weekly basis).

Plan for Implementation Fidelity

Interventionists have important but challenging roles in schools. They must identify and support students through brief and effective intervention without interrupting Tier 1 instruction. Clearly, this is a group that needs peer support and coaching to implement with fidelity.

What is implementation fidelity (IF)? It is "the extent to which an intervention was delivered as conceived and planned—to arrive at valid conclusions concerning its effectiveness in achieving the target outcomes" (Song et al., 2010, p. 673). A plan for IF could include things such as the following:

- Become trained in the use of the intervention by observing others who have successfully implemented it.
- Meet regularly with peers and or intervention coaches to ensure the intervention is being implemented in the manner it is intended. Discuss challenges and successes.
- Take notes or journal after group sessions to uncover patterns, observe student behaviors/ responses, and identify implementation challenges.
- Make accommodations to ensure fidelity of implementation each time the intervention is used, such as expanding the time allotted for each session, reducing or increasing the size of the group, or adding a coleader.

Summary

Standardizing the elements of Tier 2 kits will help interventionists adopt new content readily. Containing all of the materials needed in one, easy-to-locate bin makes it possible for school-based interventions to literally "grab and go," thereby focusing their best energy on the students in need of support.

References

American School Counselor Association. (2021). *ASCA student standards: Mind-sets and behaviors for student success.*

Song, M. K., Happ, M. B., & Sandelowski, M. (2010). Development of a tool to assess fidelity to a psycho-educational intervention. *Journal of Advanced Nursing*, *66*(3), 673–682.

■ CHAPTER 6

Culturally Affirming Tier 2 Interventions

LEARNING OBJECTIVES

1. Define culturally affirming interventions.
2. Align interventions with the student population.
3. Utilize culturally affirming Tier 2 group planning checklists.

Culturally Affirming Definition

Image 6.1

Culturally affirming practices, recognize, celebrate, and respect the diverse cultures of students. School-based interventionists using culturally affirming practices consistently demonstrate an appreciation for and desire to learn from the rich fund of knowledge their students bring to the group. They use inclusive language and asset-based planning in their work. Their goal is to cultivate a safe space where all participants have a sense of belonging. In addition, they have high expectations for all students.

In small groups, leaders can help facilitate healing of all kinds. Group members may be seeking to heal from loss, trauma, or lack of social connections. In their best form, small groups provide a place for members to have the sense they truly belong. The trust among small group members is essential for it to be effective. Unfortunately, an unhealthy group dynamic that makes one or more people feel like they do not belong or are outside of the group can arise. It is the group leader's role to establish boundaries, address transgressions, and process any language and behavior that makes a group member feel unsafe.

TABLE 6.1 Culturally Safe Spaces

Values and Knowledge	Instruction, Curriculum, and Engagement
Practice race consciousness and self-awareness. Learn what the community desires and wants to sustain through schooling. Commit to value and sustain community languages, practices, and ways of being while providing access to the dominant culture (White, middle class, and standard English speaking).	Validate students' lived experiences and identities. Integrate cultural assets into small group experience. Be active and socially engaging. Connect strategies to local racial, ethnic, and linguistic communities. Encourage critical thinking. Establish mutual respect with accountability between students and adults. Engage to empower student voice.

Sources: Alim and Paris (2017); Ferlazzo (2017); Ladson-Billings (2014); and Price-Dennis et al. (2017). Adapted from https://ies.ed.gov/ncee/edlabs/regions/west/relwestFiles/pdf/4-2-4-58_Culturally_Affirming_Spaces_Webinar_Slides_508c.pdf (slide 20).

Examples of Practices to Cultivate Culturally Affirming Spaces

When a small group facilitator engages group members as they set group norms, they attend to the unique experiences of the group members. Making time for this in the beginning of a small group process is well worth it once everyone feels confident in the boundaries that they have added to the group norms to help them to feel safe.

Incorporating students' home language whenever possible is another way to cultivate a culturally affirming space (del Carmen Salazar & Lerner, 2019). You will notice that each of the Tier 2 kits contains pre- and post-intervention correspondence and permission slips to be sent home to caregivers in both English and Spanish. In addition, group facilitators encourage students to share cultural assets (language, customs, celebrations, traditional meals, etc.). For example, prior to winter break, group members are encouraged to share what traditions they find most meaningful. We might be careful with the way we phrase the inquiry given that group members come from diverse economic backgrounds and potential family dysfunction can get in the way of gathering peacefully. In addition, it is essential that small group leaders minimize the occurrence of harm and microaggressions to maintain a culturally affirming space for all participants (Gay, 2018; Nieto & Bode, 2018). With training, facilitators can become aware of how to identify and intervene when microaggressions occur during a small group session. Table 6.2 may be helpful to you to understand the five types of microaggressions.

TABLE 6.2 Types of Microaggressions

Verbal	Behavioral	Microassaults	Microinvalidations	Microinsults
A comment or question is hurtful or stigmatizing to a certain marginalized group of people.	Someone behaves in a way that is hurtful or discriminatory to a certain group of people.	A person intentionally behaves in a discriminatory way while not intending to be offensive.	A person's comment invalidates or undermines the experiences of a certain group of people.	A comment or action is unintentionally discriminatory.
Example: "You're so smart for a girl."	Example: A group leader ignores a Black student who raised his hand first and instead calling on a White student.	Example: A person telling a racist joke then saying, "I was just joking."	Example: A White person telling a Black person that "racism does not exist in our school."	Example: A person saying to an Indian honors student, "Your people must be so proud."

Sources: Allen et al. (2013); Goodman (2011); Harrison and Tanner (2018); Nadal (2014). Adapted from https://ies.ed.gov/ncee/edlabs/regions/west/relwestFiles/pdf/4-2-4-58_Culturally_Affirming_Spaces_Webinar_Slides_508c.pdf (slide 25).

Another way to make sure a group is a culturally affirming experience is to ask for student, teacher, caregiver input before, during, and after intervention. This means that school counselors include a diverse group of educators and caregivers to preview intervention planning and to solicit essential feedback. Likewise, it is helpful to engage community members in intervention planning. For example, meeting with local religious and tribal leaders to discuss plans to support young people in a small group for those at risk for substance abuse would likely yield helpful insights into ways to make the experience culturally affirming and inclusive for young members of their congregations or tribal communities. It's also important that activities planned during intervention connect to students' lives. A good example of this is encouraging young people in a self-awareness group to compose and perform hip-hop songs to express inner feelings, struggles, and discoveries (Levy & Adjapong, 2020). It goes without saying that, in order to develop culturally affirming Tier 2 groups, the facilitator must engage in regular self-reflection about their own potential biases and debriefs with coleader weekly, if possible (Betters-Bubon et al., 2022). All data that Tier 2 facilitators review is viewed through an antiracist lens.

The following checklist was developed to provide Tier 2 group facilitators a streamlined way to select or design intentionally and thoughtfully planned culturally affirming interventions. This checklist can be utilized a template to support planning individually or as a team.

EXHIBIT 6.1: CULTURALLY AFFIRMING TIER 2 GROUP PLANNING CHECKLIST

Please ask the following questions during your planning process:

How are students identified as needing this intervention?

- ☐ Data
- ☐ Teacher referral
- ☐ Self-referral
- ☐ Caregiver referral
- ☐ Community partner referral
- ☐ All of the above

Was school data viewed from an antiracist lens? (This includes reviewing data to identify trends in student behaviors or staff bias.)

- ☐ Yes, I reviewed data to identify trends in student behaviors as well as staff bias.
- ☐ No, I reviewed data solely to identify student behaviors, attendance, graduation status, etc.

Is the intervention evidence based or research informed?

- ☐ Yes, I selected an evidence-based or research-based small group curriculum. Possible resources I reviewed were What Works Clearinghouse, CSCORE, Intervention Central, SAMHSA, and Safe Support Learning.
- ☐ No, I did not select an evidence-based or research-informed small group curriculum.

What population was utilized when piloting this intervention?

- ☐ A population similar to students in our school
- ☐ A population dissimilar to students in our school

Are students/caregivers/community partners involved in planning this Tier 2 intervention?

- ☐ Yes, I have students, caregivers, and community partners on my MTSS team.
- ☐ No, my MTSS team consists of only school staff.

Is there communication with caregivers before, during and after the Tier 2 intervention group?

- ☐ Yes, I have contacted the caregivers of all student members to gain permission, provide an update, and seek feedback on group effectiveness.
- ☐ No, I have not provided updates to student member caregivers.

Are the sessions being held in a space that permits movement and comfort for all students, regardless of ability?

- ☐ Yes, the space is open enough to accommodate all students comfortably.
- ☐ No, I need to locate another space that provides more comfort.

Are documents and conversations translated into the students' home or preferred language?

- ☐ Yes, permission slips and other papers are translated into the home language of all potential group members.
- ☐ No, all forms are in English.

Source: Peg Donohue, Stephanie Smith Durkin, and Alexandra Frank, Selection from "Strategies to Enhance Implementation Fidelity in School-Counselor-Led, Culturally Affirming Tier 2 Groups," *Professional School Counseling*, vol. 28, no. 1a. Copyright © 2024 by SAGE Publications.

EXPERIENCE FROM THE FIELD

Two 3rd-year school counselors were tasked with developing a curriculum to be used to support 10th-grade students who will become first-generation college students after graduation. They reviewed the school counseling, school psychology, and school social work literature to find information that would help them to create a research-informed approach. They prepared a slide show detailing their proposed assessment and activities to their diverse school counseling department advisory committee. They were pleased that many advisory committee members asked questions and shared helpful resources. The counselors refined their plan for the intervention and shared it with six former students who were currently first-generation college students at local community college and 4-year college institutions. After reviewing the intended activities, they encouraged the school counselors to add the following elements to the curriculum:

- asking for help to navigate bureaucracy
- discovering your passions as a high school student and pursuing them in college
- starting productive conversations with parents about affording higher education early in your high school career

The students, several of whom spoke Spanish and Korean (the two dominant languages represented at the school in addition to English) offered to take part in a panel discussion for caregivers and the students in the 10th grade and to meet with group members to share their insights and experiences in English, Spanish, and Korean.

Feedback from students, teachers, and caregivers after the group was very positive. Many highlighted the opportunity to meet students from the community who were successful college students as one of the most valuable parts of the small group experience. Several mentioned that it gave them hope that they could follow in their footsteps to pursue their passions through higher education in the future.

Summary

Planning Tier 2 interventions involves paying attention to both content and context. Small group facilitators must carefully select activities and psychoeducational lessons that address targeted skills in order to best support students. However, that is only half of the equation. They must consider the context in which the student is attempting to master the skill. Using the checklists provided in this chapter while planning a Tier 2 intervention will assist school counselors and other small group facilitators to develop culturally affirming intervention groups whereby students feel like they are seen, heard, and valued. Small groups are microcosms of the school communities where important growth and healing can take place. This chapter was designed to challenge all Tier 2 interventionists to look at their plan through the eyes of the students they will support prior to their first session. The use of the checklists will help the Tier 2 group facilitator to be proactive to develop a nurturing environment and hopefully prevent harmful behaviors such as microaggressions.

References

Alim, H. S., & Paris, D. (Eds.). (2017). *Culturally sustaining pedagogies: Teaching and learning for justice in a changing world*. Teachers College Press.

Allen, A., Scott, L. M., & Lewis, C. W. (2013). Racial microaggressions and African American and Hispanic students in urban schools: A call for culturally affirming education. *Interdisciplinary Journal of Teaching and Learning*, *3*(2), 117–129.

Betters-Bubon, J., Pianta, R., Sweeney, D., & Goodman-Scott, E. (2022). Antiracism starts with us: School counselor critical reflection within a multi tiered systems of support framework. *Professional School Counseling*, *26*(1a).

del Carmen Salazar, M., & Lerner, J. (2019). *Teacher evaluation as cultural practice: A framework for equity and excellence*. Routledge.

Donohue, P., Smith-Durkin, S. & Frank, A. (2024). Strategies to enhance implementation fidelity in school counselor-led culturally affirming tier 2 groups. *Professional School Counseling, 28(1a), 2156759X241234912.*

Ferlazzo, L. (2017, July 6). Author interview: "Culturally sustaining pedagogies." *Education Week*. https://www.edweek.org/teaching-learning/opinion-author-interview-culturally-sustaining-pedagogies/2017/07

Goodman, D. (2011). *Promoting diversity and social justice: Educating people from privileged groups*. Routledge.

Harrison, C., & Tanner, K. D. (2018). Language matters: Considering microaggressions in science. *CBE—Life Sciences Education*, *17*(1), fe4.

Ladson-Billings, G. (2014). Culturally relevant pedagogy 2.0: A.k.a. the remix. *Harvard Educational Review*, *84*(1), 74–84.

Levy, I., & Adjapong, E. (2020). Toward culturally competent school counseling environments: Hip-hop studio construction. *Professional Counselor, 10*(2), 266–284.

Nadal, K. L. (2014). A guide to responding to microaggressions. *CUNY Forum*, 2(1), 71–76.

Price-Dennis, D., Muhammad, G. E., Womack, E., McArthur, S. A., & Haddix, M. (2017). The multiple identities and literacies of Black girlhood: A conversation about creating spaces for Black girl voices. *Journal of Language and Literacy Education*, *13*(2), 1–18.

Credits

■ CHAPTER 7

Universal Screening to Identify Students With Tier 2 Needs

LEARNING OBJECTIVES

1. Define universal screening.
2. Clarify use of screening data to identify students for Tier 2 intervention.
3. Understand use of some screeners as progress monitoring tools.
4. Review common universal screening tools.

Image 7.1

Universal Screening in Schools Defined

On a typical day at schools across the country, students are screened for barriers to learning and healthy development. This takes the form of vision testing, hearing testing, and checking for scoliosis. Given the mental health challenges that preK–12 students in our country are facing, an increasing number of schools are also screening for emergent mental health concerns, social-emotional competencies mastered, resilience, and key school climate concerns, such as students' sense of hope and belonging. Screening data is used to inform

Tier 1 practices and to highlight students who may have acute needs (Tier 3) and those who could benefit from a Tier 2 small group.

Universal screening is defined as the systematic assessment of ***all*** children within a given class, grade, school building, or school district, on academic and/or social-emotional indicators that the school personnel and community have agreed are important (Ikeda et al., 2009). MTSS teams who embark on the journey of screening their students often start small with one class or one grade and scale up over time. They decide what they are looking to screen for and what validated instrument would best suit their needs and align with the cultural identities of the students they serve. Implementing universal screening takes careful planning over several school years. When done well, including universal screening in regular school practices can facilitate the following:

- more equitable access to ongoing interventions
- development of new interventions to meet student needs
- identification of students who internalize concerns. Students who externalize concerns are already known to staff.
- encouragement of greater parity between health and mental health
- reduced stigma about mental health
- gaps identified in school personnel to support students; hiring additional staff
- parent and caregiver enrichment workshops to support students with emergent mental health needs

School teams screen for emerging mental health concerns, onset of substance abuse, signs of suicidal ideation, social and emotional competencies, resilience, hope and belonging. (To peruse a comprehensive library of assessments, go to the University of Maryland's Center for School Mental Health website.)

Parents and caregivers can opt out of universal screening at any time. Most districts adopt a "passive" consent process whereby they inform the school that their student(s) will not be taking part in the screening process and should be given an alternative setting and activity while the rest of the class is screened.

Using Universal Screening Data to Identify Students Who Need Tier 2 Interventions

Once the team selects a screener and plans their pilot administration, they must determine what cut scores will make a student eligible for intervention. Validated instruments have predetermined cut scores that are readily available to users. MTSS teams develop a grid of measures used to identify students in need of intervention, including screening, attendance, academic, and behavioral data. Looking at this data together helps MTSS team members to consider the whole child and what needs are most pressing for them. Consider Table 7.1. Which students would you be most concerned about? Which students look like good candidates for a Tier 2 group focused on emotional regulation?

TABLE 7.1 Wholistic Middle School Student Data to Determine Tiered Support

	Tier 1: No support			1: No concerns	One	One
	Tier 2: Group support			2: Elevate	Two–Four	Two–Four
	Tier 3: Intensive 1:1			3: Highly Elevated	Five or more**	Five or more**
Student #	Math tiered support	Reading tiered support	Writing tiered support	SAEBRS Screener*	Office disciplinary referrals (ODRs)	Days absent as of Oct. 15
111	1	2	2	1	1	5
222	1	1	3	3	5	4
333	3	3	3	2	5	5
444	1	1	1	1	2	2
555	2	2	2	3	5	7
666	1	3	3	2	1	6
777	3	2	2	2	7	9
888	3	1	1	2	9	5
999	2	3	3	3	11	1
1010	2	3	3	2	3	4

*(SAEBRS: Social, Academic, and Emotional Behavior Risk Screener)

**By October 15

Source: Adapted from Peg Donohue, Emily Goodman-Scott, Jennifer Betters-Bubon, and Jacob Olsen, *The School Counselor's Guide to Multi-Tiered Systems of Support*. Copyright © 2023 by Taylor & Francis Group.

Meeting the Needs

If there is an overwhelming number of students who need Tier 2 interventions in a specific area, the MTSS team should consider if that need would be best met through a Tier 1 intervention. For example, if a school administers the Devereux Student Strengths Assessment (DESSA), which reveals that 40% of the fourth grade demonstrate a deficit in emotional regulation skills, teaching this skill is embedded in the Tier 1 curriculum. Often school teams are reluctant to begin screening for fear that they will uncover needs they are not prepared to address. It is important to be ready to intervene when school teams screen. Many teams prepare by developing partnerships with outside agencies, local pediatricians, and universities who can provide school-based mental health interns to increase the number of qualified personnel who are prepared to respond to student needs. Following is a case example of school using a screener to inform high school intervention groups.

EXAMPLE FROM THE FIELD

The school counselor identified ninth-grade students who scored at the elevated or highly elevated level for anxiety on the Generalized Anxiety Disorder Scale (GAD-7). After initial individual meetings with each potential group member, he met with the group. They established group norms and began discussing triggers for anxiety and strategies they might use to combat anxious feelings that get in the way of academic performance. The school counselor had created a Tier 2 kit using materials from Trails to Wellness activities and videos. Parents were informed about the group in emails that went home in English and Spanish. One session that many reported finding very helpful was the "Cognitive Coping" lesson. A video depicted a student who struggled with test-taking anxiety reframing their internal dialogue about an upcoming test. Halfway through the 8-week intervention, students took the GAD-7 (which is normed and vetted as a progress monitoring tool) for a second time. Among the eight members of the group, all but two saw their anxiety levels go down. The other two students scored the same. By the end of the 8-week intervention all eight members had GAD-7 scores in the normal or typical range. The final day of the Tier 2 group, the school counselor encouraged each student to write a letter to their future selves about what they learned in the group about what triggers their anxiety and how they can manage it in ways that are uniquely effective for them. The school counselor sent the letters to the students the week prior to their 11th-grade year. He held a booster session the 3rd week of school to see how the students were doing with their new courses and with the college selection process on the horizon. Six of the students felt comfortable taking on 11th grade on their own but promised to check in if they had any struggles. The other two students set up appointments to map out managing the anxiety that the new courses and increased responsibility were creating. The school counselor shared the data he collected with the faculty, administration and his multidisciplinary MTSS team. They decided to review the GAD-7 data in October to see how many groups like this will be needed.

Summary

Universal screening is a promising practice for identifying students needing responsive and effective Tier 2 interventions. Many MTSS teams are actively implementing or considering implementation given increased mental health needs evident in preK–12 classrooms. Universal screens take careful planning, and data collected serves as a snapshot of a student on a particular day. Thus, universal screening data should be conducted at least twice annually and considered in conjunction with attendance, academic, and behavioral data to gain a comprehensive sense of how a student is functioning overall. Universal screening makes it possible for MTSS teams to identify students who may function well academically and socially but who may be internalizing their struggles. In addition, universally screening students in the areas discussed (mental health, social emotional competencies, resiliency, hope, belonging, etc.) ensures greater equity in access to high quality interventions in all three tiers.

To learn more about universal screening in schools please refer to the following websites:

- The University of Maryland Center for School Mental Health website
- The Comprehensive Integrated Three-Tiered Model of Prevention (Ci3T) website
- The Substance Abuse and Mental Health Services Administration (SAMHSA) screening and assessment page

School counseling literature you might refer to:

- Donohue, P., Goodman-Scott, E., & Jennifer, B. B. (2015). Using universal screening for early identification of students at risk: A case example from the field. *Professional School Counseling*, *19*(1), 1096–2409.
- Goodman-Scott, E., Donohue, P., & Betters-Bubon, J. (2019). The case for universal mental health screening in schools. *Counseling Today*, *62*(3).
- Goodman-Scott, E., Donohue, P., & Betters-Bubon, J. (2023). Universal mental health screening: Steps for school counselors through multidisciplinary teaming. *Professional School Counseling*, 27(1).

Reference

Donohue, P., Goodman-Scott, E. & Crocker, J. (2023). Universal screening to support MTSS. In Goodman-Scott, E., Betters-Bubon, J., Donohue, P., & Olsen, J. A. (Eds.). (2023). *The school counselor's guide to multi-tiered systems of support*. New York, NY. (2nd ed., pp. 241–274). Routledge.

Credits

CHAPTER 8

Tier 2 Intervention Kits for Self-Awareness

Self-Awareness for Elementary School Students

Dr. Peg Donohue

Description of Skill

According to CASEL (2020), self-awareness is "the ability to understand one's own emotions, thoughts, and values and how they influence behavior across contexts. This includes capacities to recognize one's strengths and limitations with a well-grounded sense of confidence and purpose" (para. 3). In short, cultivating self-awareness makes it possible for children to be aware of their inner life and how their thoughts, emotions, values, goals, and strengths direct their behavior and choices.

The five elements of self-awareness are commonly considered:

1. **Consciousness**: Awareness of one's internal experiences including emotions and thoughts
2. **Self-knowledge**: Ability to articulate identity including beliefs, values, and motivations
3. **Emotional intelligence**: Ability to understand and manage emotions
4. **Self-acceptance**: Ability to demonstrate security in identity (i.e., showing self-compassion and engaging in regular self-care)
5. **Self-reflection**: Ability to reflect on one's feelings, thoughts, and goals

For children, self-awareness is a daily part of their learning. In supportive school and home environments, they come to understand their strengths, weaknesses, preferences (activities, foods, etc.), emotions, and physical self. Skills we are hoping to cultivate through a small group focused on self-awareness are as follows:

- identifying and analyzing emotions, and how they affect others
- understanding the relationship between one's emotions, thoughts, values, and behaviors

- demonstrating honesty and integrity
- examining prejudices and biases
- experiencing self-efficacy
- having a growth mind-set

Why focus on self-awareness? We know teaching self-awareness in an intentional way leads to future success (Yale Center for Emotional Intelligence, n.d.):

- Being able to read facial expressions of emotions and respond appropriately sets students up for better academic performance (Izard et al., 2001).
- Students with good self-awareness have fewer behavior problems (Cook et al., 1994) and demonstrate greater prosocial (kind, helpful) behavior (Denham, 1986).
- A study showed that first graders who showed little knowledge of emotions (Fine et al., 2003) were more likely to report feelings of loneliness, sadness, and anxiety in fifth grade.
- Teens who score high in emotional intelligence have greater academic success, fewer mental health issues, and better attitudes toward teachers and schools.

Clear communication with parents about the rationale for the small group intervention and details is important. In addition, it's helpful for a school-based interventionist would have a conversation with the key adults in a child's life prior to beginning the Tier 2 group.

Pre-Intervention Communication With Parents/Guardians/Teachers in Languages Represented in the School

English Version

Dear Parents/Guardians,

Your fourth or fifth grader has been selected to take part in a small group focused on developing self-awareness. This 6-week group will take place [indicate when] and will not interfere with their academic classes. The goal of this group is to identify our emotions, our strengths, our areas for growth, and ways we can further develop our overall sense of self. We will discuss our current feelings about ourselves while learning new things about our strengths and areas of the growth. This will involve reflection, sharing experiences, goal setting and taking "brain breaks." Each student will complete a pretest prior to the group and a posttest as we finish up.

Our goals are to do the following:

- Increase self-awareness.
- Improve our ability to identify our emotions.
- Make the connection between our thoughts, feelings, values, and behavior.
- Discuss the importance of being honest.
- Develop a growth mind-set.

If you have any questions about this intervention group or would like to discuss your student's participation in the group, please do not hesitate to reach out to me.

Sincerely,

Student Support Team Interventionist

Spanish Version

Queridos padres/guardianes,

Su hijo de 4.º o 5.º grado ha sido seleccionado para participar en un grupo pequeño centrado en desarrollar la conciencia de sí mismo. Este grupo de 6 semanas se llevará a cabo [indicar cuándo] y no interferirá con sus clases académicas. El objetivo de este grupo es identificar nuestras emociones, nuestras fortalezas, nuestras áreas de crecimiento y las formas en que podemos desarrollar aún más nuestro sentido general de nosotros mismos. Discutiremos nuestros sentimientos actuales sobre nosotros mismos mientras aprendemos cosas nuevas sobre nuestras fortalezas y áreas de crecimiento. Esto implicará reflexión, compartir experiencias, fijar objetivos y tomar "descansos para el cerebro". Cada estudiante completará una prueba previa al grupo y una prueba posterior cuando terminemos.

Nuestros objetivos son:

- Aumentar la autoconciencia.
- Mejorar nuestra capacidad para identificar nuestras emociones.
- Hacer la conexión entre nuestros pensamientos, sentimientos, valores y comportamiento.
- Discutir la importancia de ser honesto.
- Desarrollar una mentalidad de crecimiento.
- Si tiene alguna pregunta sobre este grupo de intervención o desea hablar sobre la participación de su estudiante en el grupo, no dude en comunicarse conmigo.

Atentamente,
Intervencionista del equipo de apoyo al estudiante

Permission Slip (If Applicable)

After reading the description of this Tier 2 small group, I ____________________, give permission for my student, ____________________, to take part in the group which will meet on ____________________ from [date] to [date]. I understand that this group is confidential and that I will be made aware if my student is making good use of this group experience. Should I need to be contacted, the best number to reach me at is____________________.

Hoja de permiso

Después de leer la descripción de este grupo pequeño de Nivel 2, yo ____________________doy permiso para mi estudiante ____________________ a participar en el grupo que se reunirá el ____________________ de [fecha] a [fecha]. Entiendo que este grupo es confidencial y que se me informará si mi estudiante está haciendo un buen uso de esta experiencia grupal. Si necesita ponerse en contacto conmigo, el mejor número para comunicarse conmigo es ____________________.

Goals of Intervention

- Increase self awareness.
- Improve our ability to identify our emotions.
- Make the connection between our thoughts, feelings, values, and behavior.
- Discuss the importance of being honest.
- Develop a growth mind-set.

CASEL Standards Addressed

- Identifying one's emotions.
- Integrating personal and social identities.
- Experiencing self-efficacy.
- Managing one's emotions.
- Linking feelings, values, and thoughts.
- Demonstrating honesty and integrity.
- Setting personal and collective goals.

ASCA Mind-Sets and Behaviors

M 1. Belief in development of whole self, including a healthy balance of mental, social/emotional and physical well-being

M 2. Sense of acceptance, respect, support and inclusion for self and others in the school environment

B-LS 7. Long- and short-term academic, career and social/emotional goals

B-SMS 1. Responsibility for self and actions

B-SMS 2. Self-discipline and self-control

B-SMS 7. Effective coping skills

B-SS 9. Social maturity and behaviors appropriate to the situation and environment

Materials Needed

Feelings journal

Books

The Empty Pot by Demi; *Sulwe* by Lupita Nyong'o

Worksheets

Pens, pencils, crayons, or colored pencils

Pre-/Post-Assessment (Teacher Completes)

Name of student: ____________________

Teacher completing assessment: ____________________ **Date:** ____________

Self-Awareness Competency	Strongly Disagree	Disagree	Agree	Strongly Agree
This student can name their emotions.	1	2	3	4
This student can name two of their strengths.	1	2	3	4
This student can name two things they need to work on.	1	2	3	4
This student is most often honest when asked a question about themselves.	1	2	3	4
This student believes they can improve.	1	2	3	4
This student treats peers with respect.	1	2	3	4
This student understands how their behavior affects others.	1	2	3	4
This student has demonstrated kindness to others in the classroom.	1	2	3	4
This student is proud of their cultural heritage.	1	2	3	4
This student is curious about individuals who are different from themselves.	1	2	3	4
This child has one or two close friends.	1	2	3	4
This child can initiate play with others.	1	2	3	4

Sessions 1–6

Session 1: Identifying and Analyzing Emotions and How They Affect Others

Objectives:

1. Students will identify two to three emotions they have had in the last day or two.
2. Students will consider how their feelings impact others.

Materials:

Emotions journal (alternate six copies of the "How Are You Feeling Page" with blank pieces of paper so that students can check in during each session)

Pens/pencils

Duration: 30–40 minutes

Instructions:

1. Welcome students and explain the purpose of the group.
2. Invite group members to provide input on group ground rules. Record them on poster paper and ask students to sign the poster paper.
3. Introduce purpose of the group. Identifying our emotions helps us to understand ourselves better. We can pause and consider how we feel and how we want to react to something.
4. Ask students to look at the first page of the emotions journal and point to the predominant feeling they are having at the moment.
5. Ask each student to share what they are feeling and why they think they might be feeling that way.
6. Explain the process of checking in about their emotions by filling out the emotions journal each day they come to group.
7. Ask them to pay attention to their emotions this week. Also, pick someone they are close to check in about how they are feeling this week. Be prepared to report back.

Emotions Journal

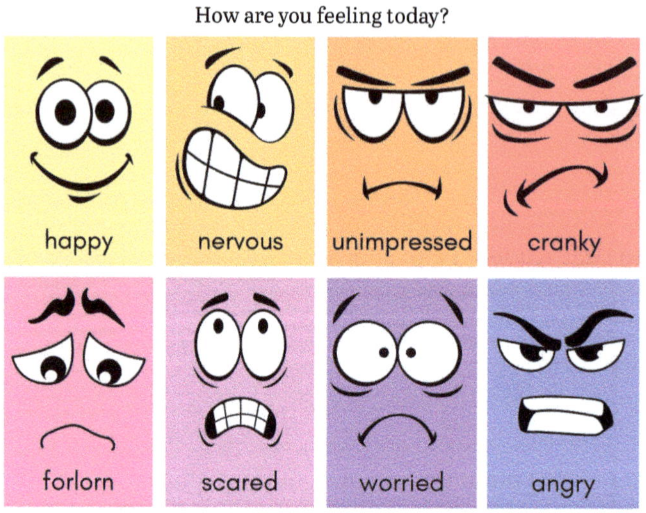

Image 8.1

Source: Sharmburg (n.d.) How are you feeling today? Retreived from https://www.pandaspeechtherapy.com/

Session 2: Understanding the Relationship Among One's Emotions, Thoughts, Values, and Behaviors

Objective(s):

1. Students will understand the difference between emotions, thoughts, values, and behaviors.
2. Students will understand how their emotions, thoughts, and values impact their behaviors.

Materials:

Feelings journal

Index cards

Worksheet

Duration: 30–40 minutes

Instructions:

1. Welcome group members. Remind them of the ground rules established during session 1.
2. Have students complete the "How Are You Feeling?" page in their journal and share with the group.
3. Introduce today's topic by showing them three pieces of paper each with one of the emotions (How do I feel?), thoughts (What do I think?), values (What is important to me?), and behaviors (What did I do?)
   a. Share the following scenario and ask them to imagine it is happening to them or a close friend: You are working on a project in science class with three other people. One person is playing with the materials instead of following the directions and getting the assignment done.
   b. How do you feel? (Ask for answers: frustrated, worried, angry, impatient.)
   c. What do you think? (Ask for answers: We are going to get a bad grade; that person does not care about school; I am going to have to do their work as well; this isn't fair.)
   d. What's important to you? (Ask for answers: We should all work together and follow the directions the teacher gave us; I want to get good grades in school; everyone should do an equal amount of the work; we all need to learn to work together.)
   e. What would you do? (Ask for answers: Talk to the classmate and ask them to help out; tell a grown-up; do the work without them, etc.)
   f. Ask them to share a scenario when they had to decide how to respond. Give prompts that it might be something that happened on the playground, during a sporting event, at home with family or friends, and so on. Next, fill out the self-awareness worksheet.

Name: ______________________ Date: ____________

Self-Awareness Session 2

Understanding how what I feel, think, and believe impacts my behavior.

Recently this challenging thing happened:

____

____

____

Image 8.2

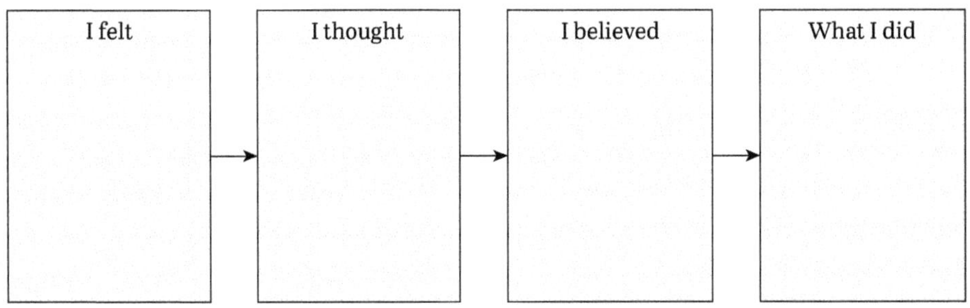

I could ask ______________________ for help with this situation if I needed to.

Session 3: Demonstrating Honesty and Integrity

Objectives:

1. Students will understand what honesty and integrity mean.
2. Students will understand why it is important to be honest.
3. Students will understand why it is important to demonstrate integrity.

Materials:

Emotions journal

Pens/pencils

Book: *The Empty Pot* by Demi

Empty pot worksheet

Duration: 30–40 minutes

Instructions:

1. Welcome students back and remind them of the ground rules.
2. Ask the students complete the "How Are You Feeling?" page in their journal and share with the group.
3. Introduce the topic for today. What do we mean by being honest? Who knows what integrity means?
4. Read the book *The Empty Pot* by Demi.
    a. Synopsis: *The Empty Pot* is a story set in China, a long time ago. An honest schoolboy, Ping, was given some flower seeds by the emperor. He tended to them every day but eventually had to return to the emperor with an empty flower pot. Kids learn the importance of honesty and how it pays off in the end.
    b. Discussion questions:
        - Why do you think Ping felt bad about his empty pot?
        - Have you ever tried something and not succeeded? How did that make you feel?
        - How did the other children grow beautiful flowers? Was that right or wrong for them to try other seeds? Encourage discussion about right versus wrong.
        - Can anyone tell the class the morale of this book? How does this morale relate to us?
5. Fill out the following worksheet.

Name: ______________________________ Date: __________

Next to each of the pots, write down a reason it is better to tell the truth.

Image 8.3

6. Ask students to keep track this week of when they had a choice about telling the truth or lying and what they did.

Session 4: Examining Prejudices and Biases

Objectives:

1. Students will understand the importance of checking themselves for prejudices and biases.
2. Students will identify their current feelings.

Materials:

Feelings journal

Pens/pencils

Book: *Sulwe* by Lupita Nyong'o

Duration: 30–40 minutes

Instructions:

1. Welcome group members. Remind them of the ground rules established during session 2. Ask students to complete the "How Are You Feeling?" page in their journal and share with the group.
2. Follow up on last week's lesson. Ask them to share about a time when they had a choice about telling the truth or lying and what they did.
3. Introduce today's lesson about prejudices and biases
   a. When you are hungry for a snack, do you usually want something sweet or something salty? Make a list on the board with who likes each. This shows what each person's preference is.
   b. Ask, "Is it okay that __________ likes salty things, not sweet things?"
   c. Define what a prejudice is: having an opinion or idea about a member of a group without really knowing that individual. A dislike is based on information about and experiences with a specific individual. Does that sound fair?
   d. Define what a bias is: prejudice in favor of or against one thing, person, or group compared with another, usually in a way considered to be unfair.
4. Read the book *Sulwe* by Lupita Nyong'o.
   a. Synopsis: *Sulwe* is a children's fiction picture book about a young girl who wishes for her dark skin to be lighter. The story is about learning to love oneself, no matter one's skin tone. *Sulwe* is an engaging story about the importance of standing up for what is right.
   b. Prereading questions:
      - Have you ever felt self-conscious or uncomfortable with how you look?
      - What can you do to feel more confident when you are self-conscious?
      - Who makes you feel better when you are feeling self-conscious?

- Have you heard someone make fun of the color of someone's skin, hair, or weight? What can you do if you see that happen?

c. Postreading questions:

- People at Sulwe's school made fun of her for the color of her skin. How did this make Sulwe feel? How did it affect her self-confidence?
- Sulwe's mom tells Sulwe, "Real beauty comes from your mind and your heart. It begins with how you see yourself, not how others see you." Did Sulwe see herself as beautiful? How did that change?
- You are beautiful just the way you are. What about you makes you beautiful inside and out?
- How do you celebrate your beauty?
- Activity: Invite students to draw a self-portrait. Ask them to draw themselves from shoulders up. Invite them to add favorite things (wearing their favorite shirt, add favorite book, color, food, etc.). Encourage students to share their self-portrait with the other students.

Session 5: Experiencing Self-Efficacy

Objectives:

1. Students will understand definition of self-efficacy.
2. Students will identify strengths.
3. Students will identify areas of challenge where they need to grow.
4. Students will create two to three goals.

Materials:

Emotions journal

Pens/pencils

Handout: "I Can Do It!"

Duration: 30–40 minutes

Instructions:

1. Welcome group members. Remind them of the ground rules established during the first session.
2. Have students complete the "How Are You Feeling?" page in their journal and share with the group.
3. Share definition of self-efficacy: the ability to define a goal, persevere, and see oneself as capable.
4. Underline the most important words in that sentence (ability, goal, persevere, capable).
5. Ask students to fill out worksheet; invite students to share their responses.

Session 5: I Can Do It!

Name: ______________________________ Date: ____________

I have abilities:	I have goals:
I have kept trying when:	**I have accomplished:**

Session 6: Having a Growth Mind-Set and Wrap-Up

Objectives:

1. Students will understand definition of a growth mind-set.
2. Students will understand benefits of using positive self-talk instead of negative.
3. Students will identify areas of growth during 6-week group session.
4. Students will create to to three goals for the future.

Materials:

Emotions journal

Pens/pencils

Worksheets: Growth Mind-Set

Duration: 30–40 minutes

Instructions:

1. Welcome group members. Remind them of the ground rules established during session 1.
2. Have students complete the "How Are You Feeling?" page in their journal and share with the group.
3. Discuss the difference between a growth mind-set and a fixed mind-set.

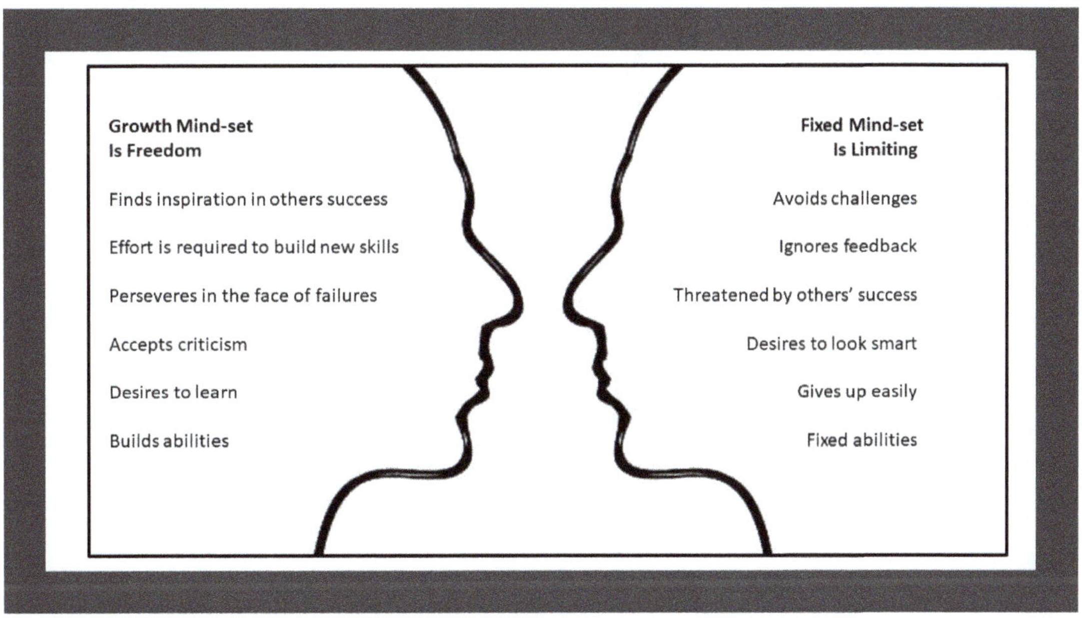

Image 8.4

a. What does it sound like? Remind students about the power of "yet."

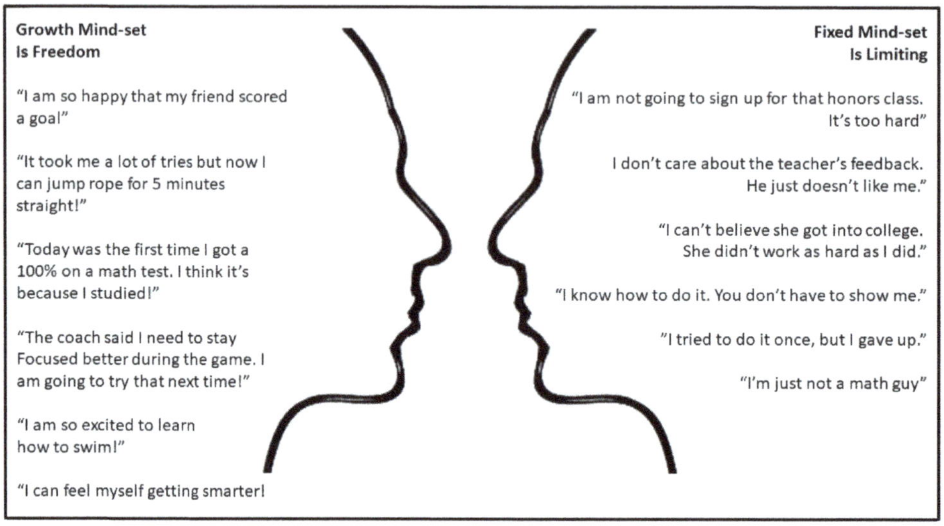

Image 8.5

b. What has your self-talk been like in the past week? List phrases either in the growth mind-set or fixed mind-set side.

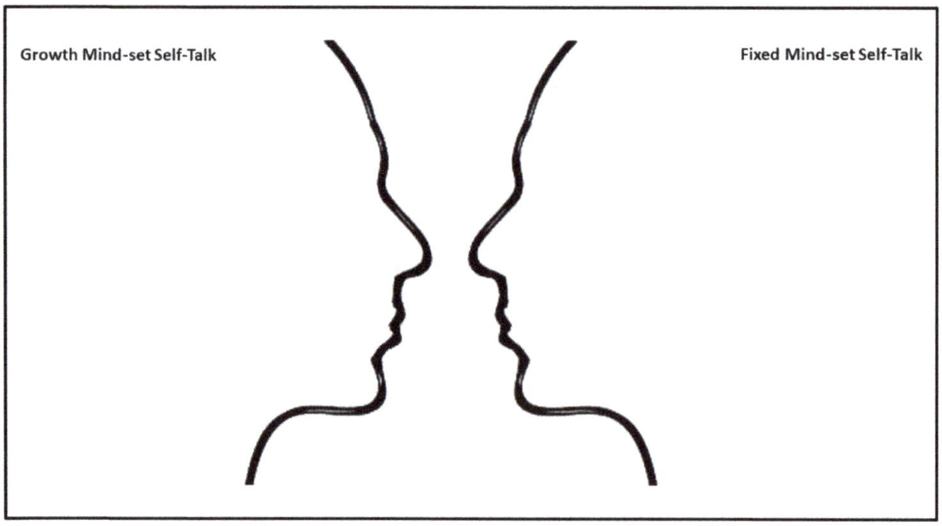

Image 8.6

c. What do you notice? Share this with your partner. Bring home and share with a parent or caregiver.

4. Reflect on their experience in the small group.
5. Set goals moving forward. Plan a "booster session" in a month's time so that we can reconnect and see how you are doing.

Books to share with students that highlight a growth mind-set:

A World Without Failures

The Lion, The Witch and The Wardrobe

The Mysterious Benedict Society

Post-Intervention Communication to Parent/Guardian

English Version

Dear Parents/Guardians,

This week we completed our small group focused on developing self-awareness. This 6-week group was designed to identify our emotions, our strengths, our areas for growth, and ways we can further develop our overall sense of self. We discussed our current feelings about ourselves while learning new things about our strengths and areas of growth. This involved reflection, sharing experiences, goal setting, and taking "brain breaks." Each student completed a pretest prior to the group and a posttest.

Our goals were to do the following:

- Increase self-awareness.
- Improve our ability to identify our emotions.
- Make the connection between our thoughts, feelings, values, and behavior.
- Discuss the importance of being honest.
- Develop a growth mind-set.

Make sure to review the journal and worksheets your student is bringing home today. There will be lots of things to discuss! If you have any questions about this intervention group or would like to discuss your student's participation in the group, please do not hesitate to reach out to me.

Sincerely,

Student Support Team Interventionist

Spanish Version

Queridos padres/guardianes,

Esta semana completamos nuestro pequeño grupo enfocado en desarrollar la autoconciencia. Este grupo de 6 semanas fue diseñado para identificar nuestras emociones, nuestras fortalezas, nuestras áreas de crecimiento y las formas en que podemos desarrollar aún más nuestro sentido general de nosotros mismos. Discutimos nuestros sentimientos actuales sobre nosotros mismos mientras aprendimos cosas nuevas sobre nuestras fortalezas y áreas de crecimiento. Esto implicó reflexionar, compartir experiencias, establecer objetivos y tomar "descansos para el cerebro". Cada estudiante completará una prueba previa al grupo y una prueba posterior cuando terminemos.

Nuestros objetivos eran:

- Aumentar la autoconciencia
- Mejorar nuestra capacidad para identificar nuestras emociones
- Hacer la conexión entre nuestros pensamientos, sentimientos, valores y comportamiento.
- Discutir la importancia de ser honesto.

- Desarrollar una mentalidad de crecimiento
- Asegúrese de revisar el diario y las hojas de trabajo que su estudiante traerá a casa hoy. ¡Habrá muchas cosas que discutir! Si tiene alguna pregunta sobre este grupo de intervención o desea hablar sobre la participación de su estudiante en el grupo, no dude en comunicarse conmigo.

Atentamente,

Intervencionista del equipo de apoyo al estudiante

Plan for Implementation Fidelity

The interventionist will ask the teacher to complete the following survey after week 3 to determine if the student is making progress because of the group. Interventionists will adhere to the lessons in the Tier 2 kit to ensure it is implemented with fidelity and make note of any challenges to implementation that they experience. This data and pre-/post-intervention should be reviewed with the MTSS team prior to utilizing this Tier 2 kit again.

Small Group Process Notes

References

Cook, E. T., Greenberg, M. T., & Kusche, C. A. (1994). The relations between emotional understanding, intellectual functioning, and disruptive behavior problems in elementary-school-aged children. *Journal of Abnormal Child Psychology*, 22, 205–219.

Denham, S. A. (1986). Social cognition, prosocial behavior, and emotion in preschoolers: Contextual validation. *Child Development*, 194–201.

Fine, S. E., Izard, C. E., Mostow, A. J., Trentacosta, C. J., & Ackerman, B. P. (2003). First grade emotion knowledge as a predictor of fifth grade self-reported internalizing behaviors in children from economically disadvantaged families. *Development and Psychopathology*, *15*(2), 331–342. https://doi.org/10.1017/S095457940300018X

Izard, C., Fine, S., Schultz, D., Mostow, A., Ackerman, B., & Youngstrom, E. (2001). Emotion knowledge as a predictor of social behavior and academic competence in children at risk. *Psychological Science*, *12*(1), 18–23.

Yale Center for Emotional Intelligence. (n.d.). *Emotions matter*. https://medicine.yale.edu/childstudy/services/community-and-schools-programs/center-for-emotional-intelligence/

Middle School Self-Awareness

Jaclyn Pierce and Emma Bee Schwarz

Description of Skill

Our friends at CASEL (2020) define *skill* as "the abilit[y] to understand one's own emotions, thoughts, and values and how they influence behavior across contexts. This includes capacities to recognize one's strengths and limitations with a well-grounded sense of confidence and purpose" (para. 3). In middle school, students are discovering new things about themselves every day. Often this essential learning happens in the context of peer interactions. Middle and high school students often compare themselves to peers and gauge their reactions to those of their peers. Developing self-awareness in the middle grades helps students to name their emotions, develop a more accurate perception of who they are, and acquaint themselves with their strong areas and ways they can grow. The hope is that, by doing this, middle schoolers can grow in self-confidence as they take responsibility for their actions and change course when necessary.

Pre-Intervention Communication With Parents/Guardians/Teachers in Languages Represented in the School

English Version

Dear Parents/Guardians,

Your [sixth, seventh, eighth] grader has been selected to take part in a small group focused on developing self-awareness. This 6-week group will take place [indicate when] and will not interfere with their academic classes. The goal of this group is to identify our emotions, our strengths, our areas for growth, and ways we can further develop our overall sense of self. We will discuss our current strategies for problem solving and decision-making while learning new approaches. This will involve reflection, sharing experiences, goal setting, and taking "brain breaks." Each student will complete a pretest prior to the group and a posttest as we finish up.

Our goals are to do the following:

- Increase self-awareness.
- Reduce attention problems.
- Improve executive functioning.
- Reduce acting-out behaviors.
- Increase awareness of stress while also improving well-being.

If you have any questions about this intervention group or would like to discuss your student's participation in the group, please do not hesitate to reach out to me.

Sincerely,

Student Support Team Interventionist

Spanish Version

Queridos padres/guardianes,

Su hijo de [6º, 7º, 8º] grado ha sido seleccionado para participar en un grupo pequeño centrado en desarrollar la conciencia de sí mismo. Este grupo de 6 semanas se llevará a cabo [indicar cuándo] y no interferirá con sus clases académicas. El objetivo de este grupo es identificar nuestras emociones, nuestras fortalezas, nuestras áreas de crecimiento y las formas en que podemos desarrollar aún más nuestro sentido general de nosotros mismos. Discutiremos nuestras estrategias actuales para la resolución de problemas y la toma de decisiones mientras aprendemos nuevos enfoques. Esto implicará reflexión, compartir experiencias, fijar objetivos y tomar "descansos para el cerebro". Cada estudiante completará una prueba previa al grupo y una prueba posterior cuando terminemos.

Nuestros objetivos son:

- Aumentar la autoconciencia
- Reducir el problema de atención
- Mejorar el funcionamiento ejecutivo
- Reducir las conductas de mal comportamiento
- Aumentar la conciencia sobre el estrés y al mismo tiempo mejorar el bienestar.
- Si tiene alguna pregunta sobre este grupo de intervención o desea hablar sobre la participación de su estudiante en el grupo, no dude en comunicarse conmigo.

Atentamente,

Intervencionista del equipo de apoyo al estudiante

Permission Slip (If Applicable)

After reading the description of this Tier 2 small group, I ______________________, give permission for my student ______________________ to take part in the group, which will meet on ______________________ from [date] to [date]. I understand that this group is confidential and that I will be made aware if my student is making good use of this group experience. Should I need to be contacted, the best number to reach me at is ______________________.

Hoja de permiso

Después de leer la descripción de este grupo pequeño de Nivel 2, yo ______________________ doy permiso para que mi estudiante ______________________ participe en el grupo que se reunirá el, ______________________ de [fecha] a [fecha]. Entiendo que este grupo es confidencial y que se me informará si mi estudiante está haciendo un buen uso de esta experiencia grupal. Si necesito que me contacten, el mejor número para comunicarse conmigo es ______________________.

Goals of Intervention

- Increase self-awareness.
- Reduce attention problems.
- Improve executive functioning.
- Reduce acting-out behaviors.
- Increase awareness of stress while also improving well-being.

CASEL Standards Addressed

- Identifying one's emotions
- Integrating personal and social identities
- Managing one's emotions

ASCA Mind-Sets and Behaviors

B-SMS 1. Responsibility for self and actions

B-SMS 2. Self-discipline and self-control

B-SMS 6. Ability to identify and overcome barriers

Materials Needed

Session	Materials
1	Individually wrapped candies
2	None
3	Session 3: worksheet
4	Session 4: Conflict chart
5	Session 5: Emotions chart, body scan chart
6	• One balloon per student • One cup of flour (alternatives: cornstarch, water beads, playdough, rice) • Funnel • Sharpie (optional)

Pre-/Post-Assessment

It's essential to collect data from students before and after the small group intervention in order to demonstrate the effectiveness of the intervention. When possible, it's helpful to use a norm referenced pscychometrically sound instrument.

Five Facet Mindfulness Questionnaire

Ruth A. Baer

Please rate each of the following statements using the scale provided. Write the number in the blank that best describes *your own opinion* of what is *generally true for you*.

1	2	3	4	5
Never or very rarely true	Rarely true	Sometimes true	Often true	Very often or always true

_________ When I'm walking, I deliberately notice the sensations of my body moving.
_________ I'm good at finding words to describe my feelings.
_________ I criticize myself for having irrational or inappropriate emotions.
_________ I perceive my feelings and emotions without having to react to them.
_________ When I do things, my mind wanders off and I'm easily distracted.
_________ When I take a shower or bath, I stay alert to the sensations of water on my body.
_________ I can easily put my beliefs, opinions, and expectations into words.
_________ I don't pay attention to what I'm doing because I'm daydreaming, worrying, or otherwise distracted.
_________ I watch my feelings without getting lost in them.
_________ I tell myself I shouldn't be feeling the way I'm feeling.
_________ I notice how foods and drinks affect my thoughts, bodily sensations, and emotions.
_________ It's hard for me to find the words to describe what I'm thinking.
_________ I am easily distracted.
_________ I believe some of my thoughts are abnormal or bad and I shouldn't think that way.
_________ I pay attention to sensations, such as the wind in my hair or sun on my face.
_________ I have trouble thinking of the right words to express how I feel about things.
_________ I make judgments about whether my thoughts are good or bad.
_________ I find it difficult to stay focused on what's happening in the present.
_________ When I have distressing thoughts or images, I "step back" and am aware of the thought or image without getting taken over by it.
_________ I pay attention to sounds, such as clocks ticking, birds chirping, or cars passing.
_________ In difficult situations, I can pause without immediately reacting.
_________ When I have a sensation in my body, it's difficult for me to describe it because I can't find the right words.

_________ It seems I am "running on automatic" without much awareness of what I'm doing.
_________ When I have distressing thoughts or images, I feel calm soon after.
_________ I tell myself that I shouldn't be thinking the way I'm thinking.
_________ I notice the smells and aromas of things.
_________ Even when I'm feeling terribly upset, I can find a way to put it into words.
_________ I rush through activities without being really attentive to them.
_________ When I have distressing thoughts or images I am able just to notice them without reacting.
_________ I think some of my emotions are bad or inappropriate and I shouldn't feel them.
_________ I notice visual elements in art or nature, such as colors, shapes, textures, or patterns of light and shadow.
_________ My natural tendency is to put my experiences into words.
_________ When I have distressing thoughts or images, I just notice them and let them go.
_________ I do jobs or tasks automatically without being aware of what I'm doing.
_________ When I have distressing thoughts or images, I judge myself as good or bad, depending what the thought/image is about.
_________ I pay attention to how my emotions affect my thoughts and behavior.
_________ I can usually describe how I feel at the moment in considerable detail.
_________ I find myself doing things without paying attention.
_________ I disapprove of myself when I have irrational ideas.

FFMQ Scoring Instructions

For all items marked "R," the scoring must be reversed. Change 1 to 5, 2 to 4, 4 to 2, and 5 to 1 (3 stays unchanged). Then sum the scores for each subscale.

Observing

1, 6, 11, 15, 20, 26, 31, 36

Describing

2, 7, 12R, 16R, 22R, 27, 32, 37

Acting with awareness

5R, 8R, 13R, 18R, 23R, 28R, 34R, 38R

Nonjudging of inner experience

3R, 10R, 14R, 17R, 25R, 30R, 35R, 39R

Nonreactivity to inner experience

4, 9, 19, 21, 24, 29, 33

Sessions 1–6

Week (Enter Dates)	Beginning of Week	End of Week
0/pre-intervention / /		Administer FFMQ pretest; teachers complete teacher survey
1 / /	Lesson 1	
2 / /	Lesson 2	Teachers complete teacher survey
3 / /	Lesson 3	
4 / /	Lesson 4	Teachers complete teacher survey
5 / /	Lesson 5	
6 / /	Lesson 6	Administer FFMQ posttest; teachers complete teacher survey

Session 1: Attention—Mindful Eating

Objective:

1. Students will exercise their attention "muscle" by learning how to practice mindful eating.

Materials:

Individually wrapped candies

Duration: 10–15 minutes

Instructions:

1. Welcome students and explain the purpose of the group.
2. Invite group members to provide input on group ground rules. Record them on poster paper and ask students to sign the poster paper.
3. Conduct icebreaker.
4. Explain to students that attention is something that can be practiced and trained like a muscle, and you can do this by focusing deeply on one thing. Put on some quiet, soothing music. Pass out candy and use the following script: "For this activity, I want you to focus on observing. Try not to think in words, just notice. Let's take three deep breaths as we begin. In, hold, out (three times).
5. Say, "Look at your candy in the wrapper. This is the most important thing right now. Observe the colors and shape. Reach out and notice what it feels like to use your arm. Feel the wrapper in your fingers. Is it slippery, crinkly?" (pause).
6. "Slowly open the wrapper, and resist any urge to tear into it. Take a deep breath. Look at the candy. Bring it to your nose and notice its scent" (pause).
7. "Take a small bite and close your eyes if comfortable. Hold it on your tongue for a bit" (pause).
8. "Begin to slowly chew. How does it feel between your teeth? Flavor, texture? As you swallow, notice the physical sensations. Take a deep breath. Return when ready."
9. Ask students to share their experience of participating in this exercise.

Session 2: Attention—Awareness of Distractibility

Objective:

1. Students will know what to do when they are distracted and utilize breathing spaces. Over time these will help them recognize when they need to hit "restart."

Materials: N/A

Duration: 15 minutes

Instructions:

1. Welcome students and remind them of the group ground rules.
2. Check in about the past week.
3. Teach students how to use a breathing space. When distracted, or feeling any strong emotion, they can use this to gather themselves and start fresh. Direct them to close their eyes or gaze softly at a point a few feet away and take three deep breaths. Slowly direct "in, hold, out" (three times).
4. Next, ask students to scan their body to find where they feel their emotion. Direct them to kindly say to themselves, "It is okay to feel this way" as they focus on breathing into that part of their body. If they get distracted, that is okay; just return to the breath. Have them take a few more breaths, then have them open their eyes. Tell them that the more they practice this, the more they will recognize when they need it.
5. Finally, have students discuss when and how this might be useful. Ask for specific examples.

Session 3: Conflict Prevention

Objective:

1. Students will be more aware of their emotions and learn to respond instead of reacting.

Materials:

Session 3 worksheet

Duration: 15 minutes

Instructions:

1. Welcome students and remind them of the group ground rules.
2. Check in about the past week.
3. Start the group with five deep breaths (in, hold, out).
4. Pass out the "Lesson 3: Recognizing When We Need to Step Away" worksheet and explain that we can prevent fights by learning more about ourselves and responding mindfully rather than reacting.
5. Remind students that they can take breathing spaces as needed and not to judge themselves or their feelings.
6. Guide two deep breaths. Ask students to each offer one thing they could have done differently when they realized the situation was going to escalate.
7. (Look for "Leave the room," "Take a breathing space," "Say no thanks")
8. Ask them to practice this skill between now and next group.

Session 3: Recognizing When We Need to Step Away

Even while doing this, take breathing spaces as needed. Think back to a time you had an argument or fight with another student. Briefly describe the argument in two sentences:

____

____

Take a deep breath. What were you doing right before the argument started?

____

What were your thoughts right before it?

____

____

What did it feel like in your physical body? Where (i.e., chest, stomach, hands, etc.)?

____

____

What does it feel like in your body when thinking about it now?

____

____

Session 4: Conflict Resolution

Objective:

1. Students will learn to solve problems without needing a teacher's assistance by understanding conflicts and how to resolve/de-escalate them.

Materials:

Session 4 conflict resolution chart

Duration: 15 minutes

Instructions:

1. Welcome students and remind them of the group ground rules.
2. Check in about the past week.
3. With a small group of students, ask them to describe different conflicts that might occur at school. Hand out the conflict chart. Select a few examples and discuss how the steps from their conflict chart would apply to each situation.
4. Have the students role-play example situations, either as themselves or with toys, action figures, or puppets.
5. Introduce the idea of using their words to express feelings in place of blaming someone else or using physical aggression.
6. Optional: Have students create/draw/color their own conflict chart that matches the example. Bonus points for adding their own creative examples/scenarios.

Conflict Resolution Chart

Pause	Take a moment before you lose control of your temper It could make the conflict worse
Share	Share what you feel is the problem What is causing the disagreement? What do you want?
Listen	Listen to the other person's ideas and feelings
Think	Think of solutions that will support both your needs

Image 8.7

Session 5: Behavior Awareness and Aggression Management

Objective:

1. Students will use a chart to indicate what emotions they are feeling and then pinpoint where it is on the body they feel it. Once they can name and identify their emotions, they will then use mindfulness techniques to tame their emotions.

Materials:

"Name It to Tame it!"

Emotions chart and body scan chart

Duration: 15 minutes

Instructions:

1. Welcome students and remind them of the group ground rules.
2. Check in about the past week.
3. Introduce topic for the week: behavior awareness and aggression management.
4. Explain that the first step is to label the emotion. Have students use the example emotion chart to find which one (or two) best describes what they are feeling in that moment.
5. Have them said it or describe it out loud: "I am angry," "I am frustrated," and so on.
6. After labeling the emotion, have them focus on where they feel that in their body. Ask them questions such as these: "Do you feel tension or tightness?" "Are you clenching your teeth?" "Are you holding/making a fist?" "Does your skin feel hot?"
7. Take a moment to discuss and describe the emotions in detail; ask the student(s) to tell a story using these emotions and feelings.
8. Explain how labeling our emotions can help to externalize them, allowing us to see more clearly and have a sense of control over those feelings.
9. When helping the student to identify these emotions, be sure to validate them and help them feel understood.

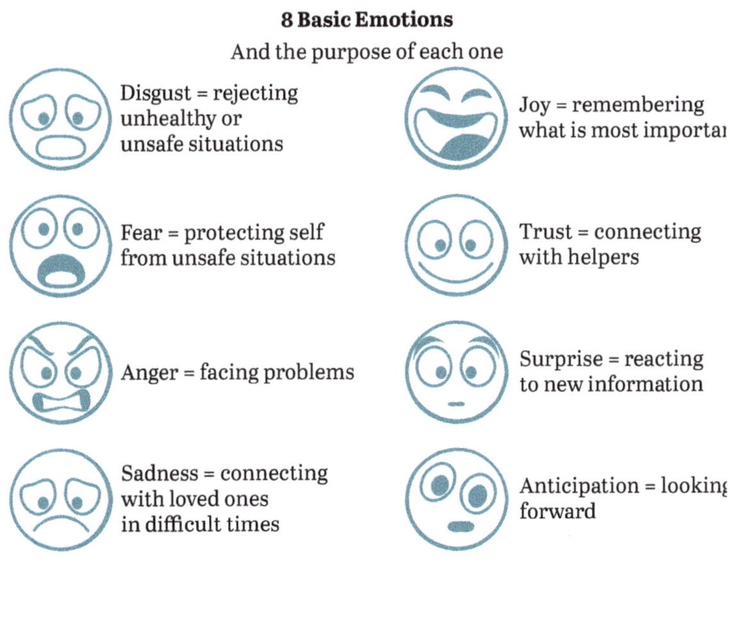

Image 8.8

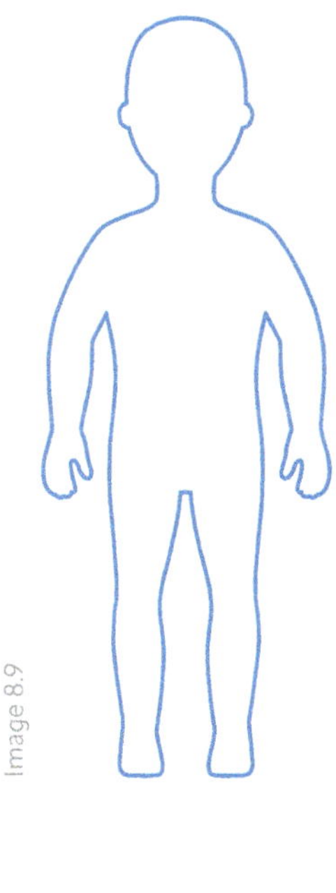

Image 8.9

Session 6: Aggression Prevention

Objective:

1. Students will learn to recognize their warning signs of aggression, tension, anxiety, and so forth and will utilize their coping techniques such as using a stress ball. They will make their own stress ball as a stimulus to help maintain focus and prevent negative behavior during class.

Materials:

One balloon per student

One cup of flour (alternatives: cornstarch, water beads, playdough, rice)

Funnel

Sharpie (optional)

Duration: 15–20 minutes

Instructions:

1. Welcome students and remind them of the group ground rules.
2. Check in about the past week.
3. Students will review the ways they recognize their warning signs (e.g., losing temper, fidgeting, chewing on pencils/pens, etc.) when behaviors such as aggression or anger start to emerge during class. To avoid these, students will learn to use appropriate replacement behaviors such as playing with a stress ball. Having a tangible item to hold and manipulate is a helpful coping tool to maintain focus.
4. Stress ball–making instructions:
    a. Blow up the balloon, then deflate before starting (this stretches it out, making it easier to fill).
    b. Pull the opening of the balloon over the small end of funnel.
    c. Gently pour flour into the funnel. Shake/tap the funnel to guide the flour down into the balloon. Pro-tip: Use a pen or pencil to help push more flour through if it gets stuck.
    d. Add more flour until the desired size is reached, typically the size of a tennis ball.
    e. Remove the funnel and tie a knot in the balloon. Get the knot as close as possible to the base of the balloon.
    f. Have students write their names or decorate with the Sharpie.
    g. *Optional: Cut the neck off a second balloon and wrap over the stress ball to hide the knot and it adds a double layer of durability.
5. Summarize the activities they took part in during the group. Ask them to share favorite activities.

6. Invite students to set a goal for their self-awareness moving forward.
7. Invite students to share gratitude for someone in the group for something specific that they did during their time together.
8. Explain that a booster session will take place in one month's time to see how they are doing.

Post-Intervention Communication to Parent/Guardian

Interventionist(s) and or teachers will speak with parent/guardian after the group is finished to discuss their student's specific goals for the group experience and their progress toward the goals. Parents/guardians will be asked if the student is generalizing these skills at home, in after-school activities, and in other environments. A plan will be made for further intervention if necessary.

Plan for Implementation Fidelity

The interventionist will ask the teacher to complete the survey below after week 3 to determine if the student is making progress because of the group. Interventionists will adhere to the lessons in the Tier 2 kit to ensure it is implemented with fidelity and make note of any challenges to implementation they experience. This data and pre-/post-assessment should be reviewed with the MTSS team prior to utilizing this Tier 2 kit again.

Small Group Process Notes

Teacher Survey: Progress Monitoring

Student #: ______________ Teacher: ______________

Week # (circle one) 0 2 4 6

Mark an x for each behavior, 1 being least frequently displayed and 5 the most.

The student ...	1	2	3	4	5
Talks out of turn					
Argues with peers					
Argues with adults					
Is visibly distracted					
Needs redirection					
Lashes out in anger					
Makes careless mistakes in work					
Avoids or resists hard work					
Interrupts activities, conversations					

Resources

Bluth, K., & Blanton, P. W. (2013). Mindfulness and self-compassion: Exploring pathways to adolescent emotional well-being. *Journal of Child and Family Studies*, *23*(7), 1298–1309. https://doi.org/10.1007/s10826-013-9830-2

Cheang, R., Gillions, A., & Sparkes, E. (2019). Do mindfulness-based interventions increase empathy and compassion in children and adolescents: A systematic review. *Journal of Child and Family Studies*, *28*(7), 1765–1779. https://doi.org/10.1007/s10826-019-01413-9

Martinez, T., & Zhao, Y. (2018). The impact of mindfulness training on middle grades students' office discipline referrals. *RMLE Online : Research in Middle Level Education*, *41*(3), 1–8. https://doi.org/10.1080/19404476.2018.1435840

Sanger, K. L., Thierry, G., & Dorjee, D. (2018). Effects of school based mindfulness training on emotion processing and well being in adolescents: Evidence from event related potentials. *Developmental Science*, *21*(5), e12646. https://doi.org/10.1111/desc.12646

Van de Weijer-Bergsma, E., Formsma, A., de Bruin, E., & Bögels, S. (2012). The effectiveness of mindfulness training on behavioral problems and attentional functioning in adolescents with ADHD. *Journal of Child and Family Studies*, *21*(5), 775–787. https://doi.org/10.1007/s10826-011-9531-7

Self-Awareness for High School Students

Dr. Peg Donohue

Description of Skill

For teens, self-awareness becomes increasingly important as they mature. The high school years are a time when students begin to develop a sense of self. During this time of great change, students are often more self-conscious about themselves and their new-found "identity" than at any other time in their lives. People can identify with multiple social groups. For example, adolescents may focus on individuals who share their same gender, sexual preference, race, nationality, or political party. In time, adolescents discover personal identity, which becomes a cohesive sense of self. This cohesive self includes ideas about all of their group identities, as well as their values and goals. If asked about their identity, an adolescent might say something like "I'm an African American male; I want to give back to my community, make the world a better place, and take care of my family."

While developing a sense of identity, adolescents will reflect on the age-old question, "Who am I?" It is a process of trial and error. Many teens will switch social groups, try a new sport, change their look, or explore a new subject area as they search for an identity. This is a time when some adolescents might experiment with risky behaviors, including using drugs or alcohol. Even though identity development often begins during the teen years, it is a life-long process. The exercises in this Tier 2 kit are meant to support healthy identity development and can be used in either small group counseling or as part of an advisory program.

Pre-Intervention Communication With Parents/Guardians/Teachers in Languages Represented in the School

English Version

Dear Parents/Guardians,

Your [ninth, 10th, 11th, or 12th] grader has been selected to take part in a small group focused on fostering self-awareness. This 6-week group will take place [indicate when] and will not interfere with their academic classes. The goal of this group is to delve into clarifying students' values, goals, strengths, and weaknesses. This will involve reflection, sharing experiences, and completing thought provoking handouts. Each student will complete a pretest prior to the group and a posttest as we finish up.

Our goals are to explore and master how to do the following:

- Support a healthy sense of self and positive identity development.
- Identify strengths, areas that they need to improve.
- Identify role models to support their growth.
- Clarify values and goals.
- Identify and follow through on commitments they make.

If you have any questions about this intervention group or would like to discuss your student's participation in the group, please do not hesitate to reach out to me.

Sincerely,

Student Support Team Interventionist

Spanish Version

Queridos padres/guardianes,

Su hijo de [9.º, 10.º, 11.º o 12.º] grado ha sido seleccionado para participar en un grupo pequeño centrado en fomentar la autoconciencia. Este grupo de 6 semanas se llevará a cabo [indicar cuándo] y no interferirá con sus clases académicas. El objetivo de este grupo es profundizar en clarificar los valores, objetivos, fortalezas y debilidades de los estudiantes. Esto implicará reflexionar, compartir experiencias y completar folletos que inviten a la reflexión. Cada estudiante completará una prueba previa al grupo y una prueba posterior cuando terminemos.

Nuestros objetivos son explorar y dominar cómo:

- Apoyar un sentido saludable de uno mismo; desarrollo de identidad positiva
- Identificar fortalezas, áreas que necesitan mejorar.
- Identificar modelos a seguir para apoyar su crecimiento.
- Aclarar valores y objetivos.
- Identificar y cumplir los compromisos que asumen.
- Si tiene alguna pregunta sobre este grupo de intervención o le gustaría hablar sobre la participación de su estudiante en el grupo, no dude en comunicarse conmigo.

Atentamente,

Intervencionista del equipo de apoyo al estudiante

Permission Slip (If Applicable)

After reading the description of this Tier 2 small group, I ______________, give permission for my student ________________ to take part in the group which will meet on ______________ from [date] to [date]. I understand that this group is confidential and that I will be made aware if my student is making good use of this group experience. Should I need to be contacted, the best number to reach me at is ________________ .

Hoja de permiso

Después de leer la descripción de este grupo pequeño de Nivel 2, yo ________________ , doy permiso para que mi estudiante ________________ participe en el grupo que se reunirá el ________________ de [fecha] a [fecha]. Entiendo que este grupo es confidencial y que se me informará si mi estudiante está haciendo un buen uso de esta experiencia grupal. Si necesito que me contacten, el mejor número para comunicarse conmigo es ________________ .

Goals of Intervention

- Support a healthy sense of self and positive identity development.
- Identify strengths, areas that they need to improve.
- Identify role models to support their growth.
- Clarify values and goals.
- Identify and follow through on commitments they make.

CASEL Standards Addressed

- Identifying one's emotions
- Integrating personal and social identities
- Experiencing self-efficacy
- Setting personal and collective goals

ASCA Mind-Sets and Behaviors

B-SMS 1. Responsibility for self and actions

B-SMS 2. Self-discipline and self-control

B-SMS 6. Ability to identify and overcome barriers

Pre-/Post-Assessment

Statement	
I feel like I know who I am.	Very true 5 4 3 2 1 Not true at all
I can name three to four strengths of mine.	Very true 5 4 3 2 1 Not true at all
I can name three to four weaknesses of mine.	Very true 5 4 3 2 1 Not true at all
I feel confident I can improve in areas where I still need to grow.	Very true 5 4 3 2 1 Not true at all
I have a role model who I look up to because of the personal and professional choices they have made.	Very true 5 4 3 2 1 Not true at all
I can clearly state my five most important values.	Very true 5 4 3 2 1 Not true at all
I can state two to three goals I have for my future.	Very true 5 4 3 2 1 Not true at all
I am dependable when it comes to following through on commitments I have made.	Very true 5 4 3 2 1 Not true at all

Sessions 1–8

Session 1: Supporting a Healthy Sense of Self—Positive Identity Development

Objectives:

1. Students will understand what it means to develop their sense of self.
2. Students will understand benefits of developing a positive identity.

Materials:

"Where I'm From" worksheet

Large poster paper for ground rules

Duration: 30–40 minutes

Instructions:

1. Welcome students and explain the purpose of the group.
2. Invite group members to provide input on group ground rules. Record them on poster paper and ask students to sign the poster paper.
    a. Share the story of your name with the group.
    b. Do you like your name? Why or why not?
    c. Do you have any nicknames? What do they mean to you?
    d. "Where I'm From" introduction

Where I'm From

Name: ____________________

I am from ____ (specific ordinary item), from ____________________ (product name) and ______________________________ ____.

I am from the _______________________________________ (home description: two adjectives and sensory detail)

I am from the _______________________________________ (plant, flower, natural detail)

I am from ____ (family tradition) and __________________________ (family trait) from ____________________ (family member name) and ________________________ (*another family member*) and ________________ (family name) and ____________________ (another family name).

I am from ______________________________________ and ______________________________ ______________________________________ (descriptions of family tendency).

From ____________________ and ____________________ (two things you were told as a child).

I am from ____ (place of birth and family ancestry), ____ (two food items representing family) ____ (specific family story about specific person and detail) ____________________ (another detail) and the ____________________ (another specific detail about another family member).

I am from ______________________ (special memory, location of family picture, and detail about its worth). I am ____________________ (name), and I am __________________________.

Mind Mapping Exercise

Encourage students to complete a mind map whereby they write down who they perceive themselves to be in various areas of life. Spend a few minutes on each of the following mind map topics:

Relationships: List all the different relationship roles that they have, such as brother, son, grandson, nephew, student, employee, boyfriend, and so on.
Cultural Identity: List cultural aspects of their life, such as religion/faith, ethnicity, language, nationality, and so on.
Likes: List their favorite activities, hobbies, music, sports, TV shows, and so on.
Dislikes: List the activities, music, sports, TV shows, and so on that they don't care for.
Hopes: List things that they want to do in the future, such as jobs, how many kids they want, and so on.
Dreams: List things they want to see happen for themselves in the future, such as graduating from college, earning a living, traveling, and so on.

Some young people will prefer to visualize these rather than simply writing their answers down. Therefore, have colored pens or pencils on hand so that they can draw/sketch/doodle their answers instead.

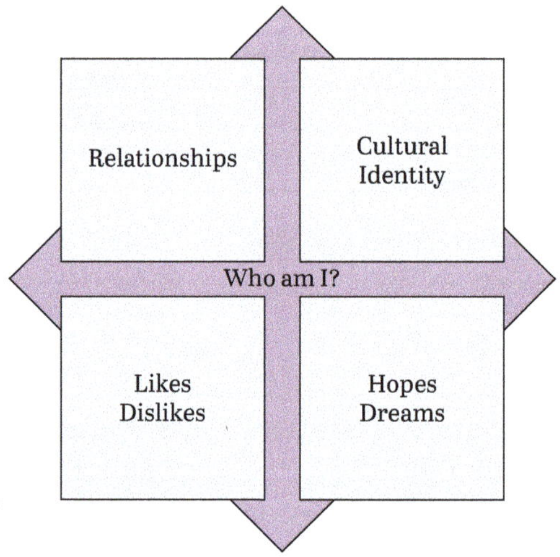

Image 8.10

Session 2: Identify Strengths, Areas That Need Improvement

Objective:

1. Students will understand their strengths.
2. Students will understand areas that need improvement.

Duration: 30–40 minutes

Instructions:

1. Welcome students and remind them of the group ground rules.
2. Check in about their week. Did they use the skill we taught last week?

Ask teens to complete the handout. They will take inventory of areas of strength and weakness. For each area they check off whether it is a strength or weakness and jot down either how it became an area of strength or how they might improve in that area.

Twenty Strengths and Weaknesses Activity

Characteristic	Strength or weakness?	If this is an area of strength, how did you become strong in this area? If this is an area of growth, how could you improve?
I enjoy learning.	S W	
I am courageous.	S W	
I love my family.	S W	
I am good to my friends.	S W	
I take care of my health.	S W	
I am respectful of others.	S W	
I am kind to strangers.	S W	
I follow rules.	S W	
I manage most of my responsibilities independently.	S W	
I persevere when things get difficult.	S W	
I can identify my emotions.	S W	
I can control my emotions.	S W	
I am good at_______ (hobbies).	S W	
I would like to know more about _______.	S W	
Other	S W	
Other	S W	
Other	S W	

Invite students to share three to four of their items with the group.

Session 3: Identify Role Models to Support Their Growth

Objectives:

1. Students will understand the purpose of seeking role models.
2. Students will identify a role model in their community.

Materials:

Chart paper and marker

Half sheet of paper per student

Pens/pencils

Duration: 30–40 minutes

Instructions:

1. Welcome students and remind them of the group ground rules.
2. Check in about their week. Did they use the skill we taught last week?
3. Invite students to help brainstorm the definition of a role model. Keep a list of attributes that students share for role models.
4. Give each student a half sheet of paper. On one side, ask them to write down (at the top) the name of a role model they interact with in their town or family. This is someone they could reach out to.
5. On the other side, ask them to write down (at the top) the name of a role model who is a celebrity or a figure in history.
6. Ask the students to name three to four qualities that make that person a role model and to brainstorm four to five questions they would ask that person.
7. Share in pairs or as a whole group.
8. Encourage students to ask their local/family role model the questions they posed and report back during the next group meeting.

Session 4: Forced Identities

Objectives:

1. Students will consider and discuss different key aspects of their identities.
2. Students will explore what elements of their identities they identify with most.

Materials:

Paper signs

Markers

Duration: 30–40 minutes

Note: This activity is best suited for groups who have already established trust with one another.

Instructions:

1. Hang up signs around the room with space for students to move near. Each sign should list one of the following words: *race*, *ethnicity*, **sexual orientation*, *gender*, *first language*, *religion*, *body size/shape*, *physical ability*, *mental illness*, *socioeconomic status*, *education*, and *age*. Feel free to add or change identity markers to fit your group. (*Note: Be aware of what students have already shared or feel comfortable sharing about their sexual orientation. This activity is not meant to "out" any students who are not comfortable doing so. Only include this category if students have already shared freely about their sexual identity.)
2. Welcome students and remind them of the group ground rules.
3. Check in about their week. Did they interview a role model? Ask them to share highlights of their interview.
4. Explain purpose: "Our identities are multifaceted. We are not just teenagers or high school students. Today we are going to explore those multiple identities. You will be given options and can choose to share about that aspect of your identity or, as always, pass."
5. Take time to review each of the identity signs on the wall.
6. To play, ask students to move closest to the identity that resonates the most with them as you read a series of statements one-by-one.

Here are some suggested statements:

This is the identity I most like to share with others.
This is the identity I am less inclined to share with others.
This is the identity that I have most in common with my close friends.
This is the identity I am having trouble discussing.
This is the identity that I think most people judge me by.
This is the identity that brings me joy.
This is the identity that causes me the most pain.
This is the identity I believe is the most important to me right now, in this room.

7. After reading each statement, invite volunteers to share why they settled on that identity marker. Sharing their specific identities is optional.
8. Debriefing questions: What was it like to have to choose only one identity from around the room? Which question(s) were easiest for you to respond to? Which ones did you struggle with? Process as a whole group or in pairs.

Source: Adapted from Tandet, J., "7 Easy Activities that Encourage Students to Open Up About Identity and Privilege," Modern Campus, 2022, https://sapro.moderncampus.com/blog/7-easy-activities-that-encourage-students-to-open-up-about-identity-and-privilege.

Session 5: Clarifying Values and Goals

Objectives:

1. Students will understand the definition of "values" and be able to name three to five core values.
2. Students will understand the benefits of setting goals for their personal growth.

Materials:

Core values word list and personal values chart

Pens/pencils

Duration: 30–40 minutes

Instructions:

1. Welcome students and remind them of the group ground rules.
2. Check in about their week. Any leftover thoughts, feelings, or reactions to our activity last week?
3. Review the list of values and ask students to give examples of five to seven of them.
4. Invite students to circle five that they think are most important to them.
5. Write those on the center most circle on the worksheet.
6. Discuss the next circle: family. What values might they put there?
7. Discuss the next circle: friends. What values might they put there?
8. Discuss the next circle: society. What values might they put there?
9. Give the students time to work independently.
10. Discuss answers. What similarities and differences do you see?
11. How might conflicting values impact you and your key relationships?

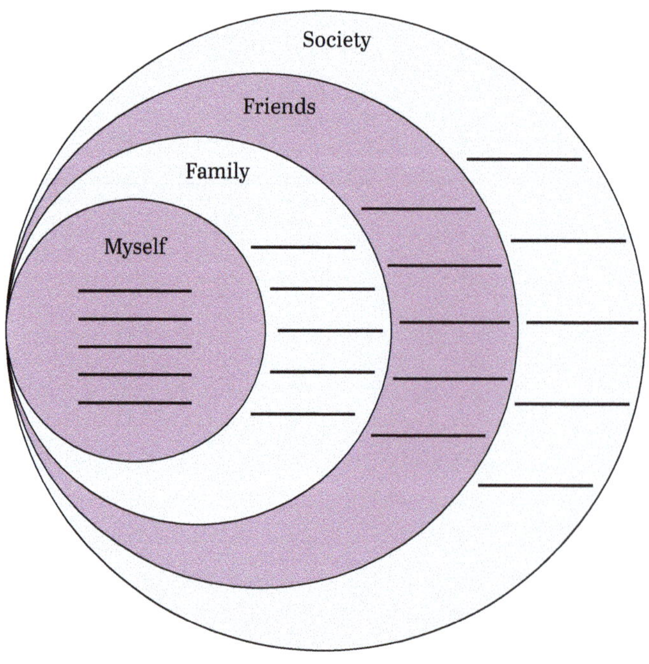

Image 8.11

Core Values List

Authenticity	Achievement	Adventure	Authority	Autonomy
Balance	Beauty	Boldness	Compassion	Challenge
Citizenship	Community	Competency	Contribution	Creativity
Curiosity	Determination	Fairness	Faith	Fame
Friendships	Fun	Growth	Happiness	Honesty
Humor	Influence	Inner harmony	Justice	Kindness
Knowledge	Leadership	Learning	Love	Loyalty
Meaningful work	Openness	Optimism	Peace	Pleasure
Poise	Popularity	Recognition	Religion	Reputation
Respect	Responsibility	Security	Self-respect	Service
Spirituality	Stability	Success	Status	Trustworthiness
Wealth	Wisdom			

Session 6: Identifying and Following Through on Commitments They Make

Objectives:

1. Students will identify three to five commitments they currently have.
2. Students will understand the importance of following through on their commitments.

Materials:

Worksheet

Pens/pencils

Duration: 30–40 minutes

Instructions:

1. Welcome students and remind them of the group ground rules.
2. Check in about their week. Did they think about their values and goals that we discussed last week? Did they talk about the activity with any of their mentors or role models?
3. Ask students a list of commitments they have in their day-to-day life.
4. Using the worksheet, indicate if these commitments are easy or difficult to keep and why.
5. Ask students to reflect on a time when someone did not keep a commitment they made and how it made them feel.
6. Pair-share or share with the group.

My Current Commitments

Name: ______________________________ Date: ________________

Commitment(s)	Easy to Keep	Hard to Keep	Why?

Share about a time when someone kept a commitment they made to you.

How did it make you feel?

Share about a time when someone did not keep a commitment they made to you.

How did it make you feel?

Session 7: How Do I Share Who I Am With Others?

Objectives:

1. Students will understand which aspects of their identity they share freely with others and which they keep hidden.
2. Students will understand the impact their social media presence or regular posts have on the way others view them.

Duration: 30–40 minutes

Instructions:

1. Welcome students and remind them of the group ground rules.
2. Check in about their week. Did they think about their commitments and their ability to follow through on them? Do they have any new insights on this?
3. Ask students to share a recent post they made on social media in which they shared something about themselves. If they don't regularly post, ask them to share some ways they tell others who they are through other avenues (dress, choice of activities, engagement in class, friends, etc.).
4. Discuss ways that we can misunderstand someone's image based on those things (social media, dress, choice of activities, engagement in class, friends, etc.).
5. Ask group participants to discuss a time when they felt misunderstood because of the way they were projecting their image.
6. Give students time to share in pairs and as a group.

Session 8: Write a Letter to Your Future Self

Objectives:

1. Students will synthesize their personal learning over the past 8 weeks in a letter to themselves.
2. Students will set goals for their continued self-awareness growth.
3. Students will acknowledge support they received from each member of the group.

Materials:

Self-awareness goals sheets

Blank cards (optional for final activity)

Duration: 30–40 minutes

Instructions:

1. Welcome students and remind them of the group ground rules.
2. Check in about their week. Did they use the skill we taught last week?
3. Complete pre-/post-assessment.
4. Discuss what they learned about themselves in the group.
5. Discuss how the group was similar or dissimilar to what they thought it would be.
6. Ask students to write themselves a letter, including things that they learned about themselves during the group and things they want to remember moving forward. The letter should have an encouraging tone.
7. Invite students to share excerpts from their letters with group members.
8. Letters should be sent to participants 6 months after the group is completed.
9. Students will set goals for continuing to develop their self-awareness.
10. Closure activity: Invite students to identify one thing they have appreciated about each group member (e.g., the support they have given, their ability to listen, a way they have been challenged or served as a role model, their courage to share openly, etc.). This activity can be completed through whole group conversation or by asking students to sign a card to each person.

Self-Awareness Goals

Name: ______________________________ Date: ________________

Three things I learned about myself during this group:

1.
2.
3.

Two ways I can challenge myself to continue to improve:

1.
2.

Please finish these statements:

1. I am proud of myself because ______________________________.
2. A role model I can turn to is ______________________________.
3. Knowing myself better helps me to ______________________________.
4. One way I can support others to become more self aware is to ________________.
5. ____.

Post-Intervention Communication to Parent/Guardian

English Version

Dear Parents/Guardians,

We have had an exciting time discussing what goes into developing one's identity as a high school student. As you will remember, answering the question "Who am I?" can be a confusing part of growing up. The students in the group were respectful to one another as they shared their answers and explored the following topics:

Dislikes and likes
Values (ours, our families, etc.)
Goals
Role models
Commitments

Make sure to spend some time with your child discussing some of the things they may have learned about themselves during the 8-week group. This learning is an essential part of their high school experience and can be very instructive as they begin developing a postsecondary plan. As always, we are here to answer any questions you might have. Thank you for sharing your very special young person with us!

Sincerely,

Student Support Team Interventionists

Spanish Version

Queridos padres/guardianes,

Hemos pasado un momento emocionante discutiendo lo que implica desarrollar la identidad de uno como estudiante de secundaria. Como recordarás, responder a la pregunta "¿quién soy yo?" puede ser una parte confusa del crecimiento. Los estudiantes del grupo fueron respetuosos unos con otros mientras compartían sus respuestas y exploraban los siguientes temas:

Gustos y disgustos
Valores (nuestros, nuestras familias, etc.)
Objetivos
Modelos a seguir
Compromisos

Asegúrese de pasar algún tiempo con su hijo/hija discutiendo algunas de las cosas que pudo haber aprendido sobre sí mismo durante el grupo de 8 semanas. Este aprendizaje es una parte esencial de su experiencia en la escuela secundaria y puede ser muy instructivo cuando comienzan a desarrollar un plan postsecundario. Como siempre, estamos aquí para responder cualquier pregunta que puedas tener. ¡Gracias por compartir con nosotros a tu joven tan especial!

Atentamente,

Intervencionistas del equipo de apoyo estudiantil

Plan for Implementation Fidelity

To achieve the intended outcomes of this intervention, it is helpful to colead the small group with a colleague, reflect on student responses to the activities, and seek support to keep engagement in the group high. Tier 2 small group facilitators should seek peer coaching and ask for feedback to make sure the intervention is implemented with fidelity.

Small Group Process Notes

Reference

CASEL. (2020). *CASEL's Framework: What are the Core Competence Areas and Where are They Promoted?* CASEL Framework Briefs. https://casel.org/casel-sel-framework-11-2020/?view=true

Credits

CHAPTER 9

Tier 2 Intervention Kits for Coping Skills

Coping Skills for Elementary School Students

Breanna Soto

Description of Skill

Self-management skills help students cope with challenging events throughout their day. The skills that create the centerpiece of this Tier 2 kit are essential for students as they progress through elementary, middle, and high school. Managing one's emotions and responses to stress is a lifelong challenge. Any efforts to create space between stimulus and response gives students more coping strategies to draw from when they experience adversity. Coping strategies are important for students of all ages when it comes to dealing with different situations that occur during the school day. We need to first define coping, which is "the ability with which one handles a stressful event" (Maykrantz & Houghton, 2020, p. 89). A stressful event can be defined differently by different students, meaning that a stressful event for one student may not be as stressful for another. This Tier 2 kit is designed for students in grades 3–6 to help learn differences in levels of situations while also helping them learn about helpful coping strategies.

Grades 2 through 6 were chosen for this kit because this is a time when students may be struggling to navigate through some situations but are still open to learning how to cope. A study by Eacott and Frydenberg (2009) found that young people experience a slump in their ability to cope between the ages 14–16 years suggesting that having students learn about coping skills sooner than later is beneficial. The purpose of this Tier 2 kit is to help students identify potential coping skills to use during stressful times. Some people may think that students in elementary school may not be faced with stressful situations; however, they can still be affected by stress in their own ways. Helping students be able to cope with stress is key to helping them grow because "typically-developing youth who have well developed coping skills have been shown to be more resilient to traumatic events" (Katz et al., 2020, p. 4070). Traumatic events like COVID-19 can take a toll on students and helping them sooner than later should be one of our top priorities. Our students and their mental health should be one of our top priorities, and helping them with coping skills can help in the long run.

Pre-Intervention Communication With Parents/Guardians/Teachers in Languages Represented in the School

English Version

Dear Parents/Guardians,

Your [fourth, fifth or sixth] grader has been selected to take part in a small group focused on self-management skills. This 6-week group will take place [indicate when] and will not interfere with their academic classes. The goal of this group is to delve into how to best manage stress and emotionally charged situations. We will discuss our current strategies for problem solving and managing emotions while learning new approaches. This will involve reflection, sharing experiences, and learning new coping strategies and case scenarios. Each student will complete a pretest prior to the group and a posttest as we finish up.

If you have any questions about this intervention group or would like to discuss your student's participation in the group, please do not hesitate to reach out to me.

Sincerely,

Student Support Team Interventionist

Spanish Version

Queridos padres/guardianes,

Su hijo de [4º, 5º o 6º] grado ha sido seleccionado para participar en un grupo pequeño centrado en habilidades de autocontrol. Este grupo de 6 semanas se llevará a cabo [indicar cuándo] y no interferirá con sus clases académicas. El objetivo de este grupo es profundizar en cómo gestionar mejor el estrés y las situaciones de carga emocional. Discutiremos nuestras estrategias actuales para la resolución de problemas y el manejo de emociones mientras aprendemos nuevos enfoques. Esto implicará reflexionar, compartir experiencias y aprender nuevas estrategias de afrontamiento y escenarios de casos. Cada estudiante completará una prueba previa al grupo y una prueba posterior cuando terminemos.

Si tiene alguna pregunta sobre este grupo de intervención o desea hablar sobre la participación de su estudiante en el grupo, no dude en comunicarse conmigo.

Atentamente,

Intervencionista del equipo de apoyo al estudiante

Permission Slip (If Applicable)

After reading the description of this Tier 2 small group, I ____________________, give permission for my student ____________________ to take part in the group which will meet on ____________________ from [date] to [date]. I understand that this group is confidential and that I will be made aware if my student is making good use of this group experience. Should I need to be contacted, the best number to reach me at is ____________________.

Hoja de permiso

Después de leer la descripción de este grupo pequeño de Nivel 2, yo ____________________, doy permiso para que mi estudiante ____________________ participe en el grupo que se reunirá el ____________________ de [fecha] a [fecha]. Entiendo que este grupo es confidencial y que se me informará si mi estudiante está haciendo un buen uso de esta experiencia grupal. Si necesito que me contacten, el mejor número para comunicarse conmigo es ____________________.

Goals of Intervention

- Define what causes stress for participants.
- Define levels of stress.
- Learn positive coping skills.

CASEL Standards Addressed

- Identifying one's emotions
- Linking feelings, values, and thoughts
- Identifying and using stress-management strategies

ASCA Mind-Sets and Behaviors

M 1. Belief in development of whole self, including a healthy balance of mental, social/emotional and physical well-being

M 2. Sense of acceptance, respect, support and inclusion for self and others in the school environment

B-SMS 2. Self-discipline and self-control

B-SMS 1. Responsibility for self and actions

B-SMS 7. Effective coping skills

Materials Needed

Pre-/post-assessment

Lessons

Envelope with scenarios

Handouts

Pencils

Bingo cards

Bingo chips

Pre-/Post-Assessment: Coping Skills

Name: ______________________ Date: ________________

Circle the box that is true for you for each coping skill.

Coping Skill	Always	Sometimes	Never
I use words to hurt someone's feelings.	Always	Sometimes	Never
I take a "timeout" from the situation.	Always	Sometimes	Never
I use my body to hurt others (hit, push, etc.).	Always	Sometimes	Never
I yell or scream.	Always	Sometimes	Never
I use deep breathing and count to 10.	Always	Sometimes	Never
I make threats or look threatening.	Always	Sometimes	Never
I talk to my friends about my feelings.	Always	Sometimes	Never
I talk to my siblings about my feelings.	Always	Sometimes	Never
I talk to a caregiver about my feelings.	Always	Sometimes	Never
I talk to an adult at school about my feelings.	Always	Sometimes	Never
I get mad at myself.	Always	Sometimes	Never
I express my feelings in a positive way.	Always	Sometimes	Never
I find something to distract me.	Always	Sometimes	Never
I throw objects.	Always	Sometimes	Never
I cry.	Always	Sometimes	Never
I run away from adults.	Always	Sometimes	Never
Other	Always	Sometimes	Never

Sessions 1–6

These sessions are designed to teach and reinforce skills. Make note of which sessions students respond well to and which they are less responsive to. Make additions or improvements to maximize student engagement and optimize desired outcomes. Ask students for specific feedback at the end of sessions.

Session 1: Identifying Different Levels of Situations

Objectives:

1. Students will rank the intensity of the emotion experienced during different situations.
2. Students will explain their *thoughts* and *justification behind* their rankings.

Materials:

Different situations provided in the envelopes (one envelope per student)

Levels meter

Pens/pencils

Duration: 20 minutes

Instructions:

1. Welcome students and explain the purpose of the group.
2. Invite group members to provide input on group ground rules. Record them on poster paper and ask students to sign the poster paper.
3. Give each student an envelope and have them pick one group of scenarios to work with; there is blue, green, yellow, and red.
4. Have the students rate the emotional situations from 1 to 5 (1 being the lowest intensity and 5 being the highest) to express the level of emotional intensity of the situation; students can place the situation on the levels meter.
5. When students are done rating the situation, have the students explain their thought process and their justification for their answer.
6. Repeat until the group has gone through all the different situations.
7. When the group is all done labeling which level the situations go on, ask the students at which level they think they would need to start using a coping skill.

    a. Levels 1 and 2 situations should be emotional times when they can manage their emotions and easily allow them to wash away and move on after just a little time.
    b. Levels 3–5 situations students may recognize they need a coping skill/strategy.

Different Situations

- You were entering a raffle to win a new iPad and someone else's raffle ticket got called, so you didn't win.
- You were playing soccer and were about to dribble the ball down the field and score but someone on the other team was running by and tripped you. It seemed like it was just a mistake, but you fell and the other team got the ball and scored a goal.
- You're watching television by yourself and are in the middle of a really good show that you enjoy, but your sibling came into the living room and stole the remote and switched it to their show. You tell them that you were watching something, and they tell you that they don't care because they don't want to watch it and have their own show they want to watch right now.
- You are sitting at lunch, eating your sandwich and someone comes over to your desk, grabs all of your food, and throws it into the trash for no reason. Now you have no lunch.
- You are out at recess playing kickball and someone jumps ahead of you in line and takes your turn. When you tell them it was your turn, they tell you it is *their* turn and shove you on to the ground. You stand up and they try to hit you again.
- You were very excited to watch the new episode of your favorite TV show, and you get ready to watch the show only to find out that it will be on tomorrow night and not tonight.
- Your team has made it to the championship, and you have been practicing really hard. The day before the championship game, you break your arm when you fall off your bike. Now you can't play at the championship game.
- You have a test/quiz coming up in class, and you studied really hard for it. You take the test/quiz and find out you didn't do as great as you thought you did.
- You get to school and think that your favorite hot lunch is being served in the cafeteria. When you get to the lunchroom you find out that they changed the lunch menu for the day and don't have your favorite hot lunch.
- You get home from school, and you find out that there will be pizza and ice cream for dinner tonight.
- You have been working really hard this year in school and showing that you're a great friend. You go to school one day and find out that you are the student of the month.
- You get home from school and getting ready for your long vacation from school. You thought you were just staying home during the school vacation, but you find out you are going to Disney World for vacation.
- You are outside at recess, and you couldn't find your friends to play with, so you go to the swings and find your friends there, and they saved you a swing.
- When you get to the gym, the gym teacher lets you choose which activity you want to play that day.
- You thought you left your homework at home, but when you get to school you find it in your backpack.
- You get home and find out you left your favorite water bottle on the bus. When you go to get on the bus the next day, the bus driver hands it to you.

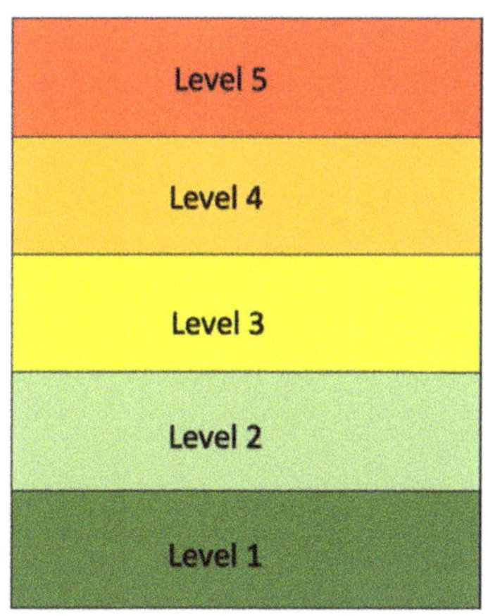

Image 9.1

Session 2: Positive versus Negative Coping Skills

Objectives:

1. Students will know the difference between positive and negative coping skills.
2. Students will identify potential alternatives to negative coping skills.

Materials:

T-chart for positive versus negative coping skills

Pencils

Duration: 20 minutes

Instructions:

1. Welcome students back and remind them of the group ground rules. Check in.
2. Give each student a T-chart and a pencil.
3. Allow the students a few minutes to fill in the T-chart by themselves with different coping skills.
4. Come together as a group to go over different coping skills the students came up with.
5. Ask students to look at their negative side of the T-chart; have the students work as a group to come up with positive alternatives to the negative coping skills that came up.
    a. Negative: Punch a wall; positive: punch a pillow/punching bag
    b. If students are struggling, try offering suggestions.

My Positive and Negative Coping Skills

Name: ______________________ Date: ________________

My Positive Coping Skills	My Negative Coping Skills

Session 3: Identifying Potential Coping Skills

Objective:

1. Students will reflect on the situations from Session 1 and pair them with some of the positive coping skills they came up with in Session 2.

Materials:

Situation cards from Session 1

Duration: 20 minutes

Instructions:

1. Welcome students back and remind them of the group ground rules. Check in.
2. Take out the envelopes from Session 1 containing the different situations.
3. Read each one of the situations; allow students a few minutes to think of a coping skill they think could help during that situation.
4. Invite the students to share what coping skill they came up with to the group; reflect on whether it is a positive or negative coping skill.
    a. If thc coping skill is negative, help students come up with a positive alternative. Repeat with each situation.

Session 4: Create a Coping Skills List for the School

Objective:

1. Students will help create a "master" list of coping skills to post around the school; this will help students think of different coping skills to use while at school.

Materials:

Folded poster paper

Pencils/markers/coloring utensils

*Optional: Students work as a team to create a poster on a computer

Duration: 20 minutes

Instructions:

1. Welcome students back and remind them of the group ground rules. Check in.
2. Ask students to brainstorm different ideas of coping skills; try to have each student come up with at least two different coping skills.
3. Once a list of 10–15 coping skills are decided on as a group, write down the coping skills on the poster and try to create a picture of that coping skill to go along with it.
4. When the poster is done, create copies to post around the school to encourage other students to use these coping skills.

Session 5: Personalized Coping Skills Booklets

Objective:

1. Students will create a list of coping skills they know work for them or they would like to try.

Materials:

Coping skill booklets

Pencils or coloring utensils

Duration: 20 minutes

Instructions:

1. Welcome students back and remind them of the group ground rules. Check in.
2. Give each student a booklet.
3. Place coloring utensils in the middle of the table.
4. Allow students to draw and write out their favorite coping skills that they have learned and think they will use in the future.
    a. Make sure to encourage positive coping skills only in the booklets.
5. Remind teachers that the students have these booklets and should be allowed to carry them around when at school.

My Coping Skills Booklet

Name ______________________________

Image 9.2

My favorite coping skill when I am angry or frustrated:

My favorite coping skill when I am sad or disappointed:

Image 9.2 (Continued)

My favorite coping skill when I am lonely:

My favorite coping skill when I feel misunderstood:

Image 9.2 *(Continued)*

My favorite coping skill when I am overwhelmed:

My healthy coping skills list:		
	1. Talk to someone I trust	21. Use an "I feel" statement
	2. Talk to the school counselor	22. Exercise
	3. Ask for help	23. Smile in the mirror
	4. Think of ways to solve the problem with an adult	24. Spend time with people I enjoy being with
	5. Try to identify my emotions	25. Set small achievable goals
	6. Try to draw out my emotions	26. Separate myself from the situation
	7. Express my emotions	27. Do a word search or crossword puzzle
	8. Take a few slow deep belly breaths	28. Do my favorite hobby
	9. Take a time out	29. Build something
	10. Practice some yoga	30. Play a game
	11. Take a walk	31. Create a piece of art
	12. Make a list of pros and cons	32. Take a walk
	13. Make a list of choices	33. Think of a time I had fun
	14. Create an action plan	34. Look at my favorite picture
	15. Slowly count to 10	35. Think of my favorite place to be
	16. Do some gentle stretches	36. Think of something funny
	17. Drink some water	37. Meditate
	18. Play outside	38. Read a book
	19. Think about my strengths	39. Get some rest
	20. Write in my journal	40. Cook or bake

Image 9.2 *(Continued)*

Session 6: Coping Skills Bingo

Objective:

1. Students will synthesize the coping skills they have learned.

Materials:

Bingo cards and chips

Callers card and calling cards

Duration: 20 minutes

Instructions:

1. Welcome students back and remind them of the group ground rules. Remind them that this is the final group meeting. Check in.
2. Give posttest.
3. Give each student a Bingo card and some chips.
4. Use the calling card bag to randomly call out coping skills; students then place a chip on their card if they have that coping skill.
5. Continue to call out coping skills until a student gets Bingo.
6. When a student wins, have them tell (and if possible, act out) their favorite coping skill they like to use.
7. Continue to play Bingo as time allows.

Coping Skills Bingo

Bingo callers card (use a second copy to cut up as Bingo calling cards)

Use a fidget	Listen to music	Draw a picture	Write a letter	Hug a stuffed animal	Think of something happy
Think about my pet	Take a breather	Talk to someone I trust	Read a book	Cook or bake	Try to identify my emotions
Talk to the school counselor	Think of a positive	Play an instrument	Get some rest	Garden	Meditate
Practice breathing exercises	Give myself a compliment	Express my emotions	Make a list of things I'm thankful for	Watch my favorite movie	Think of something funny
Take a timeout	Practice some yoga	Think of a time I had fun	Look at my favorite picture	Think of my favorite place to be	Take a few slow, deep belly mindful breaths

Take a walk	Slowly count to 10	Ask for help	Create a piece of art	Play a game	List pros and cons
Think of ways to solve the problem with an adult	Build something	Do some gentle stretches	Say "I can do this"	Smile in the mirror	Drink some water
Play outside	Do my favorite hobby	Try to draw out my emotions	Make a list of choices	Think of my strengths	Create an action plan
Spend time with people I like/ enjoy being with	Exercise	Do a wordsearch/ crossword puzzle	Use an "I feel" statement	Practice journaling	Set small achievable goals
Separate self from the situation					

Coping Skills Bingo

Practice journaling	Use a fidget	Look at my favorite picture	Cook or bake
Think of my strengths	Solve a puzzle	Separate self from the situation	Garden
Try to identify my emotions	Think of ways to solve to the problem with an adult	Hug a stuffed animal	Talk to the school counselor
Practice some yoga	Think of a positive	Exercise	List pros and cons

Coping Skills Bingo

Try to draw out my emotions	Use a fidget	Make a list of choices	Think of something funny
List pros and cons	Practice breathing exercises	Think about my pet	Get some rest
Set small achievable goals	Draw a picture	Look at my favorite picture	Think of a time I had fun
Exercise	Take a walk	Take a time out	Watch my favorite movie

Image 9.3

Coping Skills Bingo

Make a list of choices	Read a book	Write a letter	Give myself a compliment
Separate self from the situation	Go to my happy place	Listen to music	Use an "I feel..." statement
Think of my strengths	Practice some yoga	Say "I can do this"	Drink some water
Think of something funny	Take some deep breaths	Smile in the mirror	Express my emotions

Coping Skills Bingo

Play a game	Write a letter	Take some deep breaths	Think of my favorite place to be
Take a walk	Read a book	Slowly count to 10	Garden
Get some rest	Name 3 things I'm grateful for	Practice some yoga	Create an action plan
Give myself a compliment	Use a fidget	Build something	Practice breathing exercises

Image 9.4

Coping Skills Bingo

Ask for help	Play a game	Create an action plan	Garden
Go to my happy place	Do my favorite hobby	Practice some yoga	Spend time with people I enjoy
Try to identify my emotions	Say "I can do this"	Take a breather	Take a time out
Think of ways to solve to the problem with an adult	Make a list of choices	Take a walk	Draw a picture

Coping Skills Bingo

Take a breather	Cook or bake	Think of something happy	Use an "I feel..." statement
Garden	Set small achievable goals	Read a book	Look at my favorite picture
Create a piece of art	Separate self from the situation	Solve a puzzle	Play outside
Say "I can do this"	Use a fidget	List pros and cons	Think of ways to solve to the problem with an adult

Image 9.5

Coping Skills Bingo

Play an instrument	Name 3 things I'm grateful for	Create a piece of art	Try to identify my emotions
Play outside	Think of a positive	Hug a stuffed animal	Talk to the school counselor
Say "I can do this"	Slowly count to 10	Read a book	Take some deep breaths
List pros and cons	Smile in the mirror	Write a letter	Make a list of choices

Coping Skills Bingo

Play an instrument	Separate self from the situation	Look at my favorite picture	Talk to the school counselor
Exercise	Think about my pet	Draw a picture	Think of my strengths
Ask for help	Take some deep breaths	Smile in the mirror	Use an "I feel..." statement
Create a piece of art	Go to my happy place	Think of a time I had fun	Take a time out

Image 9.6

Post-Intervention Communication to Parent/Guardian

English Version

Dear Parents/Guardians,

As you know, your student, [name], took part in a 6-week group that focused on coping skills and emotional regulation. We encourage you to ask [name] to share what they learned and how they are planning to address stressful situations moving forward. Any encouragement at home supports the learning your student has done as part of this small group. Here is a list of some of the coping strategies we addressed. Please ask your student to share which strategy or strategies seem to work best for them:

Try to identify my emotions.
Express my emotions calmly with a caring adult.
Take a break.
Practice breathing exercises.
Listen to or play music.
Make a list of things I am thankful for.
Think of something funny.
Get some rest.

Since the ability to identify and manage emotions in times of stress is an important life skill, it's helpful to spend time meeting in small groups to discuss these strategies and others for our well-being and safety.

If you have any questions, please do not hesitate to contact us.

Sincerely,

Student Support Team Interventionist

Spanish Version

Estimados padres/tutores,

Como usted sabe, su estudiante, [nombre], participó en un grupo de 6 semanas que se centró en habilidades de afrontamiento y regulación emocional. Le recomendamos que le pida a [nombre] que comparta lo que aprendió y cómo planea abordar situaciones estresantes en el futuro. Cualquier estímulo en casa respalda el aprendizaje que su estudiante ha realizado como parte de este grupo pequeño. Aquí hay una lista de algunas de las estrategias de afrontamiento que abordamos. Pídale a su estudiante que comparta qué estrategia o estrategias parecen funcionar mejor para él:

Intenta identificar mis emociones.
Expresar mis emociones con calma con un adulto comprensivo.
Tomar un descanso
Practica ejercicios de respiración.
Escuchar o reproducir música
Haz una lista de cosas por las que estoy agradecido
Piensa en algo gracioso
Descansar un poco

Dado que la capacidad de identificar y gestionar las emociones en momentos de estrés es una habilidad importante para la vida, es útil dedicar tiempo a reuniones en grupos pequeños para discutir estas estrategias y otras para nuestro bienestar y seguridad.

Si tiene alguna pregunta, no dude en contactarnos.

Atentamente,

Intervencionista del equipo de apoyo al estudiante

Plan for Implementation Fidelity

To achieve the intended outcomes of this intervention, it is helpful to colead the small group with a colleague, reflect on student responses to the activities, and seek support to keep engagement in the group high. Tier 2 small group facilitators should seek peer coaching and ask for feedback to make sure the intervention is implemented with fidelity.

Small Group Process Notes

References

Eacott, C., & Frydenberg, E. (2009). Promoting positive coping skills for rural youth: Benefits for at-risk young people. *The Australian Journal of Rural Health*, *17*(6), 338–345. https://doi.org/10.1111/j.1440-1584.2009.01109.x

Katz, J., Knight, V., Mercer, S. H., & Skinner, S. Y. (2020). Effects of a universal school-based mental health program on the self-concept, coping skills, and perceptions of social support of students with developmental disabilities. *Journal of Autism and Developmental Disorders*, *50*(11), 4069–4084. https://doi.org/10.1007/s10803-020 04472-w

Maykrantz, S. A., & Houghton, J. D. (2020). Self-leadership and stress among college students: Examining the moderating role of coping skills. *Journal of American College Health*, *68*(1), 89–96. https://doi.org/10.1080/07448481.2018.1515759

Mind, P. L. (n.d.). *Coping skills assessment*. Teachers Pay Teachers.

myfreebingocards.com. (n.d.). *Bingo card generator*. https://myfreebingocards.com/bingo-card-generator

Stress Management for Middle Schoolers

Gaby Granitto and Lucia Greene

Image 9.7

Description of Skill

The purpose of this Tier 2 intervention kit is to help students in middle school (grades 6–8) who are experiencing heightened levels of stress. This could be related to many different factors, including academic expectations, social pressure, transition to high school, stressors in extracurricular activities, stressors at home, underlying anxiety, and more. Students who are experiencing heightened levels of stress can be included in Tier 2 small counseling groups. To determine eligibility for this Tier 2 group, school counselors will implement a pretest that asks students about stressors in their everyday lives. These students can either be referred from teachers or parents or be identified from previous observation from school counselors. This pretest asks basic questions about how stress impacts their everyday lives and how stress manifests in their bodies. Based on these self-assessments, school counselors can determine if they are appropriate for this Tier 2 intervention on stress management.

Stress management is essential to academic success because students are more than students; they are humans with home lives, personal lives, and stressors. When students are presented with a stressful situation or traumatic event, the amygdala signals a flight, fight, or freeze response throughout the body, taking full control over the brain (Lee, 2020). When this occurs, students are unable to access their executive functioning skills and are solely focused on the body's stress response. Additionally, when they are in this heightened state, feelings of helplessness and anxiety are more common, and memory is impaired (Willis, 2014). Since there are a variety of stress triggers, it is likely that a student will be triggered in classrooms.

Research shows that when a student is triggered, they are not likely to be accessed via conversation and thus are better off getting a drink of water, pressing against a wall, taking a walk, or engaging in other practices to notice their physical sensations, (Lee, 2020). Once a student can notice these symptoms, they can be accessed once again. This stresses the importance of learning stress management skills. Students will experience significant stresses throughout their entire life, and it is important they learn how to cope with these feelings. Lee (2020) shares multiple strategies for the classroom so that teachers can continue to reinforce these coping skills. She reports that teachers who facilitate these practices in their classrooms are better equipped to handle escalated behaviors in class. Furthermore, students can regulate themselves once they learn and practice the strategies.

Furthermore, these Tier 2 interventions are effective based on previous experiences in other schools. According to Truluck (2019), her stress-buster group intervention allowed students to decrease their stress symptoms for 90% of students and improve attendance rates by 80%. This indicates that these groups work for this age group. Other positive effects of the group included self-regulation and more in-class time due to the ability to process one's stress and return to class after a trigger. These activities are based on cognitive behavior therapy practices and mindfulness. Research shows that mindfulness practices such as relaxation techniques increase oxygen flow to the brain, which in turn triggers a relaxation response (Truluck, 2019). This will allow students to learn better because they will be able to feel present in the classroom. According to Willis (2014), research supports that learning in a positive environment allows more information to be retained. This is important to consider because if school counselors can build the foundation in a Tier 2 group, students will respond even better in the classroom.

Pre-Intervention Communication With Parents/Guardians/Teachers in Languages Represented in the School

English Version

Dear Parents/Guardians,

Your [sixth, seventh, or eighth] grader has been selected to take part in a small group focused on self-management skills. This 6-week group will take place [indicate when] and will not interfere with their academic classes. The goal of this group is to delve into how to best manage stress and emotionally charged situations. We will discuss our current strategies for problem solving and managing emotions while learning new approaches. This will involve reflection, sharing experiences, and learning new coping strategies and case scenarios. Each student will complete a pretest prior to the group and a posttest as we finish up.

If you have any questions about this intervention group or would like to discuss your student's participation in the group, please do not hesitate to reach out to me.

Sincerely,

Student Support Team Interventionist

Spanish Version

Queridos padres/guardianes,

Su hijo de [6º, 7º u 8º] grado ha sido seleccionado para participar en un grupo pequeño centrado en habilidades de autocontrol. Este grupo de 6 semanas se llevará a cabo [indicar cuándo] y no interferirá con sus clases académicas. El objetivo de este grupo es profundizar en cómo gestionar mejor el estrés y las situaciones de carga emocional. Discutiremos nuestras estrategias actuales para la resolución de problemas y el manejo de emociones mientras aprendemos nuevos enfoques. Esto implicará reflexionar, compartir experiencias y aprender nuevas estrategias de afrontamiento y escenarios de casos. Cada estudiante completará una prueba previa al grupo y una prueba posterior cuando terminemos.

Si tiene alguna pregunta sobre este grupo de intervención o desea hablar sobre la participación de su estudiante en el grupo, no dude en comunicarse conmigo.

Atentamente,

Intervencionista del equipo de apoyo al estudiante

Permission Slip (If Applicable)

After reading the description of this Tier 2 small group, I ______________________ , give permission for my student ______________________ to take part in the group which will meet on ______________________ from [date] to [date]. I understand that this group is confidential and that I will be made aware if my student is making good use of this group experience. Should I need to be contacted, the best number to reach me at is ______________________ .

Hoja de permiso

Después de leer la descripción de este grupo pequeño de Nivel 2, yo ______________________, doy permiso para que mi estudiante ______________________ participe en el grupo que se reunirá el ______________________ de [fecha] a [fecha]. Entiendo que este grupo es confidencial y que se me informará si mi estudiante está haciendo un buen uso de esta experiencia grupal. Si necesito que me contacten, el mejor número para comunicarse conmigo es ______________________ .

Goals of Intervention

- Understand what stress looks like and feels like for each individual.
- Explore what triggers stress and challenging emotions.
- Identify current ways of managing stress and challenging emotions.
- Acquire and practice new strategies to manage in stressful situations.

CASEL Standards Addressed

- Identifying one's emotions
- Managing and expressing one's emotions productively
- Identifying and using stress-management strategies

ASCA Mind-Sets and Behaviors

M 1. Belief in development of whole self, including a healthy balance of mental, social/emotional and physical well-being

B-SMS 1. Responsibility for self and actions

B-SMS 2. Self-discipline and self-control

B-SMS 7. Effective coping skills

Materials Needed

Hand outs

Colored pencils

Two packages of sticky notes (different colors)

Pre-/Post-Assessment

Name: ______________________ Date: ______________

Circle the answers you most identify with for each question.

1. I can identify when I feel stressed.	Never	Rarely	Sometimes	Often	Always
2. I know how stress impacts my body.	Never	Rarely	Sometimes	Often	Always
3. My stress levels get in the way of schoolwork.	Never	Rarely	Sometimes	Often	Always
4. I can identify positive coping strategies.	Never	Rarely	Sometimes	Often	Always
5. I practice stress management strategies.	Never	Rarely	Sometimes	Often	Always
6. I shut down when I get stressed.	Never	Rarely	Sometimes	Often	Always
7. I get angry or burst out when I get stressed.	Never	Rarely	Sometimes	Often	Always
8. I know how to calm myself down in stressful situations.	Never	Rarely	Sometimes	Often	Always
9. I understand how stress influences my academic success.	Never	Rarely	Sometimes	Often	Always
10. School stresses me out.	Never	Rarely	Sometimes	Often	Always

Progress Monitoring: Student's Self-Reported Weekly Stress Log

Stress Ruler

On a scale of 1 – 6, how intense has your stress been this week?

Image 9.8

Date	Stress Level (0–6)	What was I doing?	What was I thinking?	How did I feel?	My response was:

Progress Log for Staff Working With Student

Date	Precipitating event	Did the student reach out to you?	How did the student handle it?	What coping skills were used? Were they helpful?	Other notes

Sessions 1–6

These sessions are designed to teach and reinforce skills. Make note of which sessions students respond well to and which they are less responsive to. Make additions or improvements to maximize student engagement and optimize desired outcomes. Ask students for specific feedback at the end of sessions.

Session 1: How Stress Affects Me and Goal Setting

Objective:

1. Identify how the student experiences stress in their feelings, body, thoughts, and behaviors, and to set goals on how to deal with stress in the future.

Materials:

"How Stress Affects Me" worksheet

"Goal Setting" worksheet

Duration: 15–30 minutes

Instructions:

1. Welcome students and explain the purpose of the group.
2. Invite group members to provide input on group ground rules. Record them on poster paper and ask students to sign the poster paper.

Activity 1: How Stress Affects Me

Students will identify how they experience stress in four different areas:

1. Identify how stress affects their feelings.
2. Identify how stress affects their body.
3. Identify how stress affects their thoughts.
4. Identify how stress affects their behaviors and actions.

Students should aim for three responses per category.

Activity 2: Goal Setting

Students will identify and set goals on how to manage stress in four different areas:

1. Set goals for how they will feel when dealing with stress.
2. Identify coping strategies they can use when feeling stressed.
3. Identify positive thoughts to think about when they are stressed.
4. Identify positive behaviors they will engage in when they are stressed.

Students should aim for three responses per category.

How Stress Affects Me

Name: ______________________________ Date: ____________________

When we are stressed, we typically experience it in our emotions, bodies, thoughts, and behaviors. Fill in the boxes to describe how stress affects you in each area.

When I am stressed, I feel ...

Image 9.9

When I am stressed, my body feels ...

Image 9.10

When I am stressed, I think about ...

Image 9.11

When I am stressed, I (actions/behaviors) ...

Image 9.12

Goal Setting: How I Will Handle Stress

Name: ______________________________ Date: __________________

When we are stressed, we can manage our emotions, bodies, thoughts, and behaviors. Fill in the boxes to describe how you will cope with stress in each area.

When I am stressed, I will feel (positive emotion) ...	When I am stressed, I will (physical coping strategy) ...
Image 9.13 	Image 9.14 
When I am stressed, I think about (positive thoughts) ...	**When I am stressed, I (positive behaviors or actions) ...**
Image 9.15 	Image 9.16 

Session 2: Where Do I Feel Stress?

Objective: Identify how the body responds to stress and coping strategies to reduce symptoms of the body's stress response.

Materials:

Blank body outline

Markers or colored pencils (optional)

Blank sheets of paper (can be colored or white)

Duration: 30 minutes

Instructions:

1. Welcome students back and remind them of the group ground rules. Check in.

Activity 1: Where Is Stress?

1. Provide all students receive a blank sheet of a body outline.
2. Students are asked to recall a time where they felt stressed. Students are prompted to draw where stress lives in their body and to draw what it feels like. They are invited to use different colors and shapes or designs to showcase what it looks like for them.
3. Facilitator debriefs the exercise and students share their pictures.
   Reflection questions: What was that like for you? Where does everyone experience stress? What does it feel like? What do you do when you feel these feelings?
4. Facilitator explains that these feelings occur because of our bodies going into fight or flight mode as a response to a stressor. Everyone copes in their own way. Our goal when we manage stress is to not let stress take over our bodies. We can honor our feelings while staying connected to the body.

Activity 2: Draw Your Breath

1. Students receive a sheet of paper and colored pencils or markers.
2. Students place their writing tools on paper.
3. Instruct them to notice their breath, to imagine their breath as a line, and then to represent it on the paper. Students can speed up their breath and notice how it changes the line. They can slow down their breath to draw what that might look like.
4. On the other side of the sheet of paper, students focus on slow, deep breathing. Have them draw lines that represent their "calm breath." Remind them that there is no wrong or right way to complete this exercise.
5. Discuss the impact of breath on the body's stress response. Ask them to compare their feelings when they breathe quickly and shortly versus long, deep breaths.
6. Closure: When can you practice deep breathing?

Source: Adapted from "Drawing Your Breath," by C. Mehlomakuu, 2017, https://creativityintherapy.com/2017/08/drawing-your-breath-a-mindful-art-exercise/.

Where Do I Feel Stress?

Directions: Think about a time when you felt really stressed out. Draw where you felt the stress in your body. Draw what the stress felt like in your body. Be as creative as you want!

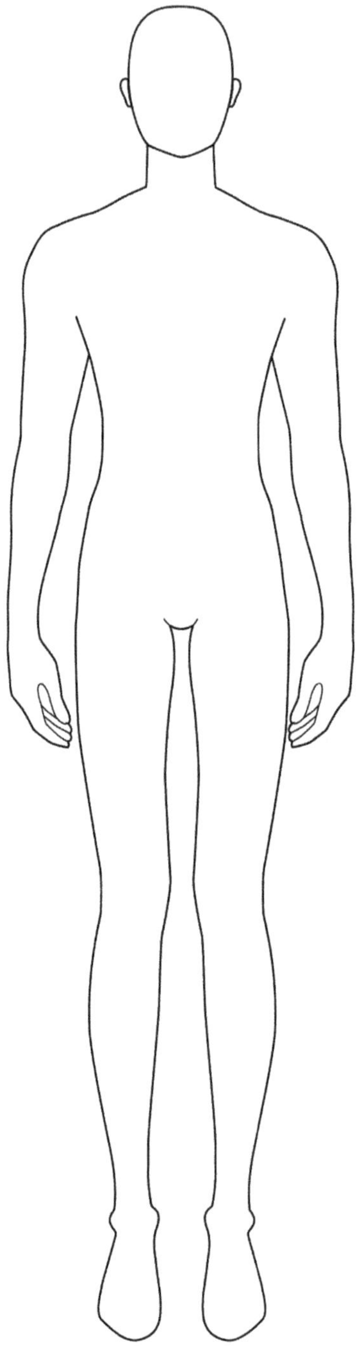

Image 9.17

Session 3: Locus of Control

Objective:

1. Identify stressors and triggers for stress responses and create action plans to address them.
2. Identify negative self-talk and replace with positive thoughts.

Materials:

Two different colored packs of sticky notes

Paper

Writing utensils

Duration: 30–40 minutes

Instructions:

1. Welcome students back and remind them of the group ground rules. Check in.

Activity 1: Locus of Control

1. Ask students, "What stresses you out?" Make a list of all the stressors.
2. Have students pick one that is their biggest stressor.
3. On a sheet of paper, students draw a big circle and a smaller one in the middle.
4. In the big circle, they write factors about that stressor that are outside of their control.
5. The inner circle is for things that are within their control about the situation.
6. The group discusses the importance of discerning these items and identifying action steps and resources to manage their situation.

Activity 2: Take Out the Trash Talk

1. Each student gets two sticky notes with different colors.
2. Explain to students that sometimes when we are stressed, our mind starts racing.
3. Ask students to write down their negative thoughts on one sticky note.
4. Invite people to share what they feel comfortable with. Ask, "Where do we feel these thoughts come from?" Explain that sometimes we have negative thoughts as gut reactions, but it doesn't mean they're true. For example, if you see a rollercoaster, some people might get scared and have scary thoughts, but then they change their minds.
5. On the other sticky note, write a positive/kinder spin on your negative comments.
6. Ask, "What is it like to see this mental reframe?"
7. Close the session by having students crumple up their negative comments and throw them in the trash.

Session 4: Managing School Stress

Objective: Identify coping strategies to manage academic overwhelm and test-taking anxiety.
Materials:

"Weekly Study Plan" worksheet

"Managing Test Anxiety" worksheet

Duration: 30–40 minutes

Instructions:

1. Welcome students back and remind them of the group ground rules. Check in.

Activity 1: Breaking It Down

2. The facilitator explains that sometimes stress or academic overwhelm can lead to procrastination with schoolwork.
3. Students complete the Weekly Study Plan worksheet for each class this week.
4. They write their due dates and practice splitting up their assignments into smaller chunks rather than waiting until the last minute.
5. This can be used to record their homework each day.

Activity 2: Managing Test Anxiety

1. Students complete the Managing Test Anxiety worksheet. First, they identify what they feel when they think about the test.
2. Next, they identify what they worry most about when they think of the test.
3. Then, they review the different coping strategy categories: preparation, relaxation techniques, test-taking skills, and mind-set.
4. They check off what they currently do and draw a star what they would like to try.
5. The facilitator ensures that all students understand the strategies before closing the discussion.
6. Close by asking what the students want to implement and how they will do so.

Weekly Homework Plan

Academic to-do-list for the week of: ____________________

	Days of the Week	Due Dates	Test/Quizzes	Assignments	Papers	Presentations	Readings	Homework
Classes								

Image 9.18

Weekly Study Plan

Name: ______________________________ Date: ____________

Quizzes and Tests this week:

Day of the week	Sunday	Monday	Tuesday	Wednesday	Thursday	Friday	Saturday
Prep for test in							
Prep for quiz in							
Reread notes for							
Other							

Managing Test Anxiety

Name: ______________________________ Date: ____________

How do I feel when I think about taking a test?

Image 9.19

Image 9.20

What do I worry about while I am taking a test?

Coping Tools	
Be Prepared	**Use Relaxation Techniques**
Ask the teacher what is going to be on the test. Ask the teacher about the test format. Self-test yourself. Say information out loud to test your memory. Use active learning strategies like practice quizzes, flash cards, teaching material to someone else, or rewriting information in your own words. Try to predict and answer possible test questions.	Practice deep breathing. Get a drink of water and take a short walk before the quiz. Tighten and relax your hand and arm muscles. Take 10–15 minutes of quiet in a peaceful location. Think about something else before the quiz or test that you are looking forward to in the future.
Master Test Taking Skills	**Be Optimistic**
Read all directions carefully Scan your test/quiz: What is each section worth? Which sections will take longer? Manage your time. Work on one question at a time. Mark difficult questions and return later. Focus only on what you are doing.	Encourage yourself with positive thoughts such as "All I can do is my best." Even if you didn't do well before, remember this is a new chance. Think of a test as a chance to show your teacher all you know. Envision yourself finishing the test and feeling proud of yourself.

Session 5: Coping Skills Spinner

Objective:

1. Identify coping skills for stress and create a tactile resource that can be used as needed.

Materials:

Coping skills list

"Coping Skills Spinner" worksheet

Paper fastener

Optional: Markers, colored pencils, crayons, or art supply of choice

Duration: 45 minutes

Instructions:

1. Welcome students back and remind them of the group ground rules. Check in.

Activity 1: Identifying Coping Skills

1. Students will receive a list of positive coping skills.
2. Students will check off coping skills that they feel may help them in stressful times. Students should check a minimum of eight coping skills.

Activity 2: Crafting the Coping Skills Spinner

1. Students will construct and decorate their coping skills spinners.
2. Following the instructions on the worksheet:
    a. Write eight coping skills on the bottom layer.
    b. Decorate the coping spinners as desired.
    c. Cut out the three pieces.
    d. Fasten them together with the paper fastener.

Source: Adapted from Counselor Clique, n.d., https://counselorclique.com/.

Name: ______________________________ Date: __________

Positive Coping Skills	
• Read a book. • Hug or climb a tree. • Journal. • Use kind and compassionate self-talk. • Make a collage or scrapbook. • Rest, nap, or take a break. • Go on a hike, walk, or run. • Take good care of the earth. • Drink water. • Play a board game. • Do something kind. • Make art. • Take a shower or bath. • Get exercise. • Drink a warm cup of tea or cocoa.	• Ride a bike or scooter. • Create origami. • Cook or bake a treat. • Ask someone for help. • Talk to someone you trust. • Weave, knit or crochet. • Build something. • Get a hug. • Visualize your favorite peaceful place. • Stretch. • Write a letter to yourself. • Use positive affirmations. • Take slow, mindful breaths. • Clean or declutter an area. • Use aromatherapy.

Notes:

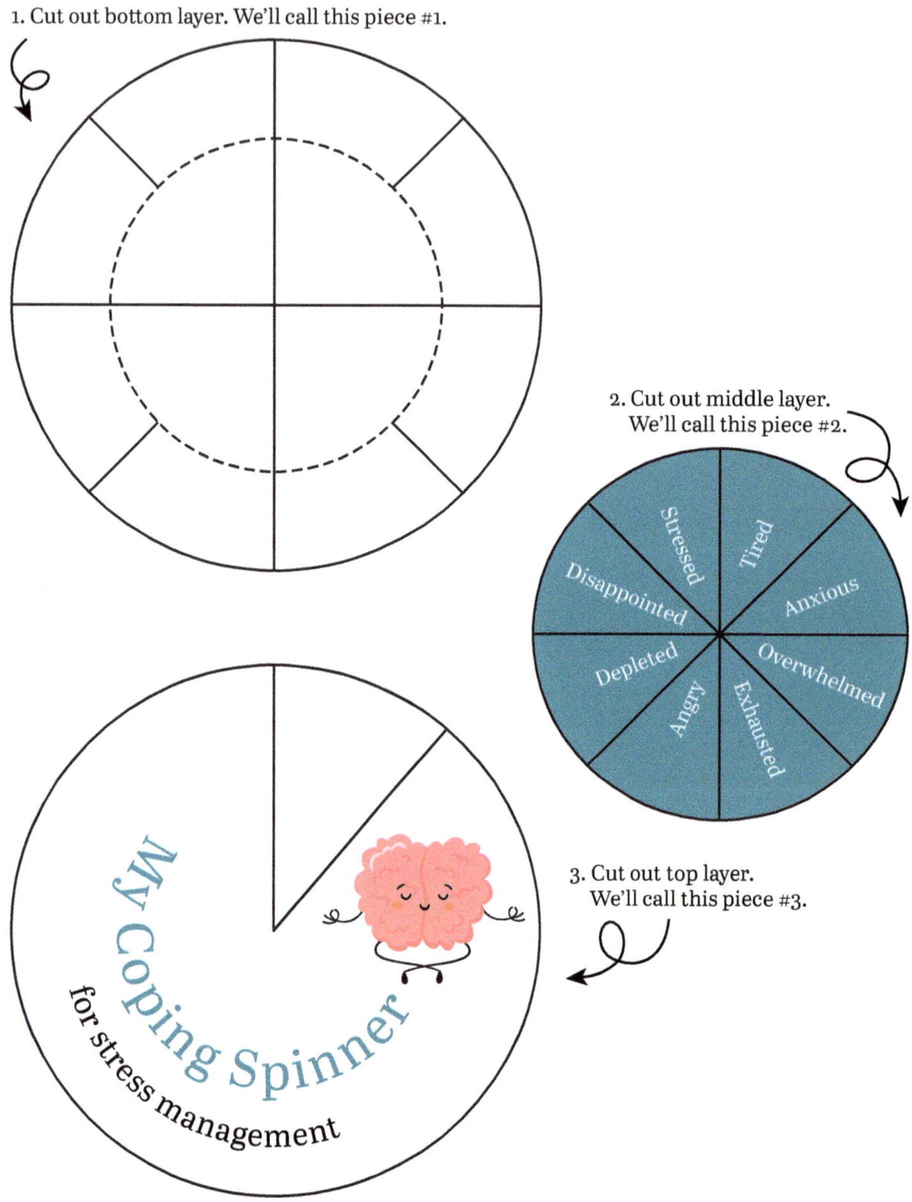
1. Cut out bottom layer. We'll call this piece #1.
2. Cut out middle layer. We'll call this piece #2.
Stressed
Tired
Anxious
Overwhelmed
Exhausted
Angry
Depleted
Disappointed
3. Cut out top layer. We'll call this piece #3.
My Coping Spinner
for stress management

Image 9.21

Session 6: Revisiting Our Goals—Letter to Oneself

Objective:

1. Students will participate and share how they are progressing with their stress management goals.

Materials:

Completed "Goal Setting" worksheet

Blank sheet of lined paper

Duration: 15 minutes

Instructions:

1. Welcome students back and remind them of the group ground rules. Check in.
2. Ask students to identify positive strategies that they have used during the course. Encourage them to give specific examples of how they used the strategies and why.
3. The group leader will give the student helpful feedback and encourage other group members to do the same if the student is open to it.
4. Each member gets time to reflect on one or two of the goals they set during the 6 weeks of the group.
5. Ask group members to write a letter to their future self. This letter should contain reminders of why they struggled with managing stress and uncomfortable emotions and the new strategies they learned. They should be encouraged to complete some or all of the following sentences:
    a. I hope that you are ...
    b. Remember stress or uncomfortable feelings ...
    c. Applying what you have learned in this group will ...
    d. When others around me have difficulties handling stress, I will ...
6. Send letter to student in 3–6 months.
7. Complete posttest.

Post-Intervention Communication to Parent/Guardian

English Version

Dear Parents/Guardians,

As you know, your student, [name], took part in a 6-week group that focused on coping skills and emotional regulation. We encourage you to ask [name] to share what they learned and how they are planning to address stressful situations moving forward. Any encouragement at home supports the learning your student has done as part of this small group. Here is a list of some of the coping strategies we addressed. Please ask your student to share which strategy or strategies seem to work best for them:

Try to identify my emotions.
Express my emotions calmly with a caring adult.
Take a break.
Make a weekly schedule to complete my homework.
Listen to or play music.
Talk to a friend.
Think of something funny.
Go outside for some fresh air.

Since the ability to identify and manage emotions in times of stress is an important life skill, it's helpful to spend time meeting in small groups to discuss these strategies and others for our well-being and safety.

If you have any questions, please do not hesitate to contact us.

Sincerely,

Student Support Team Interventionist

Spanish Version

Estimados padres/tutores,

Como usted sabe, su estudiante, [nombre], participó en un grupo de 6 semanas que se centró en habilidades de afrontamiento y regulación emocional. Le recomendamos que le pida a [nombre] que comparta lo que aprendió y cómo planea abordar situaciones estresantes en el futuro. Cualquier estímulo en casa respalda el aprendizaje que su estudiante ha realizado como parte de este grupo pequeño. Aquí hay una lista de algunas de las estrategias de afrontamiento que abordamos. Pídale a su estudiante que comparta qué estrategia o estrategias parecen funcionar mejor para él:

Intenta identificar mis emociones.
Expresar mis emociones con calma con un adulto comprensivo.
Tomar un descanso
Hacer un horario semanal para completar mi tarea
Escuchar o reproducir música
Hablar a un amigo
Piensa en algo gracioso
Sal a tomar un poco de aire fresco

Dado que la capacidad de identificar y gestionar las emociones en momentos de estrés es una habilidad importante para la vida, es útil dedicar tiempo a reuniones en grupos pequeños para discutir estas estrategias y otras para nuestro bienestar y seguridad.

Si tiene alguna pregunta, no dude en contactarnos.

Atentamente,

Intervencionista del equipo de apoyo al estudiante

Plan for Implementation Fidelity

To achieve the intended outcomes of this intervention, it is helpful to colead the small group with a colleague, reflect on student responses to the activities, and seek support to keep engagement in the group high. Tier 2 small group facilitators should seek peer coaching and ask for feedback to make sure the intervention is implemented with fidelity.

Small Group Process Notes

References

Counselor Clique. (n.d.). *Home page*. https://counselorclique.com/

Lee, L. (2020, October 2). With stress in schools increasing, simple strategies to stay calm. *Edutopia*. https://www.edutopia.org/article/stress-schools-increasing-simple-strategies-stay-calm

Truluck, B. (2019, December). *Stress busters*. The Counseling Connection. https://www.schoolcounselor.org/newsletters/january-2020/stress-busters?st=MO

Willis, J. (2014, July 18). The neuroscience behind stress and learning. *Edutopia*. https://www.edutopia.org/blog/neuroscience-behind-stress-and-learning-judy-willis

YouthSMART. (n.d.). *Home page*. https://www.youthsmart.ca/

Stress Management for High School Students

Katherine Molinari and Kayla Snyder

Description of Skill

Stress management consists of a variety of strategies to assist an individual with being able to better cope with difficulties (adversity) and stress in their life. Learning how to manage stress can help an individual live a healthier, happier, calmer, and more balanced life (Mayo Clinic, 2021).

What exactly is stress? Stress is defined as "an automatic physical, mental and emotional response to a challenging event" (Mayo Clinic, 2021, p. 1). Stress is something everyone experiences. It can be more intense and overwhelming depending on an individual's stage of life and their knowledge of coping skills. When perceived and utilized positively, stress can facilitate growth and change in an individual. However, when viewed as negative, stress can decrease an individual's overall quality of life long-term (Mayo Clinic, 2021).

Examples of stress management techniques include these:

- learning problem-solving skills, prioritizing certain tasks, and time management (Mayo Clinic, 2021).
- strengthening an individual's ability to deal with adversity, for example, learning how to be aware of the triggers of and symptoms of stress and increase one's sense of control.
- using relaxation strategies such as yoga, deep breathing, autogenic training, progressive muscle relaxation, meditation, and mindfulness.

Pre-Intervention Communication with Parents/Guardians/Teachers in Languages Represented in the School

English Version

Dear Parents/Guardians,

Greetings! You are receiving this letter to inform you that your child will be involved in a set of activities to learn more about stress management. Stress management is a valuable topic for the students of Happy Valley High School to learn about because of the numerous benefits it can offer. When children learn to manage their stress they can find effective healthy strategies to help them cope with these overwhelming feelings and learn how to better manage their time, while balancing school and life stressors.

Over 6 weeks, your child will learn various techniques to aid them in being able to manage their stress. These techniques include being able to understand what stress means, identifying their triggers of stress, being aware of how stress impacts them physically, and learning how to make better use of their time while balancing various stressors. The lessons on stress management your child will participate in are the following:

- In or Out
- Food Scan Meditation
- Autogenic Training (AT)
- Deep Breathing (Belly Breathing) Exercise
- Progressive Muscle Relaxation (deep muscle relaxation)
- Stress Plan

These lessons will be taught by the school counselors, Kayla Snyder and Katherine Molinari. If you have questions regarding any of the activities from the Stress Management Program, please feel free to contact the School Counseling department by email at sc@happyvalley.edu or by phone at (860) 967-7288 ext. 4281. We would be pleased to hear from you and to help with any concerns or questions. Thank you for your time.

Sincerely,

Your school counselor

Spanish Version

Queridos padres/guardianes,

¡Saludos! Recibe esta carta para informarle que su hijo participará en una serie de actividades para aprender más sobre el manejo del estrés. El manejo del estrés es un tema valioso para que los estudiantes de la escuela secundaria *Happy Valley* aprendan debido a los numerosos beneficios que puede ofrecer. Cuando los niños aprenden a manejar su estrés; pueden encontrar estrategias saludables efectivas para ayudarlos a lidiar con estos sentimientos abrumadores y aprender a administrar mejor su tiempo, mientras equilibran los factores estresantes de la escuela y la vida.

Durante el período de seis semanas, su hijo aprenderá varias técnicas para ayudarlo a controlar su estrés. Estas técnicas incluyen poder entender lo que significa el estrés, identificar los desencadenantes del estrés, ser conscientes de cómo el estrés los afecta físicamente y aprender a hacer un mejor uso de su tiempo mientras equilibran varios factores estresantes. Las lecciones sobre el manejo del estrés en las que participará su hijo son las siguientes:

- Dentro o fuera
- Meditación de escaneo de alimentos
- Entrenamiento Autogénico (AT)
- Ejercicio de respiración profunda (respiración abdominal)
- Relajación Muscular Progresiva (relajación muscular profunda)
- Plan de Estrés

Estas lecciones serán impartidas por las consejeras escolares, Kayla Snyder y Katherine Molinari. Si tiene preguntas sobre cualquiera de las actividades del Programa de Manejo del Estrés, no dude en comunicarse con el departamento de Consejería Escolar por correo electrónico a sc@happyvalley.edu o por teléfono al (860) 967-7288 ext. 4281. Nos complacería saber de usted y ayudarle con cualquier inquietud o pregunta. Gracias por tu tiempo.

Atentamente,

Intervencionista del equipo de apoyo al estudiante

Permission Slip (If Applicable)

Dear Parents/Guardians,

When conducting Tier 1 interventions of stress and self-care for grades 9–12, we noticed after giving a pre-assessment that some students were presenting with higher levels of stress compared to the rest of the students. Those we identified showed signs of trouble managing their stress levels as well as struggling to find positive and effective coping mechanisms that were suggested and taught to them in Tier 1.

With your permission, your child, ______________________________, will be involved in a school counseling 6-week lesson plan based on stress management. During this time they will learn a variety of skills in a small group setting that will take place during the school day. By the end of the 6-week program your child will be able to do the following:

- Define and understand what stress is.
- Identify their triggers of stress.
- Be aware of how stress can impact them physically.
- Find effective healthy strategies to cope with stress.
- Manage their time while balancing school and life stressors.
- Create a stress management action plan.

Students partaking in this lesson plan will take a post-assessment to see if their stress has decreased by being part of this intervention. If the student's stress has increased, changes need to be made for this intervention kit, but if the student's stress decreases, we know it is successful to use in future practices. The counselors will continue to monitor the students involved in this stress-management intervention by handing out extra progress monitoring sheets, making it available online, and checking in with the students' teachers.

Student name: ______________________________

Student signature: ______________________________

Parent/guardian name: ______________________________

Parent/guardian signature: ______________________________

Hoja de permiso

Queridos padres y guardianes,

Al realizar intervenciones de Nivel 1 de estrés y cuidado personal para los grados 9 a 12, notamos después de realizar una evaluación previa que algunos estudiantes presentaban niveles más altos de estrés en comparación con el resto de los estudiantes. Aquellos que identificamos mostraron signos de problemas para controlar sus niveles de estrés, así como de luchar para encontrar mecanismos de afrontamiento positivos y efectivos que se les sugirieron y enseñaron en el Nivel 1.

Con su permiso, su hijo ______________________________ participará en un plan de lecciones de 6 semanas de Consejería Escolar basado en el Manejo del Estrés. Durante este tiempo aprenderán una variedad de habilidades en un grupo pequeño que se llevará a cabo durante el día escolar. Al final del programa de 6 semanas, su hijo podrá:

- Definir y comprender qué es el estrés.
- Identificar sus desencadenantes del estrés.
- Sea consciente de cómo el estrés puede afectarles físicamente.
- Encuentre estrategias saludables efectivas para afrontar el estrés.
- Administre su tiempo mientras equilibra los factores estresantes de la escuela y la vida.
- Crear un plan de acción para el manejo del estrés.

Los estudiantes que participen en este plan de lección realizarán una evaluación posterior para ver si su estrés ha disminuido al ser parte de esta intervención. Si el estrés del estudiante ha aumentado, entonces es necesario realizar cambios en este kit de intervención, pero si el estrés del estudiante disminuye, entonces sabemos que será exitoso usarlo en prácticas futuras. Los consejeros continuarán monitoreando a los estudiantes involucrados en esta intervención de manejo del estrés entregando hojas de seguimiento de progreso adicionales, poniéndolas a disposición en línea y comunicándose con los maestros de los estudiantes.

El nombre del estudiante: ______________________________

Firma del alumno: ______________________________

Nombre del padre de familia / guardian: ______________________________

Firma del padre / tutor: ______________________________

Goals of Intervention

- Define and understand what stress is.
- Identify their triggers of stress.
- Be aware of how stress can impact them physically.
- Find effective healthy strategies to cope with stress.
- Manage their time while balancing school and life stressors.
- Create a stress management action plan.

CASEL Standards Addressed

- Managing one's emotions
- Identifying and using stress-management strategies
- Establishing self-discipline and self-motivation
- Setting personal and collective goals
- Showing the courage to take the initiative
- Demonstrating personal and collective agency

ASCA Mind-Sets and Behaviors

M 1. Belief in development of whole self, including a healthy balance of mental, social/emotional and physical well-being

B-LS 1. Critical thinking skills to make informed decisions

B-SMS 1. Responsibility for self and actions

B-LS 2. Creative approach to learning, tasks and problem solving

B-SMS 2. Self-discipline and self-control

B-LS 3. Time-management, organizational and study skills

B-SMS 3. Independent work

B-LS 4. Self-motivation and self- direction for learning

B-SMS 6. Ability to identify and overcome barriers

B-LS 7. Long- and short-term academic, career and social/emotional goals

B-SMS 7. Effective coping skills

B-SMS 8. Balance of school, home and community activities

Materials Needed

Session	Materials Needed
1	Paper, colored pencils/markers, pens, printed outline of hand
2	Small wrapped candy, item with texture, item with image, item with odor, item that makes a sound
3	Autogenic training script (read by facilitator)
4	Directions for deep belly breathing
5	Directions for progressive relaxation exercise
6	Stress management plan sheet, list of coping strategies, list of stressors, person outline, why stress happens sheet

Pre-/Post-Assessment

Name: ______________________________ Date: __________

Stress Management Pre-/posttest

Over the last month, how often have you been bothered by any of the following problems? Please circle your answer.

(5) Almost always **(4)** Most of the time **(3)** Some of the time **(2)** Almost never **(1)** Never

11. Little interest or pleasure in doing things you love to do?	5	4	3	2	1
12. Body feeling tense?	5	4	3	2	1
13. Experiencing little to no sleep?	5	4	3	2	1
14. Failure to see the humor in situations others find funny?	5	4	3	2	1
15. Experiencing headaches?	5	4	3	2	1
16. Upset stomach?	5	4	3	2	1
17. Get irritated quickly?	5	4	3	2	1
18. Blow up easily?	5	4	3	2	1
19. Have difficulties making decisions?	5	4	3	2	1
20. Neglecting things (HW, friends, exercising etc.)	5	4	3	2	1
21. Trying to do everything yourself?	5	4	3	2	1
22. Trouble concentrating?	5	4	3	2	1
23. Hard time feeling relaxed?	5	4	3	2	1
24. Feeling unable to control things?	5	4	3	2	1
25. Feeling confident in abilities to handle personal problems?	5	4	3	2	1

Total: (Under 20: low stress) (21 to 40: medium stress) (41 and up: high stress)

Sessions 1–6

These sessions are designed to teach and reinforce skills. Make note of which sessions students respond well to and which they are less responsive to. Make additions or improvements to maximize student engagement and optimize desired outcomes. Ask students for specific feedback at the end of sessions.

Session 1: In or Out of My Control

Objective:

1. Students will get to create a visual of what is in and out of their control when it comes to stressful things happening in their life.

Materials:

Paper

Colored pencils/markers, pens

Printed outline of hand

Duration: 30 minutes

Instructions:

1. Welcome students and explain the purpose of the group.
2. Invite group members to provide input on group ground rules. Record them on poster paper and ask students to sign the poster paper.

Activity 1: Discussion

1. Students will turn toward a person and answer the following questions as well as give an example of each: "What does 'in your control' mean? What does 'out of your control' mean?"
2. Students will give examples to a peer when it comes to everyday tasks.
3. Students will go around the room sharing what they spoke about (write some answers on the board to give people ideas).

Activity 2: Hand Exercise

1. Pass out paper with the printed hand on it. Students who have a disability or need accommodations will receive a printed hand with a word bank that is color coded so that they can match which items (things in and out of our control) go inside the hand and which words go outside the hand.
2. Have students fill it out then share with the class.

Activity 3: Exit Thought Questions

1. Pass out exit thought questions: How do you think this exercise relates to the word stress? Did it help you to visualize the things you should not be worrying about when it comes to everyday tasks? What do you take away from completing this activity?

Name: ______________________________ Date: ______________

In and out of our control: Write down stressors that are in your control inside the hand. Likewise, write down stressors outside the hand that are out of your control.

What do you notice?

Name: ______________________________ Date: ______________

Thought questions:

How do you think this exercise relates to the word *stress*?

____

____

____

Did it help you to visualize the things you should not be worrying about when it comes to everyday tasks?

____

____

____

What do you take away from completing this activity?

____

____

____

Session 2: Food Scan Meditation

Objective:

1. Students will utilize their five senses to be mindful of what is surrounding them and give them a chance to relax and have fun.

Materials:

Something you can eat for taste

Something you can feel

Something you can see

Something you can smell

Something you can hear

Duration: 15–20 minutes

Instructions:

1. Welcome students back and remind them of the group ground rules. Check in.

Activity 1:

1. Have students take out a piece of paper.
2. Ask them to write down how they are feeling at this current moment using only one word.
3. Ask them to turn it around and put it on the corner of their desks.
4. Pass out chips (or different snacks) to each student. Do not have them touch it yet!
5. Put on calming meditation music and speak slowly while you go through each of the senses, following the guided script.

Activity 2: Open Discussion

- How did this activity make you feel compared to the beginning of the exercise? Relaxed?
- What did you notice about yourself during the exercise?
- Any thoughts on how this applies to stress management?
- Would you use this in the future as a coping strategy when feeling stressed?

A Mindful Eating Script

Begin by connecting to your breath and body, feel your feet on the ground, and notice your experience in this moment. With your awareness in this moment, notice any thoughts, sensations, or emotions you are experiencing. (pause)

Tune into the awareness or sensation that you have in your body of feeling hungry, thirsty, or maybe even feeling full. If you were going to eat or drink something right now, what is your body hungry for? What is it thirsty for? Just pay attention and notice with awareness the sensations that give you this information. (pause)

Now, bring your attention to the item in your hand and imagine that you are seeing it for the first time. Observe with curiosity as you pay attention and notice the color, shape, texture, and size. Is there anything else that you notice, sense, or feel? (pause)

Imagine what it took for this item to get to your hands: sunshine, water, time, processing, and shipping. You may choose to be aware of gratitude for everyone involved in the cultivation and preparation of this item of food. You may choose to bring in your own gratitude or spiritual blessing. (pause)

Now place the item between your fingers and feel the texture, temperature, and ridges. You may notice smoothness or stickiness. Again, notice if you have any thoughts, sensations, or emotions at this time. Continue to breathe and be fully present in this moment. (pause)

Take the piece of food and bring it toward your nose and smell with your full awareness. Notice if you have any memories, sensations, or reactions in your body. Even before you eat it, you may notice that you begin to have a digestive response in your body just by noticing and smelling. (pause)

With full awareness of your hand moving toward your mouth, place the object (fruit or chocolate) into your mouth without chewing or swallowing it. Just allow it to be in your mouth; roll it around to different parts of your mouth and tongue. Notice the flavor and texture. Notice the physical sensations within your body, especially your mouth and your gut. Continue to breathe as you explore the sensation of having this item in your mouth. (pause)

Next take just one bite and notice the flavor; notice the change of texture. Then very slowly begin to chew this piece of food and notice the parts of your mouth that are involved in chewing. Notice the sound and movement of chewing, as you continue to notice the sensations and flavor. (pause)

When you are ready, swallow this item and notice the path that it follows from your mouth and throat into your stomach. Notice the sensation and taste that may linger in your mouth. Connect again to your body and your breath and notice your experience in this moment. (pause)

Next, I invite you to pick up another food item and choose to eat it however you wish. Notice your choice and your experience. Notice how it is similar or different. (Pause for 30–60 seconds, then return to large group discussion about the experience.)

Source: Christine Milovani, "A Mindful Eating Script," Whole Health for Pain and Suffering: An Integrative Approach, https://www.va.gov/WHOLEHEALTHLIBRARY/docs/Script-Mindful-Eating.pdf, U.S. Department of Veteran Affairs, 2016.

Session 3: Relaxation Through Visualization

Objective:

1. Students will learn how to alleviate their stress and reach a state of relaxation through the daily practice of visualization. The facilitator will repeat a series of visualizations and verbal cues, which will help the students feel warm and relaxed.

Materials:

Visualization script read by the facilitator

Duration: About 15 minutes for each session (30 minutes overall); one before school starts (7:00 a.m.) and one at the end of school (2:00 p.m.).

Instructions:

1. Welcome students back and remind them of the group ground rules. Check in.

Activity 1:

1. The facilitator will explain to the students what visualization is, how it works, and how it can help the students decrease their symptoms of stress. For example, the facilitator will tell the students, "Visualization helps to repair the connection between 'the activity of the sympathetic (flight or fight) and the parasympathetic (rest and digest) branches of the autonomic nervous system'" (The University of Melbourne, 2022, para. 1).
2. Complete visualization to get out of flight or fight stress mode (15 minutes).
3. Students will be guided through a visualization script by their facilitator.
4. Read the script.

Activity 2:

1. After the visualization exercise, the facilitator will ask the students to share any differences they notice in their bodies and how they feel. For example, do they feel calmer? More relaxed? Less anxious/stressed?
2. The facilitator will encourage students to use the visualization exercise on their own to help manage their stress, for example, when they wake up in the morning, before or after lunch, and before bed.
3. The facilitator will also recommend students to teach this strategy to their family or friends.

White Sandy Beach Visualization

Imagine that you are resting on a white sandy beach and feel safe, calm, and relaxed as you think about the following:

- turquoise water and a clear, blue sky
- the sound of soft waves as the tide gently rolls in
- the weight of your body sinking into your beach chair
- the warmth of the sand on your feet
- a large umbrella keeping you slightly shaded, creating just the right temperature

Relax your face and let go of any tension in your forehead, between your eyebrows, your neck, and your throat. Soften your eyes and rest. Allow your breath to slow down and match the rolling waves of the water. It is effortless to be here; spend time just taking it all in.

Image 9.24

Image 9.25

Image 9.26

Source: "How to Use Visualization to Reduce Anxiety Symptoms," by K. Star, March 10, 2022, VeryWellMind, https://www.verywellmind.com/visualization-for-relaxation-2584112

Session 4: Deep Breathing (Belly Breathing) Exercise

Objective:

1. Students will practice deep breathing techniques to help them reduce their symptoms of stress.

Duration: 5–15 minutes (depending on how many times you choose to repeat the exercise)

Instructions:

1. Welcome students back and remind them of the group ground rules. Check in.

Activity 1:

1. The facilitator will educate a small group of students on what "belly breathing" or "diaphragmatic breathing'" is, how to do it, and how it can help with decreasing stress and anxiety. For example, the facilitator will explain that belly breathing requires one's diaphragm to contract, belly to expand, and inhalation and exhalation to deepen, which lowers the frequency of breathing and increases the amount of oxygen in one's bloodstream (Ma et al., 2017). As a result, belly breathing induces a state of relaxation and has been shown to reduce depression, anxiety, and stress in various studies (Ma et al., 2017).
2. The facilitator will also emphasize that this breathing technique can be used to cope with present and future stressors.

Activity 2:

1. The facilitator will have students stand or sit comfortably, adequately spaced out from each other.
2. Provide students with the following directions:
   a. Stand straight up with feet should-width apart.
   b. Arms and hands are relaxed downward.
   c. Body is relaxed.
   d. Eyes are closed.
   e. Focus on lower abdomen (belly) and imagine a small balloon in that space.
   f. Breathe in slowly and deeply through the nostrils, imagining the balloon inflating and growing bigger slowly. Hold a few seconds.
   g. Slowly exhale through the mouth, imagining the balloon gently deflating; blow out of the mouth as if blowing out a candle.
   h. Tip: Place a hand over the lower abdomen to feel it go up and down and make sure you're not breathing with the chest.
   i. Repeat at least 10 times.

Activity 3:

1. After the breathing exercise, the facilitator will ask the students to share any differences they notice in their bodies and how they feel. For example, are they more relaxed/calm? Do they feel lighter? Great? Tired?
2. The facilitator will encourage students to use deep/belly breathing on their own to help manage their stress, for example, before bed, waiting in line to get lunch, or on the bus ride to school.
3. The facilitator will also recommend students to teach this strategy to their family or friends.

Session 5: Progressive Muscle Relaxation (Deep Muscle Relaxation)

Objective:

1. Students will learn how to achieve deep muscle relaxation as a simple stress management activity.

Duration: 5–15 minutes (depending on how many times you choose to repeat the exercise).

Instructions:

1. Welcome students back and remind them of the group ground rules. Check in.

Activity 1:

1. The facilitator will educate a small group of students on what progressive muscle relaxation (PMR) is, how it works, and how it can help students manage their stress. For example, the facilitator will explain that PMR is a strategy for decreasing stress and anxiety through the act of tensing and relaxing one's muscles alternately (Pawlow & Jones, 2002).
2. The facilitator will continue, explaining that since anxiety and stress are typically accompanied with muscle tension, anxiety can be lowered by learning how to relax and decrease muscular tension through PMR (Bracke, 2010).
3. The facilitator will tell students that they can sit or lay down, depending on what they feel comfortable with and the available space.
4. Demonstrate/model each step for students in preparation for their participation. Then read and model the following instructions to your students.

Activity 2:

1. After the muscle relaxation exercise, the facilitator will ask the students to share any differences they notice in their bodies and how they feel. For example, do they feel calmer? More relaxed? Less anxious and stressed?
2. The facilitator will encourage students to use PMR on their own to help manage their stress, for example, before bed, before taking an exam, or as a 5-minute break when doing homework.
3. The facilitator will also recommend students to teach this strategy to their family or friends.

PMR Meditation

1. Raise your eyebrows and wrinkle your forehead. Try to touch your hairline with your eyebrows. Hold for 5 seconds and relax.
2. Make a frown. Hold for 5 seconds and relax.
3. Close your eyes as tightly as you can. Draw the corners of your mouth back with your lips closed. Hold for 5 seconds and relax.
4. Open your eyes and your mouth as wide as you can. Hold for 5 seconds and relax. Feel the warmth and calmness in your face.
5. Stretch your arms out in front of you. Close your fists tightly. Hold for 5 seconds and relax. Feel the warmth and calmness in your hands.
6. Stretch your arms out to the side. Pretend you are pushing against an invisible wall with your hands. Hold for 5 seconds and relax.
7. Bend your elbows and make a muscle in your upper arm. Hold for 5 seconds and relax. Feel the tension leave your arms.
8. Lift your shoulders to your ears. Hold for 5 seconds and relax.
9. Arch your back away from the back of the chair. Hold for 5 seconds and relax.
10. Round your back. Try to push against the back of your chair. Hold for 5 seconds and relax. Feel the tension leaving your back.
11. Tighten your stomach muscles. Hold for 5 seconds and relax
12. Tighten your hip and buttock muscles. Hold for 5 seconds and relax.
13. Tighten your thigh muscles by pressing your legs together. Hold for 5 seconds and relax
14. Bend your ankles toward your body as far as you can. Hold for 5 seconds and relax.
15. Curl your toes under as far as you can. Hold for 5 seconds and relax
16. Tighten all the muscles in your whole body. Hold for 10 seconds and relax. Let your entire body be heavy and calm. Sit quietly and enjoy the feeling of relaxation for a couple of minutes.

Source: Adapted from "Progressive Muscle Relaxation Script," Therapist Aid, 2017, https://www.therapistaid.com/worksheets/progressive-muscle-relaxation-script.

Session 6: Stress Plan

Objective:

1. Students will create a stress management plan for times they are feeling overwhelmed and be able to utilize this at any convenience.
2. Students will be able to identify their stressors and ways to cope with them.

Materials:

Stress management plan sheet

List of coping strategies

List of stressors

Person outline

"Why Stress Happens" worksheet

Duration: 30 minutes

Instructions:

1. Welcome students back and remind them of the group ground rules. Check in.

Activity 1:

1. Give students a handout that discusses what stress is, what makes people stressed, signs of stress, and coping strategies.

Activity 2:

1. You will then hand out a fill in the blank sheet that the students fill out. This will create their stress management action plan.

What Are the Signs of Stress?

How you might feel:

- anxious
- afraid
- angry or aggressive
- sad
- irritable
- frustrated
- depressed

These feelings can sometimes produce physical symptoms, making you feel even worse.

How your body might react:

- headaches
- nausea
- indigestion
- digestive problems such as constipation, bloating, or diarrhea
- shallow breathing or hyperventilating
- sweating
- heart palpitations
- aches and pains

How you might behave:

- withdraw from other people or snap at them
- be indecisive or inflexible
- be tearful
- have problems getting to sleep or staying asleep
- experience sexual problems
- smoke, drink alcohol, or take drugs more than usual

If the stress is long-lasting, you may notice your sleep and memory are affected, your eating habits change, or you feel less inclined to exercise.

Students will then identify where they feel stress on their bodies using the outline of a person sheet. They will list their top stressors next to it.

I know I am stressed when...

Name: ______________________________ Date: __________

Example: Top stressor = school work

Where do you feel the stress? = in my stomach

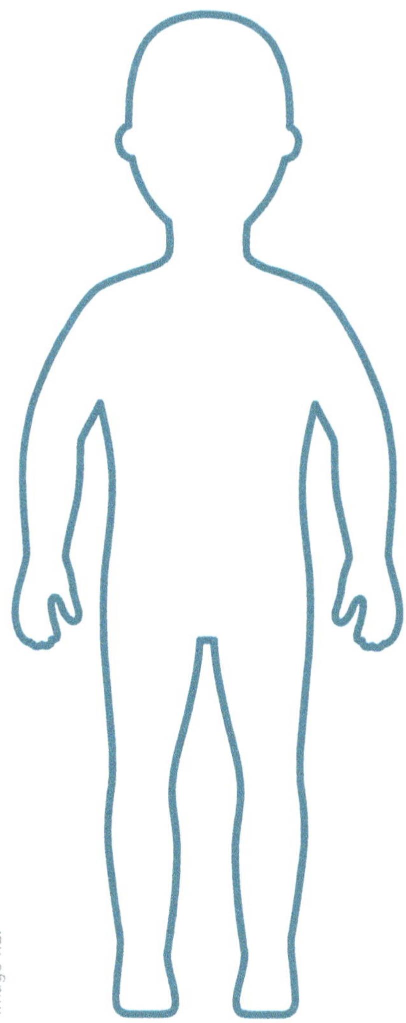

Image 9.27

Stress Management Action Plan

Name: ______________________________ Date: ____________

People who can help me	**Four activities I like to do**

Positive affirmations I can use	**In the moment coping skills (e.g., breathing)**

Image 9.28

Post-Intervention Communication to Parent/Guardian

English Version

Dear Parents/Guardians,

Your child, ______________________________, participated in a 6-week stress-management program that helped them overcome certain barriers toward their academic and/or their social emotional learning. In this process they were able to effectively manage their stress by partaking in various different activities brought to them by the counseling staff, some of which included an action plan, meditation, and autogenic training. We are proud to say that with all of your child's hard work their progress has greatly improved. Attached you will find all the work they have done throughout the course of these 6 weeks and how much growth they had from beginning to end.

We hope that in the future your child will be able to overcome stressful situations on their own utilizing the techniques we provided. If you have any questions, comments, or concerns please do not hesitate to reach out to our staff so we can set up a time to discuss further. Thank you.

Sincerely,

Counseling Intervention Team

Spanish Version

Estimados padres/tutores,

Su hijo, ______________________________, estaba participando en un programa de manejo del estrés de seis semanas que lo ayudó a superar ciertas barreras hacia su aprendizaje académico o socioemocional. En este proceso, pudieron controlar eficazmente su estrés participando en diversas actividades diferentes que les presentó el personal de consejería. Algunos de los cuales incluían un plan de acción, meditación y entrenamiento autógeno. Estamos orgullosos de decir que con todo el arduo trabajo de su hijo, su progreso ha mejorado enormemente. Adjunto encontrarás todo el trabajo que han realizado a lo largo de estas seis semanas y cuánto crecimiento tuvieron de principio a fin.

Esperamos que en el futuro su hijo pueda superar situaciones estresantes por sí solo utilizando las técnicas que le proporcionamos. Si tiene alguna pregunta, comentario o inquietud, no dude en comunicarse con nuestro personal para que podamos programar un horario para discutir más a fondo. Gracias.

Atentamente,

Equipo de intervención de asesoramiento

Plan for Implementation Fidelity

To achieve the intended outcomes of this intervention, it is helpful to colead the small group with a colleague, reflect on student responses to the activities, and seek support to keep engagement in the group high. Tier 2 small group facilitators should seek peer coaching and ask for feedback to make sure the intervention is implemented with fidelity.

Small Group Process Notes

Progress Monitoring

Name: ______________________________ Date: ______________

Are You Managing Your Stress?

Days	M	T	W	T or Th	F
Moment you felt symptoms of stress					
How you felt					
Coping strategy used					

References

Bracke, P. E. (2010, January 30). Progressive muscle relaxation. *The Corsini Encyclopedia of Psychology*. https://doi.org/10.1002/9780470479216.corpsy0712

Collaborative for Academic, Social, and Emotional Learning. (2021, December 23). *Frameworks, competencies, standards, and guidelines*. https://casel.org/state-resource-center/frameworks-competencies-standards-and-guidelines

Mayo Foundation for Medical Education and Research. (2021, October 5). *Stress management*. https://www.mayoclinic.org/tests-procedures/stress-management/about/pac-20384898

Milovani, C. (2016). *A mindful eating script: Veterans affairs*. https://www.va.gov/WHOLEHEALTHLIBRARY/docs/Script-Mindful-Eating.pdf

Pawlow, L. A., & Jones, G. E. (2002). The impact of abbreviated progressive muscle relaxation on salivary cortisol. *Biological Psychology*, *60*(1), 1–16.

The University of Melbourne. (2022). *Autogenic training exercise*. Counseling & Psychological Services. https://services.unimelb.edu.au/counsel/resources/guided-exercises/autogenic-training#:~:text=Autogenic%20training%20is%20a%20relaxation,time%2C%20and%20in%20the%20evening

Credits

CHAPTER 10

Tier 2 Intervention Kits for Social Awareness

Middle School Social Awareness/Social Skills Group

Stephanie Barbagallo and Vareesha Rahman

Description of Skill

Social awareness is defined as "the abilit[y] to understand the perspectives of and empathize with others, including those from diverse backgrounds" (CASEL, 2020, para.5). As middle schoolers mature there are several key developmental tasks:

- Build on earlier understanding of others to comprehend more complex emotional situations in self and others.
- Form a largely group-based identity with increasing independence from adults.
- Become able to resolve conflicts within dyadic and group situations (Denham, 2018).

This Tier 2 intervention is designed for students in grades 6–8 who have shown signs of poor social skills, including but not limited to lack of communication skills, lack of understanding of nonverbal cues, difficulties managing peer pressure, and challenges resolving conflicts with peers. General education teachers recommend students to the group who they feel would benefit from social skills training. It is important to teach students social skills, including how to deal with peer pressure. Students in middle school want to be accepted by peers, which is why it is imperative that students learn strategies to confront peer pressure in a healthy way. These lessons could also be shared with all students in a Tier 1 lesson. We believe that this social skills group will help students feel confident in themselves when they need to stand up for their wants and beliefs. By utilizing role-plays, students will be able to see different examples of peer pressure and discuss how they may work through those situations.

Pre-Intervention Communication With Parents/Guardians/Teachers in Languages Represented in the School

English Version

Dear Parents/Caregivers,

As you know, we take special care at our school to foster a positive and inclusive school environment for all of our learners. Your student was encouraged to join this group to share their knowledge about navigating the social world as a middle schooler and to learn new strategies. We will focus on communication, reading body language, perspective taking, and resolving conflicts peacefully. The group will last 6 weeks and will meet during ________ (time of day). The group begins on ______ (date) and concludes on ______ (date).

If you have any questions, please feel free to contact us.

Sincerely,

The Student Support Team

Spanish Version

Estimados padres/cuidadores,

Como usted sabe, en nuestra escuela ponemos especial cuidado en fomentar un ambiente escolar positivo e inclusivo para todos nuestros alumnos. Se animó a su estudiante a unirse a este grupo para compartir sus conocimientos sobre cómo navegar en el mundo social como estudiante de secundaria y aprender nuevas estrategias. Nos centraremos en la comunicación, la lectura del lenguaje corporal, la toma de perspectiva y la resolución pacífica de conflictos. El grupo tendrá una duración de 6 semanas y se reunirá a las ________ (hora del día). El grupo comienza el ______ (fecha) y concluye el ______ (fecha).

Si tiene alguna pregunta, no dude en contactarnos.

Atentamente,

El equipo de apoyo estudiantil

Permission Slip (If Applicable)

After reading the description of this Tier 2 small group, I, ____________________, give permission for my student ____________________ to take part in the group which will meet on ____________________ from [date] to [date]. I understand that this group is confidential and that I will be made aware if my student is making good use of this group experience. Should I need to be contacted, the best number to reach me at is ____________________.

Hoja de permiso

Después de leer la descripción de este grupo pequeño de Nivel 2, yo, ____________________, doy permiso para mi estudiante ____________________ a participar en el grupo que se reunirá el ____________________ de [fecha] a [fecha]. Entiendo que este grupo es confidencial y que se me informará si mi estudiante está haciendo un buen uso de esta experiencia grupal. Si necesita ponerse en contacto conmigo, el mejor número para comunicarse conmigo es ____________________.

Goals of Intervention

- Improve communication skills.
- Develop a better understanding of nonverbal cues.
- Learn new strategies for managing peer pressure.
- Practice strategies to resolve conflicts with peers in a peaceful and mature manner.

CASEL Standards Addressed

- Taking others' perspectives
- Showing concern for the feelings of others
- Demonstrating empathy and compassion
- Identifying diverse social norms, including unjust ones
- Demonstrating cultural competency
- Recognizing strengths in others
- Developing positive relationships
- Resolving conflicts constructively

Materials Needed

Hat/bowl

Slips of social skills

Check-in sheet

8" × 11" colored paper

5-minute mindfulness music video

Role-playing scenarios

Skit worksheet

Nonverbal communication chart

Three buckets

Three phrase cards (six total)

Three emotion cards (six total)

Role-play cards

Chairs organized in a circle

Board game

Card questions

Eraser caps

Spinner

Pre-/Post-Assessment: Social Skills

Please read the following questions and circle yes or no:

1. When the teacher asks the class a question, I speak without raising my hand.

   YES NO

2. I use the bathroom in the beginning and end of class.

   YES NO

3. I raise my hand when I have a question or concern in class.

   YES NO

4. When the teacher is talking, I do not talk to my peers around me.

   YES NO

5. If my peers distract me, I ignore them and listen to the teacher.

   YES NO

6. I show anger when things don't go my way.

   YES NO

7. If I am stuck on a problem, I still try my best.

   YES NO

8. I find something productive to do when I finish my work.

   YES NO

Sessions 1–6

These sessions are designed to teach and reinforce skills. Make note of which sessions students respond well to and which they are less responsive to. Make additions or improvements to maximize student engagement and optimize desired outcomes. Ask students for specific feedback at the end of sessions.

Session 1: Developing Social Skills

Objective:

1. Students will develop a basic understanding of the importance of social skills training and review multiple social situations.

Materials:

Hat/bowl

Slips of social skills

Check-in sheet

Duration: 15–20 minutes

Instructions:

1. Welcome students and explain the purpose of the group.
2. Invite group members to provide input on group ground rules. Record them on poster paper and ask students to sign the poster paper.

Activity 1: Check-In

1. When students first arrive at the group, have each member write down on a slip of paper a difficult social situation that they feel uncomfortable in or are unsure how to deal with.
2. Have students keep slips of paper at the corner of their desk.
3. At the end of the lesson, if students feel comfortable, have students share what they wrote and work together as a group to find a solution for how to deal with the social situation.

Activity 2: Fishing for Social Awareness

1. In a hat or bowl have about 15 different social skills written on slips of paper.
2. Ask students to randomly pick a card and then share the importance of that social skill. Some examples of social skills may include, but are not limited to, the following:
   - asking for help
   - active listening
   - accepting differences
   - reporting bullying
   - encouraging peers
   - sharing
   - positively resolving conflicts
   - disagreeing politely

- walking in the hallways
- following directions
- taking turns
- equal participation
- using self-control
- patience
- respecting teachers
- respecting peers

Assessment/evaluation: Do they now know the importance of social skills? Was their uncomfortable social situation addressed?

Asking for help	**Encouraging peers**
Active listening	**Sharing**
Accepting differences	**Positively resolving conflicts**
Reporting bullying	**Disagreeing politely**
Walking in hallways	**Using self-control**
Following directions	**Patience**
Taking turns	**Respecting teachers**
Equal participation	**Respecting peers**

Session 2: Communicating With Teachers

Objective:

1. Students will learn different methods of communication and explore positive interactions with teachers and peers.

Materials:

8" × 11" colored paper

5-minute mindfulness music

Duration: 20 minutes

Instructions:

1. Welcome students back and remind them of the group ground rules. Check in.

Activity: Communication Origami: How to Communicate With Teachers (10 minutes)

1. The group will start by passing out colored paper to each student. The instructor will ask the students to either close their eyes or look away from the paper.
2. Turn on the 5-minute mindfulness music as a timer and begin by instructing students to rip and fold the paper according to what is being said. Example: "Fold the paper in half" "rip a circle out the center."
3. Once the music stops, have the students open up the paper and compare it with a partner.
4. End this activity by asking the students how they felt not being able to look or ask questions.
5. Emphasize the importance of asking questions to the teacher and how everyone has a different way of interpreting what is being said. Communication is the key to getting a clear understanding of the assignment.

Assessment/evaluation: How would you ask for help if you were confused or unsure of how to do an assignment?

Session 3: Communicating With Peers

Objective:

1. Students will learn different methods of communication and explore positive interactions with teachers and peers.

Materials:

Role-playing scenarios

Skit worksheet

Duration: 20 minutes

Instructions:

1. Welcome students back and remind them of the group ground rules. Check in.

Activity: Role-Playing: How to Communicate With Peers

1. Students will be asked to role-play different methods of communication. Each student will be paired up with another student and will be given a topic for a scenario.
2. Students will be asked to take 5 minutes to write a quick skit to present about the specific topic.
3. Ask students to present them their role-play in front of the groups to practice speaking skills.
4. Let the students know to focus on the three most important aspects for the skit:
    a. They should have at least two characters.
    b. They should be at least five or more lines.
    c. Make sure you state your problem and provide a solution.

Assessment/evaluation: After watching the skits performed, how would you benefit from communicating in a new way in different situations?

Skit Topics (Cut Into Separate Topics to Pass Out)

Write a skit about receiving a compliment from a peer.
Write a skit about getting distracted from classwork.
Write a skit about asking a teacher for help.

Write a Skit

Don't forget to underline the problem and the solution. Example: "Write a skit on how to avoid peer pressure."

> Character 1: "Hey, let's skip class"
>
> Character 2: "I don't think that's a good idea"
>
> Character 1: "It'll be fine no one will know."
>
> Character 2: "I have an idea: Let's go to class and hang out after school."
>
> Character 1: "You are right; let's go."

Session 4: Nonverbal Communication

Objective:

1. Students will learn the different types of nonverbal communication and understand how things like tone and body language may portray a different message than what we communicate verbally.

Materials:

Nonverbal communication chart

Three buckets

Three phrase cards (six total)

Three emotion cards (six total)

Duration: 20 minutes

Instructions:

1. Welcome students back and remind them of the group ground rules. Check in.

Activity 1: Nonverbal Communication Chart

1. Students will each be given a copy of the three handouts.
2. The first discusses the four main components to nonverbal communication, including eye contact, body language, tone, and the physical distance between them and other individuals.
3. The second is a facial expression emotion chart, and the last is a "cat" body language chart.
4. The last chart refers to how cats show their emotions and how humans also show how they are feeling based on the way they position their body.

Activity 2: Communication Charades

1. Students will each pick a slip from the two buckets. One bucket has three different phrases (written on six slips of paper). Each individual will be paired with whoever has the same phrase. The phrases are as follows:
   a. "I can't believe this is happening."
   b. "Did you see that?"
   c. "That sounds perfect."
2. The second bucket will have six different emotions.
3. The student will work with their partner to try and say their phrase, using tone and body language to portray the emotion they picked.
4. Give students 5 minutes to prepare to allow them to refer to their charts for assistance. Once the groups are ready, have the students present and the other students guess the emotion.
5. If time permits, have students discuss what they learned from the exercise.

Assessment/evaluation: Continue to monitor students' behavior charts to ensure that social skills behavior is improving within classes.

Feelings Chart

Image 10.1

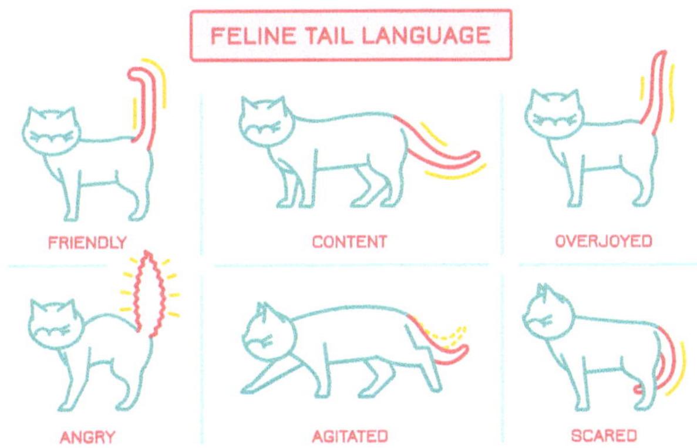

Image 10.2

"I can't believe this is happening."	"Did you see that?"	"That sounds perfect."
"I can't believe this is happening"	"Did you see that?"	"That sounds perfect."

Scared	Excited
Angry	Sad
Surprised	Happy

Session 5: Peer Pressure

Objective:

1. Students will learn how to address peer pressure, stand up for themselves and others, and avoid pressuring others.

Materials:

Role-play cards

Chairs organized in a circle

Duration: 20 minutes

Instructions:

1. Welcome students back and remind them of the group ground rules. Check in.

Activity:

1. Introduction of topic. As students get settled, ask if anyone has ever experienced peer pressure.
2. How did they deal with it? Was the experience positive or negative? Discuss the difference between positive and negative peer pressure.
3. Discuss how peer pressure, either positive or negative, can be frustrating for the individual on the receiving end and why we must respect our peers' decisions.
4. Then move into the role-plays. Peer pressure case scenarios:
    a. Students will act out and discuss the role-plays.
    b. Four different students will volunteer to act as Pablo and Marcus.
    c. Have students answer the discussion questions.
5. Read the dialogue in this scene and discuss the questions provided:

    Pablo: Is that kid new? I haven't seen him before today. He was on my bus this morning. He looks so out of place.

    Marcus: I think he's okay. He's probably a little nervous.

    Pablo: I just had class with him, and the teachers split us up in teams to study for the test tomorrow. He didn't know anything, so our team lost. I want to give him a hard time on the bus ride home. Maybe I will get some others in on it too.

    Marcus: Why?

    Pablo: Just to razz him a little. Are you in?

    Marcus: I don't know. I bet he just wants us to leave him alone.

Pablo: Oh geez. You are so afraid of getting in trouble. We sit in the back of the bus. No one will ever see us. Besides, we are the oldest ones on the bus. The younger kids are too scared to stand up for themselves.

Marcus: I don't think it's a good idea. I ...

Pablo: I "what"? You used to go along with ideas I had. Now you are afraid of everything. Fine, I will sit with the other guys on the bus from now on.

Marcus: That's not what I mean, okay?

Pablo: Marcus, what happened? You used to be so cool. I am not going to beg you to get in on it. Are you in or not?

Discussion questions:

1. How did you feel listening to the actors read these lines?
2. Does this scenario seem familiar to you? Why or why not?
3. Who is the person pressuring?
4. What kinds of words or phrases did he use?
5. What do you think it feels like to Marcus to hear those words?
6. What would you do if you were Marcus?

Assessment/evaluation: Evaluate students' progress on behavior CICO card if they are currently taking part in CICO.

Session 6: Conflict Resolution

Objectives:

1. Students will understand how conflicts develop.
2. Students will understand steps to conflict resolution.

Duration: 30–40 minutes

Instructions:

1. Welcome students back and remind them of the group ground rules. Check in.

Activity 1: Apple Arguments

1. Ask students to think about different types of conflict origins.
2. Ask how do most conflicts develop?
3. Explain to students that it is helpful to understand how a conflict began in order to arrive at solutions or resolution.
4. Share, "We know that conflicts arise for all sorts of reasons at school, at home, on the field, on the bus, anywhere. All conflicts generally have one of two origins: resources and values."
5. Explain the terms *resources* and *values*. These are the sources that drive conflict. They are intrinsically linked to human needs and satisfaction. Understanding the cause of conflict is a great way to begin resolving it. This activity will help students think about different types of conflict. Resource conflicts involve contention over a limited commodity (land, money, time, materials, labor). Resource conflicts are typically simpler to resolve and commonly settled using competition, division, sharing, and resource expanding. Value conflicts involve clashes between personal beliefs and usually center around what's right, good, or just. Value conflicts are more difficult to resolve because values are intricately tied to individual and cultural identity. Value conflicts are commonly resolved using education, exposure, interest identification, and compromise.
6. Arrange seats in a circle around a small table or desk.
7. Put an apple on the table.
8. Cut and hand out an apple position to each student. If need be, two students can share a position. Or, you can invent new ones!
9. Ask students to keep their positions secret, at first.
10. Ask two students at a time to come to the table and read or describe their positions to each other and the class.
11. For each pairing, ask the class to consider the following questions:
    a. What type of conflict has formed, if any? (Which of the class's conflict categories would you place this problem in?) Is this a resource or value conflict?
    b. What needs are at stake in this conflict?

c. Can you think of a win-win solution to this problem? For example, you want to eat the apple, but you only like the skin. You usually toss the rest. You want to use the apple to make applesauce. This is a conflict over resources.

12. Peel the apple.
13. One can eat the peel and the other can use the flesh for applesauce.
14. Continue until all students who want a turn have gone.

Apple Arguments Positions

Image 10.3

You want to eat the apple, but you only like the skin. You usually toss the rest.

You're deathly allergic to apples. You cannot touch them or anything they've recently touched.

You believe apples are demonic. They should all be burned as soon as possible.

You're certain this is the apple that was stolen from your lunchbox earlier but cannot prove it. You're an apple farmer. You want the seeds to plant in your orchard.

You're a hunger activist and think that using the apple for any purpose other than eating is wrong.

You want to use the apple to make applesauce.

Apples are sacred in your religion. They must not be eaten or otherwise defaced.

You want to put the apple in a barrel and go bobbing for apples.

You hate apples. You don't like the taste, and you don't like the texture. You'll tell anyone who asks.

You have malusdomesticaphobia, the fear of apples: You can't bear to see, be near, or even talk about apples.

You've just learned how to break an apple in half with your bare hands. You want to prove to everyone that you can do it.

You want to cut the apple in half and use it to make painting prints.

In your culture, apples are believed to have incredible healing powers, but only if you eat the whole thing, peel, seeds, and stem.

You want to take pictures of the apple at various stages of decomposition for a science project.

Discussion questions:

1. Which conflicts seemed easier to resolve, resource conflicts or value conflicts?
2. What would happen if you used the same resolution for all of these conflicts?
3. Flip a coin and the winner gets the apple? Or, split the apple and give each person half.

Post-Intervention Communication to Parent/Guardian

English Version

Dear Parents/Caregivers,

This week we completed our middle school social skills small group. We are very proud of the effort the students put forth to improve their communication skills, understand one another's perspective, better manage peer pressure, and identify two to three new strategies for handling conflicts. Make sure to ask your student about their experience in the group and their most important take aways. We will be following up with teachers to ensure that students are applying what they have learned in the group while they are in their classrooms. In a month's time we will hold a booster session to see how the group members are progressing.

It has been a pleasure to work with your student. Please do not hesitate to contact us if we can be of assistance to you in any way.

Sincerely,

The Student Support Team

Spanish Version

Estimados padres/cuidadores,

Esta semana completamos nuestro grupo pequeño de habilidades sociales de la escuela secundaria. Estamos muy orgullosos del esfuerzo que hicieron los estudiantes para mejorar sus habilidades de comunicación, comprender la perspectiva de los demás, gestionar mejor la presión de los compañeros e identificar 2 o 3 nuevas estrategias para manejar los conflictos. Asegúrese de preguntarle a su estudiante sobre su experiencia en el grupo y sus conclusiones más importantes. Haremos un seguimiento con los maestros para asegurarnos de que los estudiantes estén aplicando lo que han aprendido en el grupo mientras están en sus aulas. Dentro de un mes realizaremos una sesión de refuerzo para ver cómo van progresando los miembros del grupo.

Ha sido un placer trabajar con su estudiante. No dude en ponerse en contacto con nosotros si podemos ayudarle de alguna manera.

Atentamente,

El equipo de apoyo estudiantil

Selection from "Conflict Resolution Activities for Middle School Skill-Building," https://cpb-us-e1.wpmucdn.com/blogs.uoregon.edu/dist/8/11350/files/2015/05/Compiled-Activities-1-r5x71c.pdf, p. 28.

Plan for Implementation Fidelity

Teachers, fellow school-based mental health providers, administrators, and caregivers are briefed about the intended intervention before students are screened for the group. All constituents give feedback on the intervention, paying close attention to the cultural nuances inherent in learning and demonstrating social skills. Group leaders track students' engagement and progress during the group process while adhering closely to the activities outlined in the Tier 2 kit. Students are asked to share their thoughts about what they liked and didn't like about the group and how it could be improved for next time.

Small Group Process Notes

References

Denham, S. A. (2018). Keeping SEL developmental: The importance of a developmental lens for fostering and assessing SEL competencies. *Frameworks Briefs*, *1*(2), 127–152.

Casel. (2020). *CASEL's Framework: What are the Core Competence Areas and Where are They Promoted?* CASEL Framework Briefs. https://casel.org/casel-sel-framework-11-2020/?view=true

Collaborative for Academic, Social, and Emotional Learning. What is the CASEL framework? https://casel.org/fundamentals-of-sel/what-is-the-casel-framework/#:~:text=Social%20awareness%3A%20The%20abilities%20to,backgrounds%2C%20cultures%2C%20and%20contexts

Social Awareness for High School Students

Dr. Peg Donohue

Description of Skill

As students mature, their peers become increasingly more important to them. Peer approval and developing a sense of belonging supports students' identity develop and overall well-being. This Tier 2 kit is designed to assist students who are not demonstrating a high level of social awareness. These students may have difficulty making and maintaining friendships. They may have been disciplined for failing to respect peers whose background and culture were different from their own. In the information age when students spend a great deal of time interacting with technology, their ability to recognize and acknowledge others' emotions can be negatively impacted. Intentional instruction in a small group of this nature can improve students' self-awareness and set them on a path to developing better relationships and an improved level of social awareness. Most importantly, once students become more confident in this area, they can help contribute to a more inclusive and positive school environment.

Pre-Intervention Communication With Parents/Guardians/Teachers in Languages Represented in the School

English Version

Dear Parents/Guardians,

Your [ninth, 10th, 11th, or 12th] grader has been selected to take part in a small group focused on developing social awareness. Social awareness is the ability to take the perspective of and empathize with others from diverse backgrounds and cultures. This 6-week group will take place [indicate when] and will not interfere with their academic classes. The goal of this group is to delve into how to demonstrate empathy, improve communication, and enhance problem-solving skills in social situations. We will discuss our current strategies while learning new approaches. This will involve reflection, sharing experiences, and active listening. Each student will complete a pretest prior to the group and a posttest as we finish up.

Our goals are to explore and master how to do the following:

- Identify others' emotions.
- Contribute to an inclusive environment at our school.
- Listen actively.
- Disagree without being disagreeable.
- Recognize commonalities and respect differences in our peers.
- Act if we see someone being bullied or harassed.
- Continue to seek opportunities to develop social awareness as they mature.

If you have any questions about this intervention group or would like to discuss your student's participation in the group, please do not hesitate to reach out to me.

Sincerely,

Student Support Team Interventionist

Spanish Version

Queridos padres/guardianes,

Su hijo de [9.º, 10.º, 11.º o 12.º] grado ha sido seleccionado para participar en un grupo pequeño centrado en desarrollar la conciencia social. La conciencia social es la capacidad de adoptar la perspectiva de otras personas de diversos orígenes y culturas y empatizar con ellas. Este grupo de 6 semanas se llevará a cabo [indicar cuándo] y no interferirá con sus clases académicas. El objetivo de este grupo es profundizar en cómo demostrar empatía, mejorar la comunicación y potenciar las habilidades de resolución de problemas en situaciones sociales. Discutiremos nuestras estrategias actuales mientras aprendemos nuevos enfoques. Esto implicará reflexión, compartir experiencias y escucha activa. Cada estudiante completará una prueba previa al grupo y una prueba posterior cuando terminemos.

Nuestros objetivos son explorar y dominar cómo:

- Identificar las emociones de los demás.
- Contribuir a un ambiente inclusivo en nuestra escuela.
- Escucha activamente
- No estar de acuerdo sin ser desagradable
- Reconocer los puntos en común y respetar las diferencias entre nuestros pares.
- Actuar si vemos a alguien siendo intimidado o acosado
- Continuar buscando oportunidades para desarrollar la conciencia social a medida que maduran.

Si tiene alguna pregunta sobre este grupo de intervención o le gustaría hablar sobre la participación de su estudiante en el grupo, no dude en comunicarse conmigo.

Atentamente,

Intervencionista del equipo de apoyo al estudiante

Permission Slip (If Applicable)

After reading the description of this Tier 2 small group, I, ____________________, give permission for my student ____________________ to take part in the group which will meet on ____________________ from [date] to [date]. I understand that this group is confidential and that I will be made aware if my student is making good use of this group experience. Should I need to be contacted, the best number to reach me at is ____________________.

Hoja de permiso

Después de leer la descripción de este grupo pequeño de Nivel 2, yo, ____________________, doy permiso para mi estudiante ____________________ a participar en el grupo que se reunirá el ____________________ de [fecha] a [fecha]. Entiendo que este grupo es confidencial y que se me informará si mi estudiante está haciendo un buen uso de esta experiencia grupal. Si necesita ponerse en contacto conmigo, el mejor número para comunicarse conmigo es ____________________.

Goals of Intervention

- Identify others' emotions.
- Contribute to an inclusive environment at our school.
- Listen actively.
- Disagree without being disagreeable.
- Recognize commonalities and respect differences in our peers.
- Act if we see someone being bullied or harassed.
- Continue to seek opportunities to develop social awareness as they mature.

CASEL Standards Addressed

- Taking on others' perspectives
- Demonstrating empathy and compassion
- Identifying diverse social norms, including unjust ones
- Showing concern for the feelings of others
- Developing positive relationships
- Resolving conflicts constructively

ASCA Mind-Sets and Behaviors

M 1. Belief in development of whole self, including a healthy balance of mental, social/emotional and physical well-being

M 2. Sense of acceptance, respect, support and inclusion for self and others in the school environment

B-SMS 1. Responsibility for self and actions

B-SS 1. Effective oral and written communication skills and listening skills

B-SS 2. Positive, respectful and supportive relationships with students who are similar to and different from them

B-SS 3. Positive relationships with adults to support success

B-SS 4. Empathy

B-SS 6. Effective collaboration and cooperation skills

B-SS 9. Social maturity and behaviors appropriate to the situation and environment

B-SS 10. Cultural awareness, sensitivity and responsiveness

Materials Needed

Writing instrument

Handouts

Song lyrics

Pre-/Post-Assessment

Social Awareness Assessment

Item	Strongly Agree	Agree	Disagree	Strongly Disagree
I can identify how others may be feeling.	Strongly agree	Agree	Disagree	Strongly disagree
I include others to make them feel welcome at our school.	Strongly agree	Agree	Disagree	Strongly disagree
I use active listening skills.	Strongly agree	Agree	Disagree	Strongly disagree
I listen to my peers' opinions.	Strongly agree	Agree	Disagree	Strongly disagree
I can express disagreement in constructive ways.	Strongly agree	Agree	Disagree	Strongly disagree
I recognize commonalities and differences (e.g., racial, cultural) that exist among my peers.	Strongly agree	Agree	Disagree	Strongly disagree
I demonstrate respect for diversity among my peers.	Strongly agree	Agree	Disagree	Strongly disagree
I feel comfortable when others share their cultural backgrounds and experiences with me.	Strongly agree	Agree	Disagree	Strongly disagree
I treat others with respect.	Strongly agree	Agree	Disagree	Strongly disagree
I stand up for others when I witness bullying or harassment.	Strongly agree	Agree	Disagree	Strongly disagree
I understand our school's policy about bullying.	Strongly agree	Agree	Disagree	Strongly disagree
I understand our school's policy about harassment.	Strongly agree	Agree	Disagree	Strongly disagree
I understand our school's policy about violence.	Strongly agree	Agree	Disagree	Strongly disagree
If there was a situation I couldn't handle on my own, I would tell an adult I trust.	Strongly agree	Agree	Disagree	Strongly disagree
I believe that being aware of others is important to my future success.	Strongly agree	Agree	Disagree	Strongly disagree
I believe that being aware of others is important to my future happiness.	Strongly agree	Agree	Disagree	Strongly disagree

Sessions 1–6

These sessions are designed to teach and reinforce skills. Make note of which sessions students respond well to and which they are less responsive to. Make additions or improvements to maximize student engagement and optimize desired outcomes. Ask students for specific feedback at the end of sessions.

Session 1: Getting to Know You

Objective:

1. Create a safe space for students to discuss their emotional and social world. It's critical that all students feel seen, heard, and valued.

Materials:

"I Am From" worksheet

"Where I'm From" poem template

Pen/pencil

Duration: 30–40 minutes depending on size of the group.

Instructions:

1. Welcome students and explain the purpose of the group.
2. Invite group members to provide input on group ground rules. Record them on poster paper and ask students to sign the poster paper. Introduce members of the group: Why are we here in the group? What are our goals? What does it mean to be socially aware? How does it help us grow to be socially aware?

Activity 1: "Where I'm From" (share leaders' poem)

What we are hoping to learn about:

- diverse experiences of group members
- why it is important to demonstrate respect for the diverse experiences, feelings, and aspirations of the class members
- being able to recognize and affirm diverse cultures in the group
- encouraging interaction among students through deeper understanding of their cultural similarities and differences

    1. Ask students to complete prewriting exercise.
    2. Have students reflect on experiences writing and sharing their poems:

        a. What was it like to write this poem?
        b. What did you learn about yourself?

   c. What did you learn about other group members?
   d. How did this exercise help us to become more socially aware?

3. Group leader collects poems to make copies and add to student folders as part of their progress monitoring.

Where I Am From

Name: ______________________________ Date: ______________

Complete each box with three to five items.

I am from ...

Familiar foods, especially those associated with family gatherings:

I am from ...

Sights, sounds, and smells from your neighborhood:

I am from ...

Familiar sayings you heard growing up:

I am from ...

Familiar people, family members, friends, and ancestors:

Source: "Where I'm From Poem Template," by M. Yung, August 21, 2020, https://elabraveandtrue.com/2020/08/21/three-templates-for-where-im-from-poems/.

Please use your answers on the worksheet to create your own "Where I'm From" poem.

Where I'm From

Name: ____________________

I am from ____ (specific ordinary item), from ______________ (product name) and ______________________________________.

I am from the ____________________ (home description: two adjectives and sensory detail)

I am from the ________________________ (plant, flower, natural detail)

I am from _______________ family tradition) and

____________ (family trait) from _____________ (family member name) and

______________ (*another family member*) and ______________ (family name) and

____________________________ (another family name).

I am from ________________________ and ___________________________________

____ (descriptions of family tendency).

From ________________ and ____________________ (two things you were told as a child).

I am from ______________________ (place of birth and family ancestry),

______________________________ (two food items representing family)

______________________________ (specific family story about specific person and detail) ______________(another detail) and the ____________(another specific detail about another family member).

I am from _______________(special memory, location of family picture, and detail about its worth). I am ___________ (name), and I am __________________________________.

Session 2: Active Listening

Objectives:

1. Students will learn the definition of active listening.
2. Students will learn essential skills of active listening.

Materials:

Handout

Pen or pencil

Duration: 25–30 minutes

Instructions:

1. Welcome students back and remind them of the group ground rules. Check in.
2. Share handout of active listening skills.
3. Explain: "Active listening requires us to listen attentively to others, understand what they're saying, respond and reflect on what's being said, and retain the information for later. Both the listener and speaker are actively engaged in the conversation. Active listening is essential for healthy relationships."

Important skills of active listening are as follows:

- Pay attention. Give the speaker your undivided attention and acknowledge the message.
- Make eye contact (when culturally appropriate).
- Show that you are listening through your body language.
- Provide feedback. Say, "What I am hearing is" or "sounds like you are saying."
- Defer judgment.
- Don't interrupt.
- Respond appropriately.

4. Divide students into pairs. Ask each pair to review one of the skills in depth.
5. Ask them to create a list of things that make it challenging to practice this skill and share with the group
6. Model active listening by asking a volunteer to describe their favorite meal. Ask students to point out the active listening strategies that you demonstrated.
7. Ask the dyad to practice the skills by assigning them to each share about the person they most admire. Encourage students to use as many of the skills as possible.
8. Discuss the experience in the full group.

Active Listening Skills

1. **Pay attention.**

Give speaker your undivided attention.

Recognize nonverbal communication also "speaks" loudly.

Maintain eye contact.

Avoid distracting thoughts and environmental distractions.

Observe the speaker's body language.

2. **Show that you are listening.**

Use your body language to convey attention.

Nod occasionally.

Use comments like "Yes" and "Aha."

3. **Provide feedback.**

As a listener, your role is to understand what is being said.

Reflect what is being said and ask questions.

Paraphrase.

Ask questions.

4. **Defer judgment.**

Interrupting is a waste of time. It frustrates the speaker and limits full understanding of the message.

Allow the speaker to finish.

5. **Respond appropriately.**

Be candid in your response.

Assert your opinions respectfully.

Treat others as you would want to be treated.

You add nothing by putting down the speaker.

Source: Adapted from "Active Listening," by MindTools Content Team, https://www.mindtools.com/az4wxv7/active-listening.

Session 3: Empathy Interviews

Objectives:

1. Students will conduct an empathy interview.
2. Students will discuss a topic that is important to both the listener and the interviewer. An emphasis is placed on clarifying how the person feels or perceives the issue they are addressing.

Materials:

Pen and paper to take notes

Duration: 60 minutes

Instructions:

1. Welcome students back and remind them of the group ground rules. Check in.
2. Each student answers this question in the empathy interview: If there is one thing that you would change about our school to make it a better place to learn and feel a sense of belonging, what would it be?
3. Each person takes turns being interviewed for 20 minutes.
4. Listeners are encouraged to take notes to be prepared to share their perceptions of the interview with the group.
5. Reconvene group. Ask what the experience was like being listened to for a full 20 minutes.
6. Ask follow-up questions: Why do you think that would improve our school? How do you feel when you talk about this issue? How would you like to feel about this issue? What do you think is standing in the way of resolving this issue at our school? What concrete steps can you, our group, or adults around us take to address this issue?

Source: Safir and Dugan (2021)

Session 4: Identifying Others' Emotions

Objective:

1. Students will develop an emotional vocabulary.
2. Identify increasingly complex emotions in oneself and others.

Materials:

Handout

Pen/pencil

Duration: 30–40 minutes depending on size of the group

Instructions:

1. Welcome students back and remind them of the group ground rules. Check in.
2. Discuss the primary emotions: love, anger, fear, sadness, and joy.
    a. How would someone know when you are feeling those feelings?
    b. What does your face look like?
    c. What does your body (posture, gestures, etc.) look like?
3. Have students discuss, show, and model these emotions.
4. Share the feelings wheels. Start with the most simple wheel.
5. Ask students to write down what makes them happy, angry, excited, or sad.
6. Encourage them to share them with a partner and demonstrate what they look like when they are feeling that way.
7. With each new wheel, more complex feelings are introduced. With the second wheel, switch pairs and ask students to reflect on what makes them scared, worried, surprised, or proud.
8. Demonstrate those expressions. Ask partners to reflect back what they see.
9. With the final wheel with the most emotions included, ask the students to share one emotion with the group and see if the rest of the group can guess which emotion they are expressing.

Discussion questions:

1. Why is it challenging to identify what others are feeling based on their facial expressions?
2. What might prevent someone from showing their emotions authentically?
3. What happens when we ask someone what they are feeling?
4. What happens for you when you ask someone what they are feeling?
5. How is it for you when someone asks you how (or what) you are feeling?

Name: ______________________________ Date: ____________

Four main emotions:

Name ________________

My Emotions Wheel

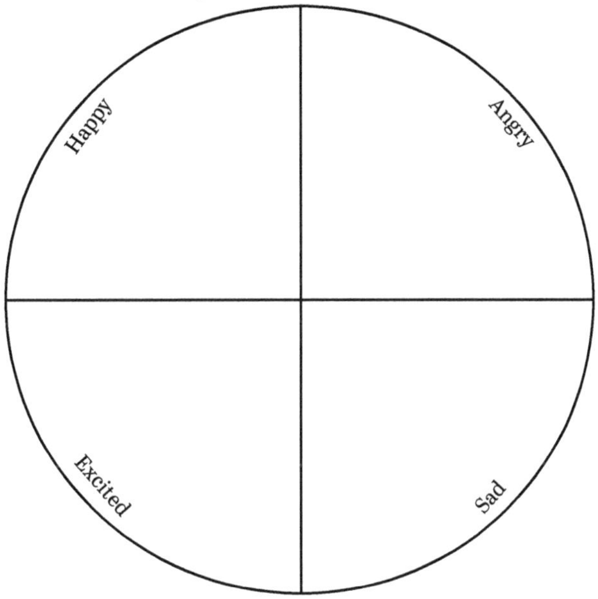

Image 10.4

Six key emotions:

Name ________________

My Emotions Wheel

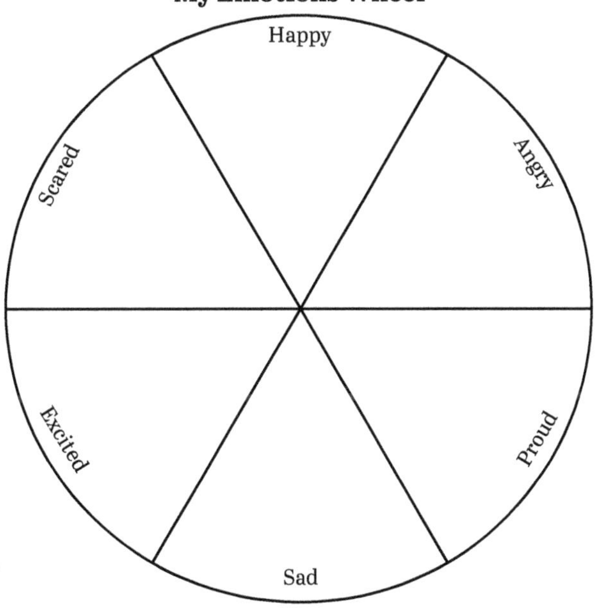

Image 10.5

Eight basic emotions:

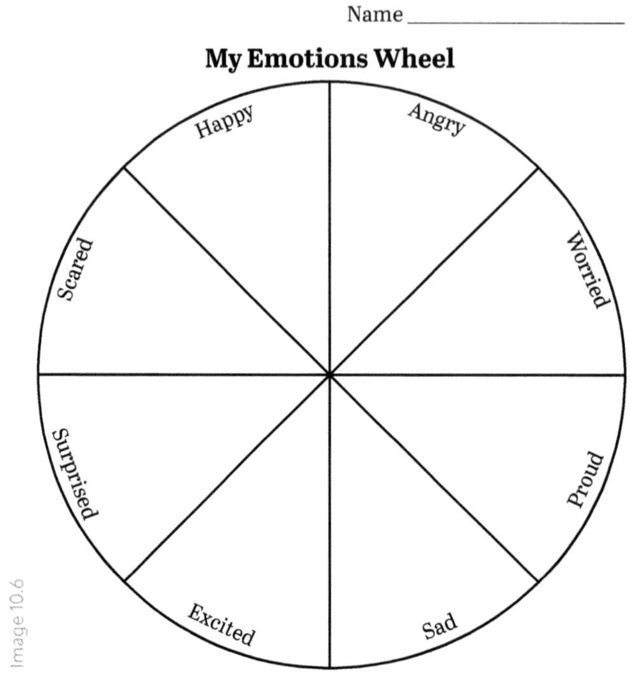

Session 5: Using Song Lyrics to Identify Our Emotions

Objective:

1. Students will identify song lyrics that help them express emotions.

Materials:

Students bring in printed song lyrics and stream their song for the group

Chart paper for group facilitator to capture emotion words

Duration: 40 minutes depending on the size of the group

Instructions:

1. Welcome students back and remind them of the group ground rules. Check in.
2. Invite students to print out the lyrics to a song they listen to when they need to be cheered up.
3. Tell the students that you are going to make a playlist for the group to listen to when they are feeling low or when they want to get in touch with how they are feeling.
4. Ask each student to play a few stanzas of their song (make sure all lyrics are rated G).
5. Invite them to share why they selected this song and perhaps how they began listening to this song.
6. Make a list of the songs to share with the group.

Session 6: Wrapping Up

Objective:

1. Group members will process feelings about/impressions of being in the group understand why reading and acknowledging others' feelings is important to them in the future.

Duration: 30–40 minutes depending on the size of the group.

Instructions:

1. Welcome students back and remind them of the group ground rules. Check in.
2. Ask the students the following questions:
    a. What was your first feeling when you found out you were being invited to be part of this group?
    b. What is your feeling about being in the group now?
    c. Why is it important to "read" others' faces during conversation?
    d. Why do good leaders know when their employees are upset or out of sorts?
    e. How could you continue to grow in being socially aware as you move through high school and into the adult world?
3. Discuss a booster meeting idea in a month or two.
4. Discuss a community service project to improve some aspect of the school community followed by time to discuss the experience.
5. Conduct the posttest.

Post-Intervention Communication to Parent/Guardian

English Version

Dear Parents/Caregivers,

We enjoyed spending the past 6 weeks discussing the importance of developing social awareness as teens. Your student took part in many activities meant to help them improve their active listening skills, identify emotions others are expressing, and understand the importance of demonstrating empathy to others. We talked about why social awareness is essential to their future success in high school and beyond. Please take a few moments to speak with your student about their experience in the group and what they think they gained from being part of it.

If you have any questions, please reach out to us. Shortly, you will be receiving a survey about the effectiveness of the group. Please take a few minutes to fill it out so that we can provide the best possible support to our students in the future.

Sincerely,

The Student Support Team

Spanish Version

Estimados padres/cuidadores,

Disfrutamos pasar las últimas 6 semanas discutiendo la importancia de desarrollar la conciencia social en la adolescencia. Su estudiante participó en muchas actividades destinadas a ayudarlo a mejorar sus habilidades de escucha activa, identificar las emociones que otros expresan y la importancia de demostrar empatía hacia los demás. Hablamos sobre por qué la conciencia social es esencial para su éxito futuro en la escuela secundaria y más allá. Tómese unos minutos para hablar con su estudiante sobre su experiencia en el grupo y lo que cree que ganó al ser parte de él.

Si tiene alguna pregunta, comuníquese con nosotros. En breve recibirás una encuesta sobre la eficacia del grupo. Tómese unos minutos para completarlo para que podamos brindar el mejor apoyo posible a nuestros estudiantes en el futuro.

Atentamente,

El equipo de apoyo estudiantil

Plan for Implementation Fidelity

Group leaders will adhere to the six lessons and reflect on students' level of engagement throughout. Student, teacher, and caregiver surveys will be distributed to measure the effectiveness of the group and to share suggestions for improving the experience for future students.

Small Group Process Notes

References

Burnett, C. (2016, March 10). *Helping children manage big emotions: My emotions printable wheel*. Childhood 101. https://childhood101.com/helping-children-manage-big-emotions-my-emotions-wheel-printable

Conflict Resolution Activities for Middle School Skill-Building. (n.d.). *Class agreements*. https://cpb-us-e1.wpmucdn.com/blogs.uoregon.edu/dist/8/11350/files/2015/05/Compiled-Activities-1-r5x71c.pdf

Safir, S., & Dugan, J. (2021). *Street data: A next-generation model for equity, pedagogy, and school transformation*. Corwin.

Credits

IMG 10.1: Copyright © 2023 Depositphotos/Meefox123@gmail.com.

IMG 10.2: Copyright © 2019 Depositphotos/annyart.

IMG 10.3: Copyright © by Microsoft. Reprinted with permission.

IMG 10.4: Source: https://childhood101.com/helping-children-manage-big-emotions-my-emotions-wheel-printable/.

IMG 10.5: Source: https://childhood101.com/helping-children-manage-big-emotions-my-emotions-wheel-printable/.

IMG 10.6: Source: https://childhood101.com/helping-children-manage-big-emotions-my-emotions-wheel-printable/.

■ CHAPTER 11

Tier 2 Intervention Kits for Relationship Skills

Elementary Relationship Skills

Dr. Peg Donohue

Description of Skill

Friendship is the cornerstone of social development throughout the life span. In childhood we learn the key skills necessary to initiate, maintain, and nourish friendships. For some students, forming friendships comes with ease. Others need support. As an elementary school counseling intern, I was asked to facilitate a structured recess area where kids could borrow cards, a game, or playground equipment to use in the area designated. I would make note of who joined me, what activities they engaged in, and any conflicts that arose. After a few weeks, I had "frequent flyers" who joined me most days. It became a safe place to connect with a peer and have fun. By the end of the year, many went off in pairs to play and only occasionally circled back to say hello and get affirmation. As a parent, my husband often reminded our two children to "just be friendly and you will have friends," which is sage advice.

Psychoeducational groups focused on friendship are commonplace in schools. Oftentimes they take the form of a lunch bunch. The activities described in this Tier 2 kit are meant to touch on the following friendship skills:

- Decide who will make a good friend.
- Smile (nonverbal communication).
- Ask questions: Do you play any sports? What do you like to do after school? What's your favorite recess game? What's in your lunch? How many brothers and sisters do you have? Who's your teacher?
- Invite others to play: "Hey, can I play the next game?"
- Share. We can teach kids that they need to learn to share about themselves in a way that doesn't sound boastful but helps others get to know them.
- Be happy for friends' victories.

- Develop coping strategies to manage difficult emotions (e.g., feeling left out, angry, or sad).
- Resolve conflicts among peers. Learn how to apologize and engage an adult if they aren't successful resolving the conflict on their own.
- Empathize.
- Practice kindness.

Pre-Intervention Communication With Parents/Guardians/Teachers in Languages Represented in the School

English Version

Dear Parents/Guardians,

I am sure you can remember those friends who made your elementary school experience memorable. We have developed classroom lessons addressing friendship skills during your child's time at [Name of School]. We are excited to add small group counseling sessions to bring students together to practice key friendship skills. Each week we will discuss a different topic and fill out a progress monitoring sheet to see if they are using the skill at recess, in the classroom, and out in the community. Make sure to ask your student about which skills they

Progress Monitoring Sheet for Elementary Friendship Group

Name: ______________________ Date: ______________

Did I?	Week 1	Week 2	Week 3	Week 4	Week 5	Week 6	Totals
Smile 😊 ?							
Ask questions?							
Invite others to play?							
Share or take turns?							
Handle my big feelings well?							
Resolve conflicts peacefully?							
Show kindness?							

Image 11.1

are working on. We will have their progress monitoring sheets ready for them each time they come to group.

If you have any questions or concerns, please do not hesitate to reach out to me to discuss your student's involvement in the group.

Sincerely,

Student support team member

Spanish Version

Queridos padres/guardianes,

Estoy seguro de que recuerdas a esos amigos que hicieron que tu experiencia en la escuela primaria fuera memorable. Hemos desarrollado lecciones en el aula que abordan las habilidades de amistad durante el tiempo que su hijo asiste a la escuela [NOMBRE]. Estamos entusiasmados de agregar sesiones de asesoramiento en grupos pequeños para reunir a los estudiantes y practicar habilidades clave de amistad. Cada semana discutiremos un tema diferente y completaremos una hoja de seguimiento del progreso para ver si están usando la habilidad en el recreo, en el aula y en la comunidad. Asegúrese de preguntarle a su estudiante en qué habilidades está trabajando esta semana. Tendremos listas sus hojas de seguimiento de progreso cada vez que vengan al grupo.

Progress Monitoring Sheet for Elementary Friendship Group

Name: ______________________ Date: ____________

Did I?	Week 1	Week 2	Week 3	Week 4	Week 5	Week 6	Totals
Smile ☺ ?	👍👎	👍👎	👍👎	👍👎	👍👎	👍👎	👍👎
Ask questions?	👍👎	👍👎	👍👎	👍👎	👍👎	👍👎	👍👎
Invite others to play?	👍👎	👍👎	👍👎	👍👎	👍👎	👍👎	👍👎
Share or take turns?	👍👎	👍👎	👍👎	👍👎	👍👎	👍👎	👍👎
Handle my big feelings well?	👍👎	👍👎	👍👎	👍👎	👍👎	👍👎	👍👎
Resolve conflicts peacefully?	👍👎	👍👎	👍👎	👍👎	👍👎	👍👎	👍👎
Show kindness?	👍👎	👍👎	👍👎	👍👎	👍👎	👍👎	👍👎

Image 11.2

Si tiene alguna pregunta o inquietud, no dude en comunicarse conmigo para analizar la participación de su estudiante en el grupo.

Atentamente,

Miembro del equipo de apoyo al estudiante

Permission Slip (If Applicable)

After reading the description of this Tier 2 small group, I, ____________________, give permission for my student ____________________ to take part in the group which will meet on ____________________ from [date] to [date]. I understand that this group is confidential and that I will be made aware if my student is making good use of this group experience. Should I need to be contacted, the best number to reach me at is ____________________.

Hoja de permiso

Después de leer la descripción de este grupo pequeño de Nivel 2, yo, ____________________, doy permiso para mi estudiante ____________________a participar en el grupo que se reunirá el ____________________ de [fecha] a [fecha]. Entiendo que este grupo es confidencial y que se me informará si mi estudiante está haciendo un buen uso de esta experiencia grupal. Si necesita ponerse en contacto conmigo, el mejor número para comunicarse conmigo es ____________________.

Goals of Intervention

- Identify qualities of a good friend.
- Practice essential skills, such as inviting others to play, asking questions, resolving conflicts, and taking turns.
- Acknowledge strengths.
- Set goals in areas where student would like to improve.

CASEL Standards Addressed

- Communicating effectively
- Developing positive relationships
- Resolving conflicts constructively

ASCA Mind-Sets and Behavior

M 1. Belief in development of whole self, including a healthy balance of mental, social/emotional and physical well-being

M 2. Sense of acceptance, respect, support, and inclusion for self and others in the school environment

B-SS 1. Effective oral and written communication skills and listening skills

B-SS 2. Positive, respectful, and supportive relationships with students who are similar to and different from them

B-SS 3. Positive relationships with adults to support success

B-SS 6. Effective collaboration and cooperation skills

B-SS 10. Cultural awareness, sensitivity, and responsiveness

Materials Needed

Handouts

Crayons or markers

Poster paper

Blank paper

Tape

Pre-/Post-Assessment

Teacher Assessment of Student

Item				
When speaking to peers, this student has good communication skills.	**Strongly agree**	**Agree**	**Disagree**	**Strongly disagree**
When speaking to adults, this student has good communication skills.	**Strongly agree**	**Agree**	**Disagree**	**Strongly disagree**
This student works well in groups.	**Strongly agree**	**Agree**	**Disagree**	**Strongly disagree**
This student works well with a partner.	**Strongly agree**	**Agree**	**Disagree**	**Strongly disagree**
This student makes positive choices about relationships most of the time.	**Strongly agree**	**Agree**	**Disagree**	**Strongly disagree**
This student contributes to a positive environment at school for students and adults most of the time.	**Strongly agree**	**Agree**	**Disagree**	**Strongly disagree**

Sessions 1–6

These sessions are designed to teach and reinforce skills. Make note of which sessions students respond well to and which they are less responsive to. Make additions or improvements to maximize student engagement and optimize desired outcomes. Ask students for specific feedback at the end of sessions.

Session 1: Why Is Friendship Important to Us?

Objectives:

1. Set ground rules for group.
2. Introduce topic of friendship and discuss its importance in our lives.
3. Set individual and collective goals for the 6-week group.

Materials:

Poster paper to record ground rules

Goal-setting worksheet

Pen/pencil

Progress monitoring sheet

Duration: 30–40 minutes depending on group size

Instructions:

1. Welcome and introductions. Ask each participant to share what would make this a great group experience for them.
2. Set ground rules. Ask for student input. Have them each sign the ground rules poster.
3. Introduce topic.
4. Discuss what it means to be a friend, strengths as a friend, things they need to work on, and so on. Mention skills we will discuss in depth that are on the progress monitoring sheet.
5. Complete goal worksheet.
6. Introduce progress monitoring sheet.

Name: ______________________________ Date: ______________

Please set goals around friendship and share them with group if you feel comfortable.

Image 11.3

Image 11.4

Image 11.5

My goals for friendship during our group:

Strengths I have as a friend: ______________________ ______________________ ______________________	Things I need to work on to be a better friend: ______________________ ______________________ ______________________
Things I can do to become a better friend: ______________________ ______________________ ______________________	Things I can do to make new friends: ______________________ ______________________ ______________________

How will you know when you have met these goals? ______________________

____

Progress Monitoring Sheet for Elementary Friendship Group

Name ____________________________________ Date _______________

Did I?	Week 1	Week 2	Week 3	Week 4	Week 5	Week 6	Totals
Smile 🙂?	👍 👎	👍 👎	👍 👎	👍 👎	👍 👎	👍 👎	👍 👎
Ask questions?	👍 👎	👍 👎	👍 👎	👍 👎	👍 👎	👍 👎	👍 👎
Invite others to play?	👍 👎	👍 👎	👍 👎	👍 👎	👍 👎	👍 👎	👍 👎
Share or take turns?	👍 👎	👍 👎	👍 👎	👍 👎	👍 👎	👍 👎	👍 👎
Handle my big feelings well?	👍 👎	👍 👎	👍 👎	👍 👎	👍 👎	👍 👎	👍 👎
Resolve conflicts peacefully?	👍 👎	👍 👎	👍 👎	👍 👎	👍 👎	👍 👎	👍 👎
Show kindness?	👍 👎	👍 👎	👍 👎	👍 👎	👍 👎	👍 👎	👍 👎

Comments:

____

____

____

Session 2: What Makes Someone a Good Friend?

Objectives:

1. Identify behaviors that are consistent with friends.
2. Identify what they are looking for in a friend.

Materials:

Chart paper

Markers

Recipe for friendship handout

Duration: 30–40 minutes depending on the size of the group

Instructions:

1. Check in on the past week: How did it go when they think about their interactions with classmates? What was a thumbs up? What was a thumbs down?
2. Remind students of ground rules for the group.
3. Take out a large piece of poster paper with the title "Recipe for Friendship."
4. Show students an actual recipe and look at the two components (ingredients and steps).
5. Give each student a different colored marker. Ask them to brainstorm on a separate piece of paper what ingredients or characteristics make someone a good friend.
6. Share out your brainstorm page after they select their two to three favorite ingredients.
7. Work together to add the ingredients to the poster paper.
8. Decide together what the steps should be.
9. Ask the students what they liked (or didn't like) about this activity. What ingredients or steps will they keep in mind in the coming week?
10. Make connections between the items and steps in the recipe and their goal(s) for friendship.

Recipe for Friendship:

Ingredients
1 cup of ________________
2 cups of ______________
½ cup of _____________
1 pint of ______________
2 T. of ________________
½ T. of _______________
Other ________________
Other ________________

Steps
1.
2.
3.
4.
5.

Image 11.7

Session 3: How Do We Have Fun, Play Fair, and Take Turns With Our Friends?

Objectives:

1. Acquaint students with appropriate turn-taking and positive behavior on playground.
2. Engage students in conversation about creating a caring and kind environment on the playground.

Materials:

Blank paper

Markers or crayons

Duration: 30–40 minutes depending on size of the group

Instructions:

1. Check in on the past week: How did it go when they think about their interactions with classmates? What was a thumbs up? What was a thumbs down?
2. Remind students of ground rules for the group.
3. Introduce topic: Who likes taking turns with friends? Who likes waiting their turn? When is it hardest for you to take turns? When is it hardest for you to share?
4. Introduce activity: Ask the students to work together to create a shared design for a new playground that could be built at the school. They need to talk for 5–6 minutes about their ideas first, and then they need to draw the plan. Only one person can draw at a time. Each person can only draw one element of the plan. Take turns until the drawing is complete. Ask them to agree on a name/theme for the playground and write it on the top. Ask both students to write their names on the bottom.
5. Tape all the playground plans to the wall.
6. Ask each team to present their plan. Encourage them to talk about how they decided what to do, how it went when they took turns, and which items they drew to complete the plan.
7. After each presentation of a playground plan, ask other students to each share either one element they liked or ask a question about the design. This may take more than one session depending on the size of group.
8. Remind students to be on the lookout for opportunities to take turns and share this week.

Session 4: What Happens When We Disagree With a Friend?

Objectives:

1. Understand emotions we experience when we are in a disagreement.
2. Learn and follow steps to conflict resolution.

Materials:

Progress monitoring sheets

Photo of two students disagreeing

Worksheet on resolving conflict

Pens/pencils/crayons/markers

Duration: 25–30 minutes

Instructions:

1. Check in on the past week: How did it go when they think about their interactions with classmates? What was a thumbs up? What was a thumbs down?
2. Remind students of ground rules for the group.
3. Introduce topic for this week by selecting a photo of two students disagreeing. (If you use Second Step, select a card that depicts students disagreeing.) Here's an example of a photo you might select.

Image 11.8

4. Ask, "What do you think is going on here? What emotions do you think they are having? What would you do in that situation? If you couldn't resolve it on your own, who would you go to for help?"
5. Remind students of steps to conflict resolution; have them complete the worksheet.
    a. Cool off.
    b. Each person tells their side of the story without interruptions using "I" messages.
    c. Repeat back what you heard the other person say.
    d. Ask each other clarifying questions.
    e. Brainstorm solutions (on paper, if possible).
    f. Select a solution you both want to try.
    g. Check back with each other in 3 days (with or without an adult) and see how the solution is working out.
6. Ask students to pay attention to how they are handling conflicts this week. Perhaps they can also observe how they see others resolving disagreements this week.

Name: __________________________________ Date: _______________

Steps to resolving a conflict: Add the steps to conflict resolution in the boxes using your own words. What do you notice about the faces above each step?

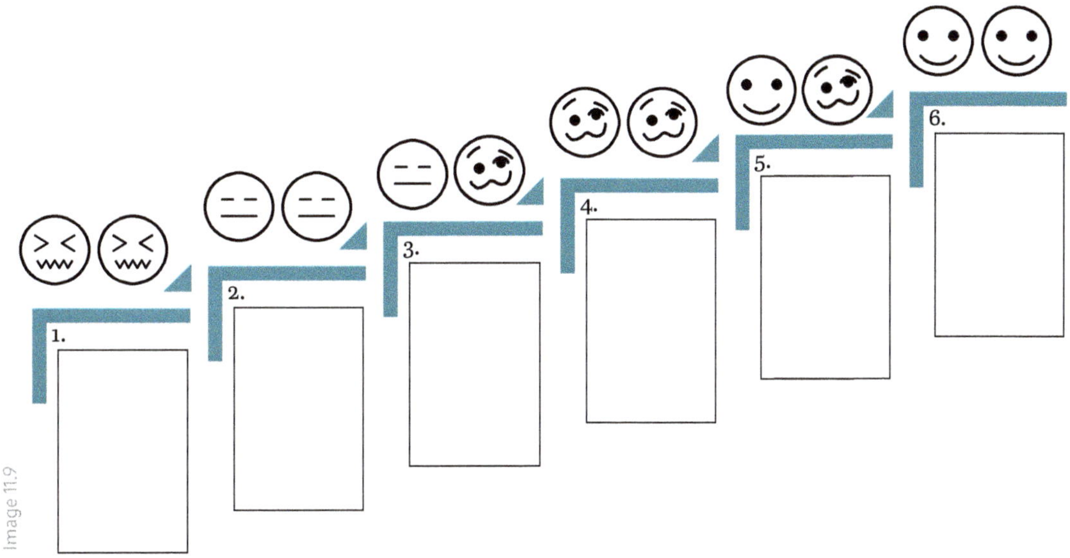

Image 11.9

Session 5: Is It Okay to End a Friendship?

Objectives:

1. Be able to discern when it is okay to give space or stop trying to initiate or maintain a friendship.
2. Identify when a friendship might not be healthy for us.

Materials:

Chart paper

Markers

Scenario card

Duration: 25–30 minutes

Instructions:

1. Check in on the past week: How did it go when they think about their interactions with classmates? What was a thumbs up? What was a thumbs down?
2. Remind students of ground rules for the group.
3. Introduce today's topic by asking if it's okay for friends to take a break in their friendship or end a friendship.
4. What are reasons why someone might end a friendship? Make a list with the students.
5. Share the scenario provided.

Leila and Sammy Break Up

At the beginning of the third-grade school year, Leila developed a friendship with another girl in her class, Sammy. Leila went home and talked about her and the games they played at school, the activities they liked to do together, and what they were planning to do the next day.

Months later, Leila's teacher called her mother. The teacher told her that both girls were beginning to have behavioral issues at recess and in class. The teacher explained that Leila was being bullied by Sammy. The mom was not surprised because she witnessed the bullying firsthand by observing them one afternoon during a play date at her house.

Sammy was hiding Leila's lunch box, taking markers away from her while she drawing her artwork, and telling the other girls mean things about her. Leila got upset, and it made her anxious to go to school sometimes. The mom went in and met with the teacher to talk about a solution. The teacher called Sammy's mom too.

1. Ask discussion questions: How do you think Leila was feeling at first? What changed? What do you think she should do? Why do you think Sammy is treating her that way? What would you do if someone treated you the way Sammy treated Leila? Have you ever seen someone treat a "friend" like this? What can we do if this happens to us or happens to others?
2. Discuss the decision between taking a break from a friendship (in the hope that their conflict is resolved) or ending the friendship (if a few attempts were made and nothing changes).
3. Remind students of friendship skills on the progress monitoring sheet.

Source: Adapted from "How to Help Your Kid (& What to Say) When a Friendship Ends," by P. Blossom, 2023, https://tinybeans.com/how-to-help-kids-with-a-friendship-breakup/.

Session 6: What Are Your Goals for Being a Good Friend in the Future?

Objectives:

1. Review goals set for the group and achievement toward them.
2. Set goals for the future.
3. Assess their own friendship goals.
4. Model gratitude for one another's friendship.

Materials:

Goal sheets

Progress monitoring sheets

Pen/pencil/markers

Duration: 30–40 minutes

Instructions:

1. Check in on the past week: How did it go when they think about their interactions with classmates? What was a thumbs up? What was a thumbs down?
2. Remind students of ground rules for the group.
3. Gratitude activity: Give each student a piece of paper with a name of one of the participants in the middle of the paper. Ask students to write something that they appreciate or are grateful for in the group. Pass them around so everyone signs each one. Invite students to share two to three examples that make them feel good about themselves.
4. Ask students to total their thumbs ups on their progress monitoring sheets for all 6 weeks.
5. Invite them to look at how (if) their progress changed in each area over the 6 weeks
6. Look at how they progressed toward their original goals (review goal sheet). Circle goals that they want to continue working at over the next month now that group is over.
7. Discuss booster session in 1 month's time. Collect goal sheets to review at that time.
8. Ask students to share two things the liked about the group and/or two things they learned.
9. Ask students what we can do to improve the group for next time.
10. Give students a certificate of participation and parent letter.
11. Complete posttest.

Post-Intervention Communication to Parent/Guardian

English Version

Dear Parents/Guardians,

Today we finished up our small group counseling sessions designed to practice key friendship skills. Each week we discussed a different topic and filled out a progress monitoring sheet to track which skills the students were using at recess, in the classroom, and out in the community. Make sure to ask your students to share the tracking sheets and which skills they will continue to work on. In a month's time we will meet to have a quick booster check-in meeting to see how things are going. As always, do not hesitate to reach out to let us know if you have any questions, comments, or suggestions. You are an essential partner in cultivating your student's friendship skills!

Sincerely,

Student Support Team Member

Spanish Version

Queridos padres/guardianes,

Hoy terminamos nuestras sesiones de asesoramiento en grupos pequeños diseñadas para practicar habilidades clave para la amistad. Cada semana discutimos un tema diferente y completamos una hoja de seguimiento del progreso para rastrear qué habilidades estaban usando los estudiantes en el recreo, en el aula y en la comunidad. Asegúrese de pedirle a su estudiante que le comparta las hojas de seguimiento y las habilidades en las que continuará trabajando. Dentro de un mes nos reuniremos para tener una reunión rápida de control de refuerzo para ver cómo van las cosas. Como siempre, no dude en comunicarse con nosotros para informarnos si tiene alguna pregunta, comentario o sugerencia. ¡Usted es un socio esencial para cultivar las habilidades de amistad de su estudiante!

Atentamente,

Miembro del equipo de apoyo al estudiante

Plan for Implementation Fidelity

Group leaders will adhere to the six lessons and reflect on students' level of engagement throughout. Student, teacher, and caregiver surveys will be distributed to measure the effectiveness of the group and to share suggestions for improving the experience for future students.

Small Group Process Notes

Reference

Blossom, P. (2023). *How to help your kid (& what to say) when a friendship ends*. Tiny Beans. https://tinybeans.com/how-to-help-kids-with-a-friendship-breakup/

Relationship Skills for Middle School Students

Erica Cumpstone, Nicole Ferreria, and Jenna Angello

Description of Skill

Friendship is the cornerstone of social development throughout the life span. In childhood we learn the key skills necessary to initiate, maintain, and nourish friendships. For some students, forming friendships comes with ease. Others need support. As a middle school counselor for 16 years, I was asked to facilitate numerous friendship groups and lunch bunches. My goal was to create a safe place to connect with a peer and have fun. After many small group experiences, students went off in pairs or small groups to play at recess and only occasionally circled back to say hello and get affirmation. They became more confident in their ability to make friends, and I tried to continue to remind them to "just be friendly and you will have friends."

The activities described in this Tier 2 kit are meant to touch on the following social habits:

- Smile and say hello.
- Be brave. Leave your comfort zone.
- Always choose kindness.
- Be genuinely interested.
- Experience empathy and see the world from different perspectives.
- Laugh and have fun!
- Be loyal, trustworthy, and honest.
- Show up.
- Be present.
- Listen intently.
- Be humble and apologize when you mess up.
- Be you.

Source: "12 Habits Every Middle Schooler Needs to Learn," Project School Wellness, https://www.projectschoolwellness.com/how-to-be-a-good-friend-12-social-habits-every--middle-schooler-needs-to-learn-with-printable/.

Pre-Intervention Communication With Parents/Guardians/Teachers in Languages Represented in the School

English Version

Dear Parents/Guardians,

Each year [School Name] provides additional services such as small group counseling. These counseling sessions occur once per week for 6 weeks. These groups focus on specific topics (e.g., social skills, bullying prevention, positive school behaviors, and increasing self-esteem) so that the participating students can be academically and socially successful at school this year. New groups and topics are formed throughout the school year.

For your student to be part of one of these small groups, they must have a permission form signed by you.

Your student has been invited to the following small group: Social Skills. In this group, students will focus on the following:

- learning how to effectively and properly communicate with peers
- understanding how to utilize conflict management and problem-solving strategies
- understanding and interpreting how to read facial and body language
- developing an understanding of perspective taking

Please return this form to the counseling office by [insert date].

Thank you for your time. If you have any questions or concerns, feel free to contact us at any time!

Sincerely,

Your School Counselors

Spanish Version

Queridos padres y guardianes,

Cada año, [NOMBRE] brinda servicios adicionales, como asesoramiento en grupos pequeños. Estas sesiones de asesoramiento se realizan una vez por semana durante seis semanas. Estos grupos se centran en temas específicos (como habilidades sociales, prevención del acoso escolar, conductas escolares positivas y aumento de la autoestima) para que los estudiantes participantes puedan tener éxito académico y social en la escuela este año. Se forman nuevos grupos y temas a lo largo del año escolar.

Para que su estudiante sea parte de uno de estos grupos pequeños, debe tener un formulario de permiso firmado por usted.

Su estudiante ha sido invitado al siguiente grupo pequeño: Habilidades Sociales

En este grupo, los estudiantes se centrarán en los siguientes elementos de acción:

- Aprender a comunicarse eficaz y adecuadamente con sus compañeros.
- Comprender cómo utilizar estrategias de gestión de conflictos y resolución de problemas.
- Comprender e interpretar cómo leer el lenguaje facial y corporal.
- Desarrollar una comprensión de la toma de perspectiva.

Por favor devuelva este formulario a la oficina de consejería antes del lunes 7 de diciembre.

Gracias por tu tiempo. Si tiene alguna pregunta o inquietud, ¡no dude en contactarnos en cualquier momento!

Atentamente,

Tu consejero escolar

Permission Slip

____ (Student Name) is

______ Given permission to participate in the Social Skills small group.

______ NOT given permission to participate in the Social Skills small group.

______________________________ __________________________

Parent/guardian signature: Date:

Hoja de permiso

____

(Nombre del estudiante) es:

______ Se le dio permiso para participar en el grupo pequeño de Habilidades Sociales.

______ NO se le dio permiso para participar en el grupo pequeño de Habilidades Sociales.

____

Firma del padre/tutor: Fecha:

Goals of Intervention

- Students will improve relationship skills by enhancing their ability to take the perspective of a peer.
- Students will improve relationship skills by enhancing their ability to resolve conflicts peacefully.
- Students will improve relationship skills by enhancing their conversational skills.
- Students will improve relationship skills by enhancing their ability to read body language.
- Students will improve relationship skills by enhancing their ability to express emotions.
- Students will improve relationship skills by enhancing their ability to respect their peer's personal space.

CASEL Standards Addressed

- Communicating effectively
- Developing positive relationships
- Demonstrating cultural competency
- Practicing teamwork and collaborative problem solving
- Resolving conflicts constructively
- Seeking or offering support when needed

ASCA Mind-Sets and Behaviors

M 1. Belief in development of whole self, including a healthy balance of mental, social/emotional and physical well-being

M 2. Sense of acceptance, respect, support, and inclusion for self and others in the school environment

B-SS 1. Effective oral and written communication skills and listening skills

B-SS 2. Positive, respectful and supportive relationships with students who are similar to and different from them

B-SS 3. Positive relationships with adults to support success

B-SS 6. Effective collaboration and cooperation skills

B-SS 10. Cultural awareness, sensitivity and responsiveness

Materials Needed

Chart paper

Pens/pencils markers

Handouts

Conversation Jenga game

Progress Monitoring Sheet for Social Skills

Name: ________________

Students should read each question carefully and respond to each question as honestly as you can.

Circle A, B, or C for each item.

A = Almost always; I am really good at this.

B = Sometimes; I am okay at this.

C = Rarely; I am not very good at this.

Questions	Always	Sometimes	Never
When someone asks me a question, I answer them.	A	B	C
I join in on conversations with other people.	A	B	C
I speak clearly so that others can understand what I am saying.	A	B	C
When I am talking to someone, I use appropriate body language. (e.g., turn body in their direction, look at them, smile, etc.).	A	B	C
When someone is talking to me, I show them that I am listening by looking toward them and nodding my head.	A	B	C
Even when I get frustrated, I am able to stay calm.	A	B	C
If someone points out that I made a mistake, I can accept it without becoming angry	A	B	C
If I disagree with someone, I still show them that I respect their ideas.	A	B	C
I am able to stay out of other people's personal space (keep an arm's length distance).	A	B	C
I apologize when I make a mistake ("I'm sorry, I should have been here at 10:00 a.m.").	A	B	C
I am comfortable working with a group.	A	B	C
I accept the ideas and suggestions of others ("That is a good idea. I might start doing that instead.")	A	B	C
I stay calm when a supervisor or teacher tells me that I have made a mistake.	A	B	C
When a supervisor or teacher tells me to correct a mistake, I do it.	A	B	C
I can handle it when someone tells me no.	A	B	C
I do not touch or use other people's belongings without their permission.	A	B	C
I offer to help others ("Hey, do you need me to fix that for you?").	A	B	C
I wear appropriate clothing to school and work (i.e., clean, neat clothing).	A	B	C
When it is break time, I do the same things that other classmates or coworkers do during their breaks (e.g., read, chat, snack).	A	B	C

Sessions 1–6

These sessions are designed to teach and reinforce skills. Make note of which sessions students respond well to and which they are less responsive to. Make additions or improvements to maximize student engagement and optimize desired outcomes. Ask students for specific feedback at the end of sessions.

Session 1: Relationship Skills: Working Through Conflict / Problem Solving

Objective:

1. Students will be able to work through conflict and to positively take control and devise a plan rather than engage in negative communication and conflict.

Materials:

Inflatable beach ball

Duration: 30 minutes

Instructions:

1. Give welcome and introductions. Ask students to share something they are hoping we talk about in the group.
2. Set ground rules for the group. Ask for student input. Make a poster of the ground rules and ask each member to sign them.
3. Introduce today' topic: managing conflict:
   a. How do they handle conflict with peers most often?
   b. What feelings come up for them when they are in a conflict?
   c. Normalize the fact that conflict is part of life.
   d. Share a time you saw two people resolve a conflict constructively (compromising).
   e. Share a time you saw two people resolve a conflict destructively (not compromising).
4. Activity: Students begin by standing in a circle.
   1. The facilitator hits the ball into the circle and tells the team that they need to hit the ball twice as many times as there are team members.

2. The only rules are that no team members can hit the ball twice in a row or volley the ball back and forth over and over with another member. Because this game is more difficult than it first appears, conflict may arise early on as the team realizes this and has to regroup and devise a plan.
3. Once the team achieves their goal number of hits, their next challenge is to hit the ball an equal number of times as there are team members. This time there is a new rule: Each team member can hit the ball only one time. Even though this is more difficult, they should be able to build on what they have already learned to achieve success without conflict.

5. After the activity, students will answer discussion questions about their experience with the game:

   a. Was this activity more difficult than you originally thought it would be?
   b. If so, did your assumptions lead to any communication challenges or conflict?
   c. How did you and your team deal with the conflict?
   d. In the second round, the goal was even more difficult. Did you experience the same communication or conflict challenges as the first round? Why or why not?
   e. In what ways can you apply what you discovered in this game to the classroom?

Session 2: Perspective Taking—We Each See the World a Little Differently

Objective:

1. Students will be able to think about how other people think and feel by using different perspective taking skills.

Materials:

Scrap paper

Pen/pencil

"We each see the world differently" perception cards

Duration: 30 minutes

Instructions:

1. Welcome everyone back to the group and remind them of the ground rules established last week.
2. Invite students to check in about how their week went.
   Activity:
   1. Students will break up into groups of three to five to play a game called "We each see the world differently."
   2. Each group will get an envelope full of perception cards with different words on them (tolerance, prejudice, morality, etc.).
   3. Each round, someone will take a card and place it on the table. That person will set a timer, and everyone has 2 minutes to write down what that word means to them.
   4. The person who selected the word will share their definition(s) of the word first and then call on others who would like to share.
   5. Each person takes a turn selecting a card and facilitating the conversation.
   6. Before sharing with the whole group, the group selects two cards they want to share with everyone. The person who led that round will share the highlights of what that conversation sparked in their group.

Perception Cards

Kindness	Frenemy	Gossip
Prejudice	Fairness	Success
Family	Justice	Injustice
Freedom	Safety	Friend
Vulnerability	Honesty	Trustworthiness

Source: Adapted from Making Choices About Conflict, Security, and Peacemaking, by Carol Miller Liebler, 1994 University of Missouri Center for International Studies.

Session 3: Conversation Skills Using Jenga

Objectives:

1. Students will be able to develop their conversation skills by having appropriate responses to questions/statements and asking follow-up questions while playing games.
2. Students will understand the importance of playing fair and taking turns.

Materials:

Jenga game with prewritten questions on each block

Duration: 50 minutes

Instructions:

1. Welcome group members back. Ask how the past week has been. Ask if there are any situations when they used their conflict resolution skills in the past week.
2. Group facilitator reminds students about group ground rules.
3. Introduce learning objectives.
4. Discuss what makes a conversation fun, interesting, and emotionally safe.
5. Introduce the "Conversation Jenga" game. Remind students of the rules. Make sure all students are prepared to be respectful and play fair during a game.
6. Discuss who should go first and why it is important to wait your turn.

Activity 1: Conversation Jenga

1. Split the students into groups of three or four.
2. On each block there is a statement or question. During each player's turn, they will pull out a block and respond to the corresponding statement or question
3. After answering, the other players must ask a follow-up question, and that person's turn is over when they answer the follow up question.

Note: This can be done with any simple board game depending on what materials you have access to. Variations may be Go Fish!, Tic-Tac-Toe, Connect Four, checkers, or chess.

Session 4: Reading Body Language

Objective:

1. Students will develop their ability to read one another's body language and apply it in everyday social situations.

Materials:

Predetermined scenarios written out on pieces of paper

Duration: 30 minutes

Instructions:

1. Check in on the past week and remind students of ground rules for the group.

Activity 1: What Am I Feeling? Charades

1. Divide students into smaller groups of three, four, or five students.
2. However, instead of acting out the traditional situations, students will focus on properly displaying emotions through facial expressions and body language in the scenario.
3. The player must appropriately depict the emotions that they believe would be evoked in the situations, and the team must accurately describe what emotions each actor is portraying in the scene to win the point within a certain amount of time.
4. After each scene, the group can discuss how they knew what the person was feeling based on body language and why the situation may provoke these emotions.
5. Depending on time constraints, the game can be played up to a certain amount of points or until time is up.

Examples of situations:

- cheating on a test and the teacher finding out
- seeing a classmate cheat off of you on a test
- being interrupted during a conversation
- sitting alone at lunch
- losing a sports game
- winning a sports game
- telling someone they look nice
- bumping into someone in the hallway
- being made fun of for a response in the classroom
- being made fun of online
- getting unwanted/inappropriate attention from a classmate
- getting a good grade on a test while your neighbor gets back a bad grade
- your group of friends ignoring you in the hallway
- making a mistake/error during gym class or during a sports game
- someone cutting you in line at lunch

Session 5: Expressing Feelings

Objectives:

1. Students will learn to process and verbalize their feelings in front of others.
2. The student will display their feelings in an appropriate manner, conveying sincerity to the listener.

Materials:

Mini M&M game boards for each student

Ten M&Ms for each student

Feelings journal

Duration: 40 minutes

Instructions:

1. Check in on the past week and remind students of ground rules for the group.
2. Have the students arrange their desks in a circle.
3. Put the M&M game board up for the students to see.
4. Provide each student with 10 M&Ms.
5. Have the students take a few moments to think about each item on the list.
6. As a group ask each student to share one of the colors with the group.
7. Participation is optional as not every student in the group will want to share, and this is okay.
8. Once everyone has gone, have the group split up into twos and have them share two other colors from the board.
9. Come back together in the circle as a group.
10. Discuss the activity with the students and ask how it made them feel to share their feelings with someone today.
11. Discuss with the students some occasions when they might want to share their feelings with someone else. And when they might not want to. Some examples are the following:
    - Working on a class project on building a mission. You have a disagreement about the materials being used.
    - You want to tell your teacher that you feel overwhelmed by the amount of homework in her class.
    - A friend has borrowed some of your school supplies without asking.

THE m&m's FEELINGS GAME		
FOR EVERY		***SHARE***
Red		*Something that makes you feel HAPPY*
Brown		*Something that makes you feel SAD*
Green		*Something that makes you feel ANGRY*
Yellow		*Something that makes you feel EXCITED*
Blue		*A POOR CHOICE you made and a better choice you could have made*
Orange		*A GOOD CHOICE you made*

Image 11.11

Optional Activity: Feelings Journal

Provide each student with the "Feelings Journal" handout to take home. Encourage the students to write their journal at home and to write about problems they may be having at school, with friends, or even with a parent.

Encourage students to share their journal with a parent or close family member to help strengthen the student's ability to share their feelings with their loved ones at home as well. The parents can take part in the feelings journal by reading the entry and then asking their child how they would like them to respond. The parent can write back with an acknowledgment, offer advice, or simply read without responding.

Name: ______________________________ Date: ________________

Image 11.12

Feelings journal:

Session 6: Social Skills: Proximity

Objective:

1. Student will learn what personal space means and how to respect their own personal space and others.

Materials:

Bubble worksheet

Duration: 30–40 minutes

Instructions:

1. Check in on the past week and remind students of ground rules for the group.
2. Provide each student a "Personal Space Bubble" worksheet.
3. Students will complete their worksheet individually or in small groups.
4. Discuss each of the bubbles together.
5. Some additional discussion topics may include the following:
    a. the physical aspects of personal space or their bubble
    b. emotional boundaries
    c. how students can protect themselves from other people's words, actions, and emotions
6. Have a discussion about the group experience:
    a. What were the key things you learned?
    b. What have you or will you apply in your day-to-day life?
    c. What could we do to make this group even better in the future?
7. Discuss plans for booster session of group in a month's time to see how they are doing using their new skills.
8. Administer posttest.

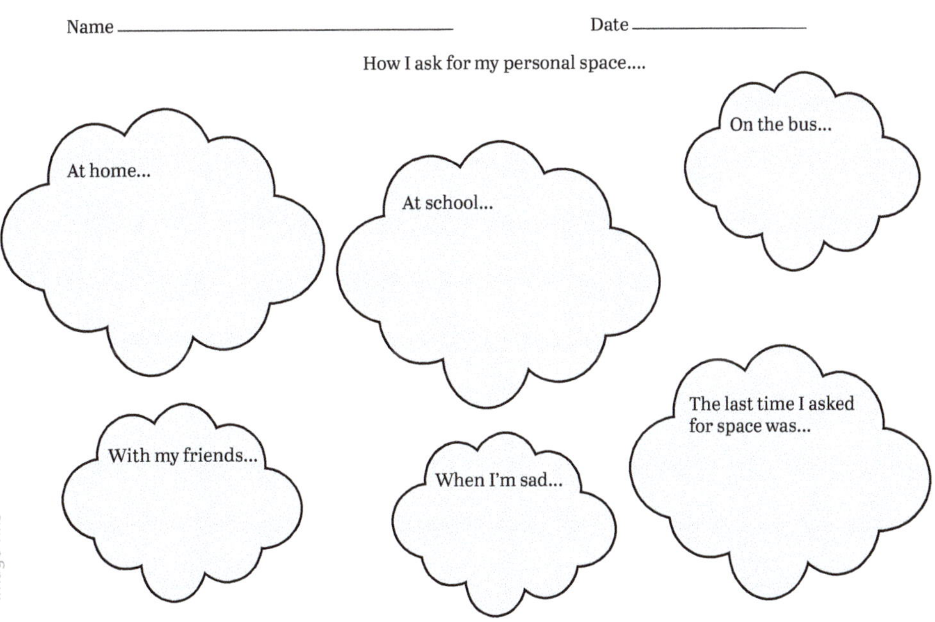

Image 11.13

Post-Intervention Communication to Parent/Guardian

English Version

Dear Parents/Guardians,

Your student just completed a small group intervention designed to help enrich their relationship skills. We set ground rules for our group and took part in activities about perspective taking, resolving conflict, conversational skills, reading body language, expressing emotions, and respecting personal space. We hope that students who participate will be even more academically and socially successful at school this year. We will meet one more time during a booster session next month to check in their skills. In the meantime, make sure to ask your student about their experience in the group.

If you have any questions or concerns, feel free to contact us at any time!

Sincerely,

Your School Counselors

Spanish Version

Queridos padres/guardianes,

Su estudiante acaba de completar una intervención en grupos pequeños diseñada para ayudar a enriquecer sus habilidades de relación. Establecimos reglas básicas para nuestro grupo y participamos en actividades sobre toma de perspectiva, resolución de conflictos, habilidades conversacionales, lectura del lenguaje corporal, expresión de emociones y respeto del espacio personal. Esperamos que los estudiantes que participen tengan aún más éxito académico y social en la escuela este año. Nos reuniremos una vez más durante una sesión de refuerzo el próximo mes para comprobar sus habilidades. Mientras tanto, asegúrese de preguntarle a su estudiante sobre su experiencia en el grupo.

Si tiene alguna pregunta o inquietud, ¡no dude en contactarnos en cualquier momento!

Atentamente,

Tus consejeros escolares

Plan for Implementation Fidelity

The interventionist will ask the teacher to complete a survey after week 3 to determine if the student is making progress because of the group. Interventionists will adhere to the lessons in the Tier 2 kit to ensure it is implemented with fidelity and make note of any challenges to implementation they experience. This data and pre-/posttest should be reviewed with the MTSS team prior to utilizing this Tier 2 kit again.

Small Group Process Notes

References

Baker, J. (2001). *The social skills picture book: Teaching play, emotion, and communication to children with autism*. Future Horizons.

Baker, J. (2006). *The social skills picture book: For high school and beyond*. Future Horizons.

Lieber, C. M. (1994). *Making choices about conflict, security, and peacemaking part I: Personal perspectives. A high school conflict resolution curriculum*. Field Test Version.

Project School Wellness. (n.d.). *12 habits every middle schooler needs to learn*. https://www.projectschoolwellness.com/how-to-be-a-good-friend-12-social-habits-every-middle-schooler-needs-to-learn-with-printable/

Healthy Relationships for High School Students: Journey to Self-Empowerment

Jennifer Estrella Vanterpool and Vanessa Rodriguez

Description of Skill

The purpose of this Tier 2 kit is to help empower students in the ninth grade who struggle with self-esteem issues, building healthy relationships and self-care interventions. These students are more likely to have been seen in the hallways skipping class, hanging with other students who are not doing well in their classes, or often isolating themselves from the rest of the students. The counselor will begin by using a screening tool to help narrow down the students who are likely to face difficulties while in school. Once the students are chosen, they will be placed in a group called STARS (Students Thriving to Achieve Rapport and Success). These students will then complete a pretest that will help evaluate the success of these interventions.

Friendship is the cornerstone of social development throughout the life span. In childhood we learn the key skills necessary to initiate, maintain, and nourish friendships. For some students, forming friendships comes with ease. Others need support. By the time students enter high school, learning about themselves through peers is second nature. Much of their academic development is taking place in the presence of peers as well. They are separating from their families and experiencing the joys and challenges of independence. As the end of high school nears, they are preparing for wholesale change after graduation and their tightly knit goes off in a multitude of directions. Throughout the 4 years of high school we make an effort to provide experiences in which they become more confident in their ability to develop high-quality friendships and explore their social world. This is the preparation they need before joining a dorm floor, a business team, a military troop, or a construction site team.

The activities described in this Tier 2 kit are meant to address the following relationship skills for high school students:

- effective communication
- strong emotional vocabulary
- good conflict resolution skills
- effective emotional regulation skills
- ability to collaborate
- ability to take on the perspective of others
- ability to demonstrate empathy

Pre-Intervention Communication With Parents/Guardians/Teachers in Languages Represented in the School

English Version

Dear Parents/Caregivers,

We are excited to provide small group counseling for our ninth-grade students to help them get their high school career off to an excellent start. As I am sure you remember, a great deal of our learning in high school happens with our peers. Students who enjoy two to three healthy friendships and feel confident when meeting new people thrive in both high school and post-secondary settings. The small groups we have designed for our ninth graders were created to help enrich our students' relationship skills. We know this effort will pay dividends in their academic progress as well. Most of our teachers assign multiple group-based projects each semester. Thus, it is critical that our students know how to communicate, resolve conflicts, set and achieve a shared goal, and have the ability to form lasting bonds with others.

This group will meet weekly during the enrichment block. If you have any questions or concerns, please do not hesitate to send one of us an email and we will get back to you.

Please return the enclosed permission slip at your earliest convenience.

We look forward to working with your student.

Sincerely,

Your school counselors

Spanish Version

Estimados padres y cuidadores,

Nos complace brindar asesoramiento en grupos pequeños a nuestros estudiantes de noveno grado para ayudarlos a que su carrera en la escuela secundaria tenga un excelente comienzo. Como estoy seguro recordarás, gran parte de nuestro aprendizaje en la escuela secundaria ocurre con nuestros compañeros. Los estudiantes que disfrutan de 2 o 3 amistades saludables y se sienten seguros cuando conocen gente nueva prosperan tanto en la escuela secundaria como en entornos postsecundarios. Los grupos pequeños que hemos diseñado para nuestros estudiantes de noveno grado fueron creados para ayudar a enriquecer las habilidades de relación de nuestros estudiantes. Sabemos que este esfuerzo también generará dividendos en su progreso académico. La mayoría de nuestros maestros asignan múltiples proyectos grupales cada semestre. Por lo tanto, es fundamental que nuestros estudiantes sepan comunicarse, resolver conflictos, establecer y lograr una meta compartida y tener la capacidad de formar vínculos duraderos con los demás.

Este grupo se reunirá semanalmente durante el bloque de enriquecimiento. Si tiene alguna pregunta o inquietud, no dude en enviarnos un correo electrónico a uno de nosotros y nos comunicaremos con usted.

Devuelva la hoja de permiso adjunta lo antes posible.

Esperamos trabajar con su estudiante.

Atentamente,

Consejeras de noveno grado

Permission Slip (If Applicable)

After reading the description of this Tier 2 small group, I, ____________________, give permission for my student ____________________ to take part in the group which will meet on ____________________ from [date] to [date]. I understand that this group is confidential and that I will be made aware if my student is making good use of this group experience. Should I need to be contacted, the best number to reach me at is ____________________.

Hoja de permiso

Después de leer la descripción de este grupo pequeño de Nivel 2, yo, ____________________, doy permiso para mi estudiante ____________________ a participar en el grupo que se reunirá el ____________________ de [fecha] a [fecha]. Entiendo que este grupo es confidencial y que se me informará si mi estudiante está haciendo un buen uso de esta experiencia grupal. Si necesita ponerse en contacto conmigo, el mejor número para comunicarse conmigo es ____________________.

Goals of Intervention

- Students will better understand how to communicate.
- Students will improve their conflict-resolution skills.
- Students will understand the steps to and value of setting and achieving shared goals.
- Students will have greater confidence in their ability to form lasting bonds with others.

CASEL Standards Addressed

- Communicating effectively
- Developing positive relationships
- Demonstrating cultural competency
- Practicing teamwork and collaborative problem solving
- Resolving conflicts constructively
- Resisting negative social pressure
- Showing leadership in groups
- Seeking or offering support when needed
- Standing up for the rights of others

ASCA Mind-Sets and Behaviors

M 1. Belief in development of whole self, including a healthy balance of mental, social/emotional and physical well-being

M 2. Sense of acceptance, respect, support and inclusion for self and others in the school environment

B-SS 1. Effective oral and written communication skills and listening skills

B-SS 2. Positive, respectful and supportive relationships with students who are similar to and different from them

B-SS 3. Positive relationships with adults to support success

B-SS 6. Effective collaboration and cooperation skills

B-SS 8. Advocacy skills for self and others and ability to assert self, when necessary

B-SS 10. Cultural awareness, sensitivity, and responsiveness

Materials Needed

Worksheets

Pens/pencils/markers

Small candies for Bingo

Pre-/Post-Assessment

Name: ______________________ Date: ____________

Item				
When speaking to my peers, I have good communication skills.	Strongly agree	Agree	Disagree	Strongly disagree
When speaking to adults, I have good communication skills.	Strongly agree	Agree	Disagree	Strongly disagree
I work well in groups.	Strongly agree	Agree	Disagree	Strongly disagree
I work well with a partner.	Strongly agree	Agree	Disagree	Strongly disagree
I make positive choices about my relationships most of the time.	Strongly agree	Agree	Disagree	Strongly disagree
I contribute to a positive environment at school for students and adults.	Strongly agree	Agree	Disagree	Strongly disagree
Self-care means staying up late, not eating, and keeping my feelings to myself.	Strongly agree	Agree	Disagree	Strongly disagree
It is acceptable to put my hands on someone when I am upset.	Strongly agree	Agree	Disagree	Strongly disagree
I can count on my friends when I need to talk about something very important and private.	Strongly agree	Agree	Disagree	Strongly disagree
It is okay to isolate myself when I feel down or angry.	Strongly agree	Agree	Disagree	Strongly disagree
Qualities of a friendship include being honest, nice, and trustworthy.	Strongly agree	Agree	Disagree	Strongly disagree

Name: ______________________________ Date: ______________

Pregroup Screening Questions

Read the following statements and select yes or no.

1. I sometimes feel alone and that I have no one to turn to.

   YES NO

2. I often find myself wondering why bad things keep happening to me at school, home, or in the community.

   YES NO

3. I feel anxious, nervous, and judged when with my friends.

   YES NO

4. I don't enjoy things like hobbies as much as I use to.

   YES NO

5. I find it difficult to make decisions at school, home, or when with my friends.

   YES NO

6. I often feel like you don't have any energy to get up in the mornings.

   YES NO

7. I have trouble sleeping at night.

   YES NO

8. I feel like the adults in my life care about me and my feelings.

   YES NO

Total yes: ______________ Total no: ________

Sessions 1–6

These sessions are designed to teach and reinforce skills. Make note of which sessions students respond well to and which they are less responsive to. Make additions or improvements to maximize student engagement and optimize desired outcomes. Ask students for specific feedback at the end of sessions.

Session 1: Who I Am

Objective:

1. Have students identify their likes and what makes them who they are.

Materials:

"Who I Am" worksheet

Pens/pencils

Poster board/paper

Duration: 25–30 minutes

Instructions:

1. Give welcome and introductions. Ask students to share something they are hoping we talk about in the group.
2. Set ground rules for the group. Ask for student input. Make a poster of the ground rules and ask each member to sign them.
3. Hand each student a "Who I Am" worksheet.
4. Review the ditto with the students prior to having them fill it out just in case they have questions.
5. Give students about 5–8 minutes to completely fill in the sections on the worksheet. Walk around the room assisting those who may need help.
6. After each student is done, have the students share three things on the worksheet with the rest of the group.
7. Write down one thing that each student shares with the group.
8. Once everyone has shared, have students look at the poster board and see all the answers they shared. Look for similarities and differences and point them out to them.

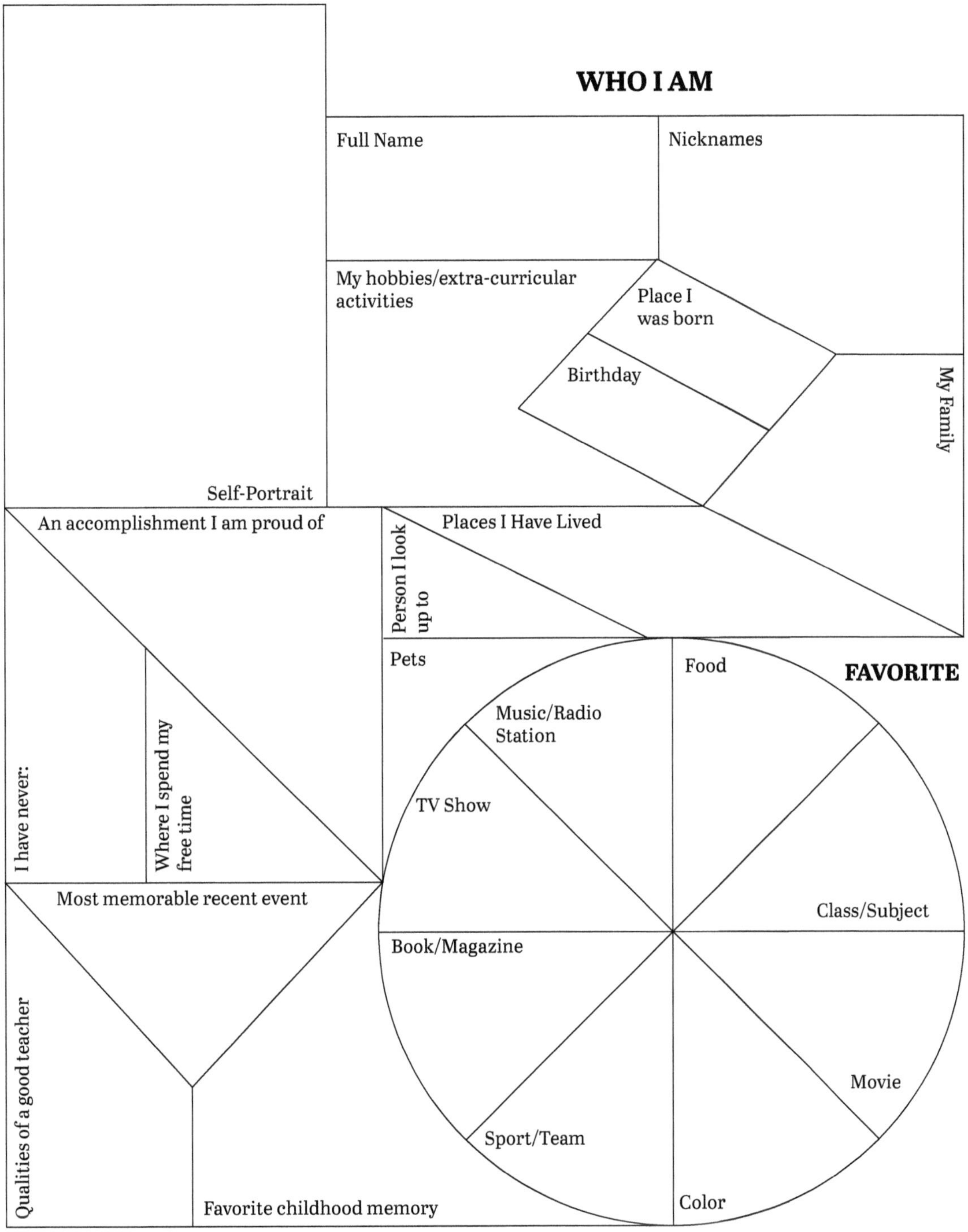
WHO I AM
Full Name
Nicknames
My hobbies/extra-curricular activities
Place I was born
Birthday
My Family
Self-Portrait
An accomplishment I am proud of
Person I look up to
Places I Have Lived
Pets
Food
FAVORITE
Music/Radio Station
TV Show
I have never:
Where I spend my free time
Most memorable recent event
Class/Subject
Book/Magazine
Movie
Qualities of a good teacher
Sport/Team
Color
Favorite childhood memory

Image 11.14

Session 2: I Have the Right to ... Bingo

Objective:

1. Reinforce positive self-image and discussion about rights in relationships.

Materials:

Bingo sheets

M&M's, Smarties, or Skittles (students can eat after playing game)

Small prizes/incentives to give the students if they win.

Duration: 20–25 minutes

Instructions:

1. Welcome everyone back to the group and remind them of the ground rules established last week. Check in.
2. Prepare before session: Make enough copies of the Bingo card so that each participant gets a Bingo board.
3. Hand each student a Bingo sheet and some candy to place on sheet as their marker.
4. Tell students not to remove their candy off their sheets if a person gets Bingo; we will continue playing. Restart the game, if necessary.
5. The facilitator calls out random "rights," and participants place markers accordingly. (They will request variations on "Bingo" such as four corners, postage stamp, etc., which you and they can decide on when you begin.)
6. When a participant gets "Bingo" they call out, "I have the right!" Check answers then award prizes to participants (lollypop, wrapped mint, gift certificate, etc.). Continue play for two more turns and reward participants.
7. Give participants the "My Declaration of Rights" handout at the conclusion and have them sign it.
8. Close the activity by making the following points (in your own words):
    a. It is not always easy to put these rights into practice. We must understand that sometimes others (friends, family, teachers) will resist our attempts to live by these rights.
    b. Standing up for our rights—while not stepping on others—can be a difficult balancing act and is a process.
    c. It's like learning anything; for some people, "taking time to meet my own needs," for example, will come very easily. For others—especially those who learn that their rights are not as important as others—becoming comfortable with this idea will take time and practice.
    d. Most adults still grapple with these issues. In fact, most of us have not been socialized—taught by our culture, society, families, friends—to live by these rules. We certainly do not mean to imply that teens should have it all figured out.

e. Ask participants if they can think of any cultural rules or sayings that run counter to the Declaration of Rights list (e.g., "Children should be seen and not heard"; "That's just the way it is"; "Do as I say, not as I do").
f. Have students sign "My Declaration of Rights" and suggest that they hang it up in their lockers or at home, somewhere special so it will remind them of their rights.

"I Have the Right to ... Bingo"

B	I	N	G	O
Not dominate or to be dominated	Change my goals whenever I want	Take time to meet my own needs	Say "no" and not feel guilty	Change a relationship when my feelings change
Not be judged or judge someone else by appear-ance	Feel good about myself without a guy's/girl's attention	Have and express my own feelings	Be treated with respect	Handle opinions different from my own
Say "no" if I don't want physical closeness	Be satisfied with my achievements	Share my true feelings with others	To have an equal relationship with a partner	Be myself with-out changing to suit others
Change my mind	Express anger in a healthy way	Be treated as a capable human being	Take time to be alone	Feel good about myself
Set limits on relationships	Stand up for my beliefs and values	To tell someone I don't like the way they are treating me	Have my needs be as important as others' needs	Say "I don't know"

B	I	N	G	O
Feel good about myself	Not dominate or be dominated	Not be judged or judge someone by appearance	Change a relationship when my feelings change	To take time to respond
Express anger in a healthy way	Be treated with respect	Say "I don't know"	Feel good about myself without a guy's\girls' attention	Say "no" and not feel guilty
To take time to think before I communicate	Handle opinions different from my own	Set limits on relationships	Share my true feelings	Stand up for my beliefs and values
Ask "Why?"	Take time to meet my own needs	Have and express my own feelings	Have my needs be as important as others' needs	Be myself without changing to suit others
Have and express my own opinions	Be satisfied with my achievements	Say "No, I don't want physical closeness"	Be treated as a capable human being	Take time to be alone

My Declaration of Rights

1. I have the right to be treated with respect.
2. I have the right to have and express my own feelings.
3. I have the right to say "no" and not feel guilty.
4. I have the right to change my mind.
5. I have the right to say "I don't know."
6. I have the right to express anger in a healthy way.
7. I have the right to be treated as a capable human being.
8. I have the right to have my needs be as important as others' needs.
9. I have the right to make mistakes.
10. I have the right to ask "Why?"
11. I have the right to have and express my own opinions.
12. I have the right to set limits on relationships.
13. I have the right to take time to respond to someone.
14. I have the right to take time to think before I communicate.
15. I have the right to take time to meet my own needs.
16. I have the right to take time to be alone.
17. I have the right to change my goals whenever I want.
18. I have the right to change a relationship when my feelings change.
19. I have the right to be myself without changing to suit others.
20. I have the right to start a relationship slowly and say, "I want to know you better."
21. I have the right to say no if I don't want physical closeness.
22. I have the right to stand up for my beliefs and values.
23. I have the right to share my true feelings with others.
24. I have the right to feel good about myself without a guy's or girl's attention.
25. I have the right to be judged only by my actions and not my appearance.
26. I have the right to handle opinions different from my own.
27. I have the right to be satisfied with my achievements.
28. I have the right to tell someone I don't like the way they are treating me.
29. I have the right to have an equal relationship with a partner.
30. I have the right to feel good about myself.

Sign: ______________________________________ Date: ____________________

http://www.ncdsv.org/images/VSDVAA_BldgHealthyRelationshipsAcrossVAFacilitator'sGuideTDVPrevention.pdf

Session 3: Personal Mission Statement

Objective:

1. Students will create a personal mission statement that will reflect the goals they wish to achieve by the end of freshman year.

Materials:

Personal mission statement sheets

Pen or pencil

Duration: 15–20 minutes

Instructions:

1. Welcome everyone back to the group and remind them of the ground rules established last week. Check in.
2. Give students a personal mission statement handout and a pen or pencil. The facilitator will explain what a mission statement is: explains who you are, who you want to be, and what you stand for. It can be used to guide you with making decisions by asking yourself, "Does it help me become who I want to be?"
3. Once the facilitator explains this, proceed with explaining each section to the students one by one. Ask the students to think of the answers to these questions while completing the sections:
    a. What is my reason for coming to school (my purpose)?
    b. What do I stand for (my values)?
    c. What accomplishments am I working toward that will help me fulfill my purpose as a freshman in a way that is consistent with my values?
4. After students fill out the handout, have them share their personal mission statement with the group. Write down each personal mission statement on a poster paper that will be displayed in the class every time the group meets. Have each student initial near their personal statement. (Have the facilitator come up with a personal mission statement that they like to accomplish and initial.)

My Personal Mission Statement

Clarify purpose: The reason why we do things

Clarify values: The importance, worth, or usefulness of something

Section A: Write three talents (skills) you have:

1. ______________________________
2. ______________________________
3. ______________________________

Section B: What makes you happy about going to school? What makes you angry about going to school?

____

____

____

____

Section C: What would a really good day at school look like for you?

I would be feeling ______________________________

I would be doing ______________________________

I would be with ______________________________

Section D: Three things I would like to accomplish by the end of my freshman year (pick one of the three you would like to work on):

1. ______________________________
2. ______________________________
3. ______________________________

Section E: Action steps to achieve my goals:

1. ______________________________
2. ______________________________
3. ______________________________

My Personal Mission Statement

I, ____, would like to ____.

I will do this by ____ and using my talents (skills) I mentioned before ______________________________,

____,

____.

Sign: ________________________________

Date: ________________________________

Session 4: Interpersonal Skills

Objectives:

1. Students will learn the definition of interpersonal skills and how these skills impact their lives and their importance.
2. Students will participate in a short activity to test their knowledge.

Materials:

Interpersonal skills activity sheet

Pencil or pen

Duration: 15–20 minutes

Instructions:

1. Welcome everyone back to the group and remind them of the ground rules established last week. Check in.
2. The facilitator will explain what interpersonal skills are: the ability of a person to interact properly with others (e.g., making eye contact, active listening, body posture).
3. The facilitator will ask students to fill out the "Using Body Language Positively" activity sheet.
4. After students are done, the facilitator will ask students to volunteer and share their answers.
5. Once students share their answers, the facilitator will ask for two volunteers to participate in a short role-play activity.

Using Body Language Positively

Goal: To be aware of our body when communicating with others.

Materials:

Role-play note cards

Duration: 30 minutes

Instructions:

1. Welcome everyone back to the group and remind them of the ground rules established last week. Check in.
2. Introduce the topic for the day.
3. Show examples (from internet or magazines) of body language and ask students to interpret them.
4. Discuss reasons an awareness of body language is important to them as they move through high school and enter adulthood.

Name: ______________________________ Date: ______________

Body Language (- and +)

Directions: Please fill in the blank with either "Positive body language" or "Negative body language." If you need help, raise your hand. When you are done, please notify the instructor.

1. Rolling your eyes when people are talking ______________.
2. Making eye contact ______________.
3. Smiling ______________.
4. Slouching ______________.
5. Sitting straight when talking with someone ______________.
6. Leaning slightly forward ______________.
7. Firm handshake ______________.
8. Frowning or scowling ______________.
9. Raising eyebrows ______________.
10. Biting lip ______________.

Role-Play

Student A: (Looks at Student B in the eyes) "Hey! I have to tell you what happened to me over the weekend. It was crazy!"

Student B: (Looking everywhere else but at Student A and slouching) "Oh yeah?"

Student A: (Looking at Student B) "Yeah, I went to the mall and the movies and to dinner with my older brother. It was so much fun!"

Student B: (Yawns) "Oh that's cool."

---

1. After students participate in the role-play, have the facilitator ask students to share their reactions.
2. Based on students' responses, the facilitator will ask for students to share something they learned from the lesson.

Session 5: Building Healthy Relationships

Objectives:

1. Students will learn qualities of healthy and unhealthy friendships.
2. Students will be able to build rapport with their peers and successful friendships.

Materials:

Wordsearch handout

Human body handout

Markers

Duration: 15–20 minutes

Instructions:

1. Welcome everyone back to the group and remind them of the ground rules established last week. Check in.
2. Have the facilitator distribute the word search handout and markers first.
3. Have the facilitator instruct students to find the words in the word search. Once everyone has found all the words, have the facilitator distribute the human body handout.
4. Students will then write inside of the body the qualities of a positive relationship and write outside of the body the qualities of a negative relationship.
5. After these two handouts are done, the facilitator will lead a conversation to teach students the meanings of the words in the puzzle. This will teach students the qualities of a positive friendship.

Word Search

Name: ________________

Health and Fitness Word Search

R	M	K	N	R	G	U	T	K	F	N	J	V	K	A	F	E
E	U	W	G	B	S	Z	E	C	C	W	B	P	T	C	E	G
A	U	M	O	T	I	V	A	T	I	O	N	E	C	T	X	O
C	X	K	R	E	N	U	T	R	I	T	I	O	N	I	E	I
T	F	C	E	O	B	U	F	I	G	L	O	T	Z	V	R	P
I	H	A	S	N	O	Y	Y	N	K	W	M	K	S	I	C	R
O	P	R	P	S	D	B	L	T	G	V	A	A	Z	T	I	O
N	X	D	I	Q	Y	M	X	E	M	Z	X	F	H	Y	S	G
T	Q	I	R	U	F	G	V	N	R	J	M	H	C	R	E	R
I	T	O	A	O	A	V	J	S	A	A	B	U	O	N	Y	E
M	F	V	T	E	T	S	J	I	A	T	V	P	O	J	I	S
E	L	A	I	K	T	S	K	T	V	H	G	E	R	R	S	S
F	E	S	O	Q	Q	V	H	Y	E	T	J	T	D	D	T	I
R	X	C	N	R	G	L	L	R	U	V	R	V	I	R	X	O
X	I	U	K	M	O	Q	E	N	D	U	R	A	N	C	E	N
D	B	L	F	R	E	Q	U	E	N	C	Y	T	A	P	H	F
G	I	A	R	F	M	T	Z	Q	T	M	F	A	T	L	Q	E
U	L	R	K	D	F	B	O	T	Q	G	F	Q	I	G	T	P
U	I	A	I	Y	J	D	O	A	X	M	S	J	O	T	C	G
B	T	Z	E	E	D	N	Y	H	L	A	G	N	N	V	X	U
Q	Y	C	R	N	F	B	C	N	B	K	R	P	P	W	J	J
D	H	O	H	R	H	E	A	R	T	R	A	T	E	H	Z	I

CARDIOVASCULAR	ACTIVITY	RESPIRATION
BODY FAT	MOTIVATION	FLEXIBILITY
NUTRITION	EXERCISE	HEART RATE
PROGRESSION	ENDURANCE	REACTION TIME
INTENSITY	FREQUENCY	COORDINATION

Image 11.15

Human Body Handout

Please write inside of the body the qualities of a positive relationship and write outside of the body the qualities of a negative relationship.

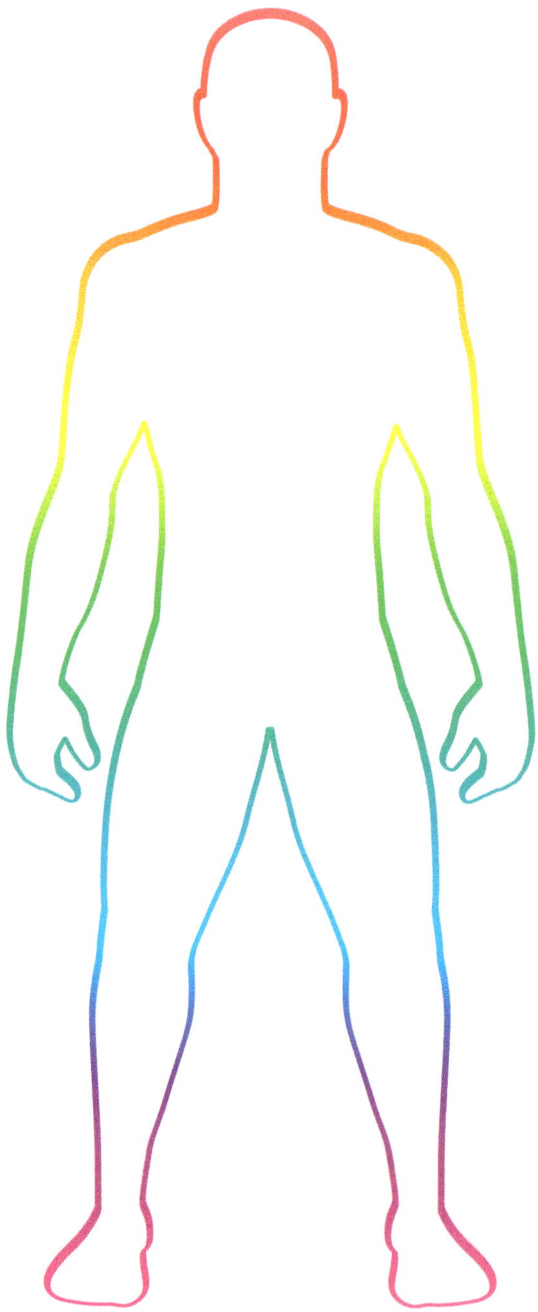

Image 11.16

Session 6: Take Care

Objective:

1. Students will engage in a guided meditation activity that will help them develop awareness and compassion toward themselves and others.

Materials:

"Just Like Me" meditation script

Duration: 15–20 minutes

Instructions:

1. Welcome everyone back to the group and remind them of the ground rules established last week. Check in.
2. Have the facilitator explain what self-care means to students: practices that you can do to develop awareness, get to know yourself better, and identify what is best for you in any situation. Also, self-care is doing what makes you happy when you are sad, stressed, or upset.
3. When the facilitator explains the definition, they should ask students if they have any questions.
4. The facilitator will say, "Now, I am going to read you a passage. For this, You need to select a partner and stand or sit face to face making eye contact."
5. After the students are in pairs, the facilitator will read the "Just Like Me" meditation.

Just Like Me

Become aware that there is a person in front of you—a fellow human being, just like you. Now silently repeat these phrases while looking at your partner.

> This person has a body and a mind, just like me.
>
> This person has feelings, emotions, and thoughts, just like me.
>
> This person has, in their life, experienced physical and emotional pain and suffering, just like me.
>
> This person has at some point been sad, disappointed, angry, or hurt, just like me.
>
> This person worries and is frightened sometimes, just like me.
>
> This person has longed for friendship, just like me.
>
> This person is learning about life, just like me.
>
> This person wants to be caring and kind to others, just like me.
>
> This person wants to be content with what life has given, just like me.
>
> This person wishes to be free from pain and suffering, just like me.
>
> This person wishes to be safe and healthy, just like me.
>
> This person wishes to be happy, just like me.
>
> This person wishes to be loved, just like me.

Now, allow some wishes for well-being to arise:

> I hope that this person has the strength, resources, and social support to navigate the difficulties in life with ease.
>
> I hope that this person will be free from pain and suffering.
>
> I hope that this person will be peaceful and happy.
>
> I hope that this person will be loved ...
>
> > because this person is a fellow human being, just like me.

1. After a few minutes, ask students to thank their partners with a bow or whatever feels appropriate.
2. *Optional: The facilitator can ask students what they learned from the time they spent in the group.
3. To conclude this session, students will participate in a pizza party and receive a "Tips for You Sheet."

Tips for You

1. Do something you love. It can be anything you love to do, such as singing, dancing, exercising, or napping.
2. Hang out with people you love to spend time with and who are positive influences in your life.
3. Practice deep breathing when you feel very upset, sad, or stressed.
4. Try to get as much sleep as your body needs. Remember, if you pay close attention to your body, it will tell you what it needs.
5. Practice self-compassion.
6. Come by my office whenever you need to.

Image 11.17

Remember: There is not a single part of you that does not deserve love and compassion.

Progress Monitoring

Please complete the following chart for each student in the group. Circle one number for the level of engagement.

Name: ____________________

	Activity	Level of Engagement	Comments
Date: Staff:	Who I Am	1 2 3 4	
Date: Staff:	I Have the Right to ... Bingo	1 2 3 4	
Date: Staff:	Personal mission statement	1 2 3 4	
Date: Staff:	Interpersonal skills lesson	1 2 3 4	
Date: Staff:	Qualities of a friendship	1 2 3 4	
Date: Staff:	Self-care	1 2 3 4	

Level of engagement key:

1 = Not engaged, 2 = Somewhat engaged, 3= Very engaged, 4 = Totally engaged

Evaluation:

Post-Intervention Communication to Parent/Guardian

English Version

Dear Parents/Guardians,

We are so pleased to share that your student, ________________________, actively participated in a 6-week relationship skills intervention group that was designed to helped them overcome certain barriers to building satisfying connections with others. Throughout this process, they were able to effectively learn new strategies for building strong peer relationships by partaking in various activities brought to them by the counseling staff. Make sure to ask your student to share what strategies seemed most helpful to them. We are proud to say that with all of your student's hard work they seem to be spending more time enjoying their peers.

We hope that in the future your student will be seek out our staff for support and will utilize the new techniques we covered during the group. If you have any questions, comments, or concerns, please do not hesitate to reach out to our staff so we can set up a time to discuss further.

Thank you. Sincerely,

Counseling Intervention Team

Spanish Version

Estimados padres/tutores,

Estamos muy contentos de compartir que su estudiante, ________________________, participó activamente en un grupo de intervención de habilidades de relación de seis semanas que fue diseñado para ayudarlo a superar ciertas barreras para construir conexiones satisfactorias con los demás. A lo largo de este proceso, pudieron aprender de manera efectiva nuevas estrategias para construir relaciones sólidas con sus pares al participar en diversas actividades que les presentó el personal de consejería. Asegúrese de pedirle a su estudiante que comparta qué estrategias le parecieron más útiles. Estamos orgullosos de decir que con todo el arduo trabajo de sus estudiantes, ellos parecen pasar más tiempo disfrutando de sus compañeros.

Esperamos que en el futuro su estudiante busque nuestro personal para recibir apoyo y

utilizando las nuevas técnicas que cubrimos durante el grupo. Si tiene alguna pregunta, comentario o inquietud, no dude en comunicarse con nuestro personal para que podamos programar un horario para discutir más a fondo.

Gracias. Atentamente,

Equipo de intervención de asesoramiento

Plan for Implementation Fidelity

To achieve the intended outcomes of this intervention, it is helpful to colead the small group with a colleague, reflect on student responses to the activities, and seek support to keep engagement in the group high. Tier 2 small group facilitators should seek peer coaching and ask for feedback to make sure the intervention is implemented with fidelity.

Small Group Process Notes

References

Borders, J. H. (2014). *Handbook on the psychology of self-esteem*. Nova Science.

Curtis, K. (2008). *Empowering youth: How to encourage young leaders to do great things*. Search Institute Press.

Glencoe. (n.d.). *MLS interpersonal skills*. McGraw-Hill. http://glencoe.mheducation.com/sites/dl/free/0078933862/822754/MLS_Interpersonal_Skills_FM_updated.pdf

National Center on Domestic and Dexual Violence. http://www.ncdsv.org/images/VSDVAA_Bldg-HealthyRelationshipsAcrossVAFacilitator'sGuideTDVPrevention.pdf

Worksheeto. (n.d.). *18 teen respect worksheets*. http://www.worksheeto.com/post_teen-respect-worksheets_295442/

Credits

CHAPTER 12

Tier 2 Intervention Kits for Decision-Making

Decision-Making for Elementary School Students

Dr. Peg Donohue

Description of Skill

By the time students reach the age of 18, they make hundreds of decisions a day. As students move through their K–12 journey their decisions become increasingly more impactful. Young children have limited choices at times. But they make daily decisions that can feel quite daunting. They have to select friends to play with at recess, pick activities to engage in during free time in the classroom, and decide to inform an adult if they see another child being harassed or bullied. Through classroom lessons and small groups interventions, we can support decision-making skills by sharing strategies such as these:

- weighing your options
- considering pros and cons
- talking to people who make good decisions
- being gentle with yourself when you make the wrong decision
- learning from mistakes or bad decisions

As educators and interventionists, we model decision-making all the time. Students watch how we respond to them, to one another, and to challenges we face. We can share our own decision-making process and ask general questions that can help them improve their decision-making skills:

- What decision do you need to make?
- What are your options, including less-preferable ones?
- What are the pros and cons of each choice?
- Are there any rules (school policy, curfew, etc.) you need to consider when making your decision?

- How will this decision impact others?
- What is your gut telling you to do?
- How does that decision make you feel?
- What's your plan B?

Pre-Intervention Communication With Parents/Guardians/Teachers in Languages Represented in the School

English Version

Dear Parents/Caregivers,

As we grow up, the decisions we make become increasingly more impactful. Starting out with good decision-making skills can put students on track for social and academic success. We are excited to provide a small group designed to help reinforce good decision-making skills by teaching and practicing helpful strategies. Your student has been selected to participate in this group, which will meet on [day of the week] and [time] from [date] to [date]. Students will not be missing any academic instructional time. If you have any questions about the group or your students' participation, please do not hesitate to call or email us at [phone and email].

We look forward to partnering with you!

Sincerely,

Student Support Team Members

Spanish Version

Estimados padres/cuidadores,

A medida que crecemos, las decisiones que tomamos se vuelven cada vez más impactantes. Comenzar con buenas habilidades para tomar decisiones puede encaminar a los estudiantes hacia el éxito social y académico. Nos complace ofrecer un grupo pequeño diseñado para ayudar a reforzar las habilidades para tomar buenas decisiones mediante la enseñanza y la práctica de estrategias útiles. Su estudiante ha sido seleccionado para participar en este grupo que se reunirá el [DÍA de la SEMANA] y las [HORA] del [FECHA] al [FECHA]. Los estudiantes no perderán ningún tiempo de instrucción académica. Si tiene alguna pregunta sobre el grupo o la participación de sus estudiantes, no dude en llamarnos o enviarnos un correo electrónico al [TELÉFONO y CORREO ELECTRÓNICO].

¡Esperamos asociarnos con usted!

Atentamente,

Miembros del equipo de apoyo estudiantil

Permission Slip (If Applicable)

After reading the description of this Tier 2 small group, I, ______________________________, give permission for my student ______________________________ to take part in the group which will meet on ______________________________ from [date] to [date]. I understand that this group is confidential and that I will be made aware if my student is making good use of this group experience. Should I need to be contacted, the best number to reach me at is ______________________________.

Hoja de permiso

Después de leer la descripción de este grupo pequeño de Nivel 2, yo, ______________________, doy permiso para mi estudiante ______________________ a participar en el grupo que se reunirá el ______________________ de [fecha] a [fecha]. Entiendo que este grupo es confidencial y que se me informará si mi estudiante está haciendo un buen uso de esta experiencia grupal. Si necesita ponerse en contacto conmigo, el mejor número para comunicarse conmigo es ______________________.

Goals of Intervention

- Demonstrate curiosity and open mindedness.
- Identify solutions for personal and social problems.
- Anticipate and evaluate the consequences of one's actions.
- Recognize how critical thinking skills are useful both inside and outside of school.
- Reflect on one's role to promote personal, family, and community well-being.
- Evaluate personal impact on others.

CASEL Standards Addressed

- Demonstrating curiosity and open mindedness
- Identifying solutions for personal and social problems
- Anticipating and evaluating the consequences of one's actions
- Recognizing how critical thinking skills are useful both inside and outside of school
- Reflecting on one's role to promote personal, family and community well-being
- Evaluating personal, interpersonal, community, and institutional impacts

ASCA Mind-Sets and Behaviors

M 1. Belief in development of whole self, including a healthy balance of mental, social/emotional and physical well-being

M 2. Sense of acceptance, respect, support and inclusion for self and others in the school environment

M 5. Belief in using abilities to their fullest to achieve high-quality results and outcomes

B-LS 1. Critical thinking skills to make informed decisions

B-LS 2. Creative approach to learning, tasks and problem solving

B-LS 9. Decision-making informed by gathering evidence, getting others' perspectives and recognizing personal bias

B-SMS 1. Responsibility for self and actions

B-SS 5. Ethical decision-making and social responsibility

Materials Needed

My Magical Choices by Becky Cummings

My Magical Choices scenario cards

Worksheets

Crayons/pencils

Pre-/Post-Assessment (Completed by Homeroom Teacher)

Item					
This student can make positive decisions in the classroom.	**Strongly agree**	**Agree**	**Disagree**	**Strongly disagree**	**N/A**
This student makes good choices about how to complete a task or learn a new concept.	**Strongly agree**	**Agree**	**Disagree**	**Strongly disagree**	**N/A**
This student believes that their thoughts and opinions are valued.	**Strongly agree**	**Agree**	**Disagree**	**Strongly disagree**	**N/A**
This student believes that others' thoughts and opinions should be valued.	**Strongly agree**	**Agree**	**Disagree**	**Strongly disagree**	**N/A**
This student is capable of evaluating their own work	**Strongly agree**	**Agree**	**Disagree**	**Strongly disagree**	**N/A**
This student responds positively when I help them to solve problems.	**Strongly agree**	**Agree**	**Disagree**	**Strongly disagree**	**N/A**
This student makes connections between success during classroom activities and accomplishing their personal goals.	**Strongly agree**	**Agree**	**Disagree**	**Strongly disagree**	**N/A**
This student can make sound decisions based on the information at hand when presented real-world scenarios	**Strongly agree**	**Agree**	**Disagree**	**Strongly disagree**	**N/A**
This student understands cause and effect.	**Strongly agree**	**Agree**	**Disagree**	**Strongly disagree**	**N/A**

Student Progress Monitoring Sheet: Self-Report

Each time you come to our group, you will be asked to complete your self-report. Circle the thumbs up icon if you think you made more good decisions in each area this week. Circle the thumbs down icon if you think you made more bad decisions in each area this week.

Name: ______________________________ Start date: ________________

Week	In Class	At Recess	At Home
1	Image 12.1 	Image 12.1 	Image 12.1 
2	Image 12.1 	Image 12.1 	Image 12.1 
3	Image 12.1 	Image 12.1 	Image 12.1 
4	Image 12.1 	Image 12.1 	Image 12.1 
5	Image 12.1 	Image 12.1 	Image 12.1 
6	Image 12.1 	Image 12.1 	Image 12.1 

Sessions 1–6

These sessions are designed to teach and reinforce skills. Make note of which sessions students respond well to and which they are less responsive to. Make additions or improvements to maximize student engagement and optimize desired outcomes. Ask students for specific feedback at the end of sessions.

Session 1: Getting Started

Objectives:

1. Establish ground rules for behavior in the group.
2. Introduce topic of decision-making skills.
3. Students will share decisions they make about taking care of themselves daily.

Materials needed:

My Magical Choices by Becky Cummings

Decision-making worksheet

Scenario cards

Duration: 30–40 minutes

Instructions:

1. Welcome and introduction; ask each student to share their favorite after-school snack when they introduce themselves.
2. Set ground rules: ask for students' input. Record rules on a poster board; ask all group members to sign it.
3. Explain the purpose of the group: "We are all here to build our decision-making muscles. What is a difficult decision you had to make? How did you go about it? Did anyone help you make the decision? What does it feel like to make a bad decision? What good decisions have you made in the last 24 hours about taking care of yourself (e.g., brushing teeth, eating vegetables, getting enough rest, getting exercise, etc.)?"
4. Read *My Magical Choices* by Becky Cummings.
5. Groups of two to four students will read a decision-making scenario and think of three different choices they could make.
6. Students draw or write their choices on the worksheet.
7. Facilitate discussion about their responses.

Group Members: **Scenario Card:**

Think about the decision making example you were provided. Brainstorm 3 choices you have as a result of this situation.

Choice 1	Choice 2	Choice 3

Image 12.2

1 Your sister wants to borrow your new bike.

What will you do?

2 You aren't invited to a friend's party.

What will you do?

3 The teacher selected another student to help pass out papers and you really wanted to do it.

What will you do?

4 You have been saving up for a new scooter. Your friend gets one for her birthday.

What will you do?

5 You are sleeping over a friend's house and don't have the stuffed animal you usually sleep with.

What will you do?

6 Your best friend wants you to say something mean to the new girl.

What will you do?

7 You accidentally spilled grape juice on your mom's new carpet.

What will you do?

8 Older players on the basketball team won't pass you the ball.

What will you do?

Image 12.3

Session 2: What Makes Someone a Good Decision-Maker?

Objectives:

1. Students see themselves as a good decision-maker.
2. Students understand what is needed to be a good decision-maker.
3. Students will set a goal about making good decisions.

Materials:

Game: Pick Up Sticks

"What Makes You a Good Decision-Maker?" worksheet

Crayons/markers/pencils

Decision-making terms cards

Duration: 30 minutes

Instructions:

1. Welcome group members and revisit group ground rules.
2. Offer two snacks to group members. (Check for allergies before purchasing snack items.)
3. Ask group members why they selected their snack. Create a pros and cons list on the board for each snack.
4. Play a game of Pick Up Sticks. Talk about why they are choosing to select each stick.
5. Introduce the topic for today: "There are qualities that make someone a good decision-maker. We are going to learn about them, and we will invite you to think about a time you used that skill or a time you might need that skill."
6. Hand out worksheet and decision-making terms cards.

Trust in myself	Trust my opinions
Self-confidence	Thoughtfulness
Concern for others	Patience

Name: ______________________________ Date: ____________

What Makes You a Good Decision-Maker?

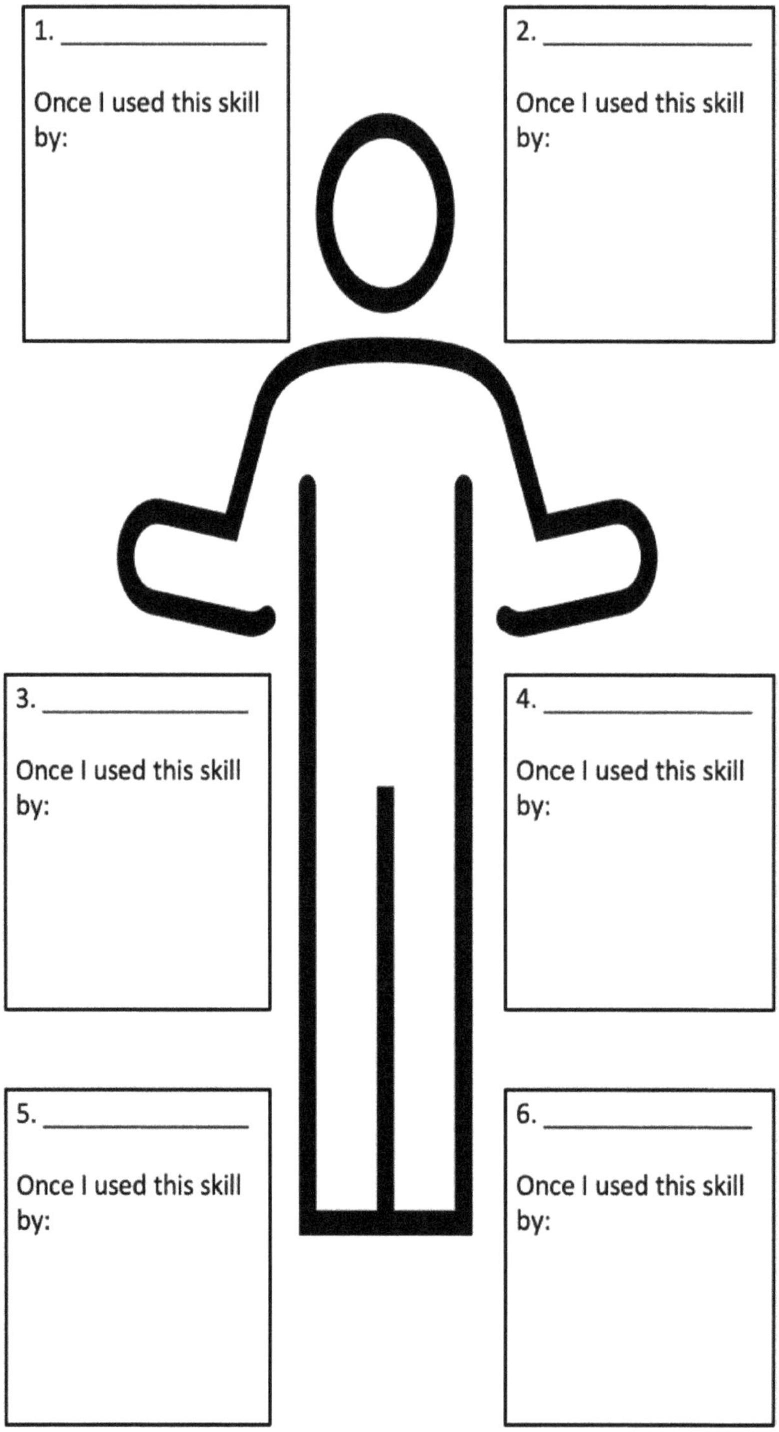

Image 12.4

Session 3: Understanding the Consequences of Our Decisions

Objectives:

1. Students will better understand how one decision impacts others.
2. Students will better understand how one decision impacts other decisions.
3. Students will practice how to take responsibility for self and actions.

Materials:

Picture of a buddy bench

Duration: 30 minutes

Instructions:

1. Welcome group members and revisit group ground rules.
2. Explain the topic for the day: understanding how our decisions impact others and understanding how one decision impacts other decisions.
3. Ask students if they have ever played Jenga. When you take one piece out of the structure, it can make the whole thing fall and the game is over. Explain that decisions we make can impact our friends.
4. Show students a picture of a buddy bench. Ask them if they know what they are for. (Answer: Schools put them next to playgrounds for a student to sit on if they have no one to play with. The other children are taught to invite someone sitting there into the game they are playing.)
5. Ask students to create a skit about what happens when someone decides to invite someone on the buddy bench to play (making sure there are at least three realistic consequences).
6. Ask the students to create a second skit about what happens when someone decides not to invite someone on the buddy bench to play (making sure there are at least three realistic consequences).
7. Discuss the differences.

Image 12.5

Session 4: Making Decisions for Yourself

Objectives:

1. Students will better understand the importance of making decisions for themselves.
2. Students will better understand the importance of resisting negative peer pressure.
3. Students will practice how to take responsibility for self and actions.

Materials:

What if Everyone Did That? by Ellen Javernick

"My Social Map" worksheet

Duration: 30 minutes

Instructions:

1. Welcome group members and revisit group ground rules.
2. Ask students to share an experience they have had when their decision was impacted by a peer and things turned out well.
3. Read *What if Everyone Did That?* by Ellen Javernick.
4. Discuss their thoughts about the book. What example in the book was like something that happened to them?
5. Ask students what they would do if they felt pressured by peers to break a rule at school.
6. Complete self-in-relationship map exercise.

My Social Map

Name: ______________________________ Date: ______________

Using initials only, add the people who belong in each of the two innermost circles. Add groups that you belong to. Next to each person or group, put a + next to those who you experience positive or no peer pressure. Place a - next to those who make you feel pressured about your decisions. Perhaps these are friends you get into trouble with from time to time.

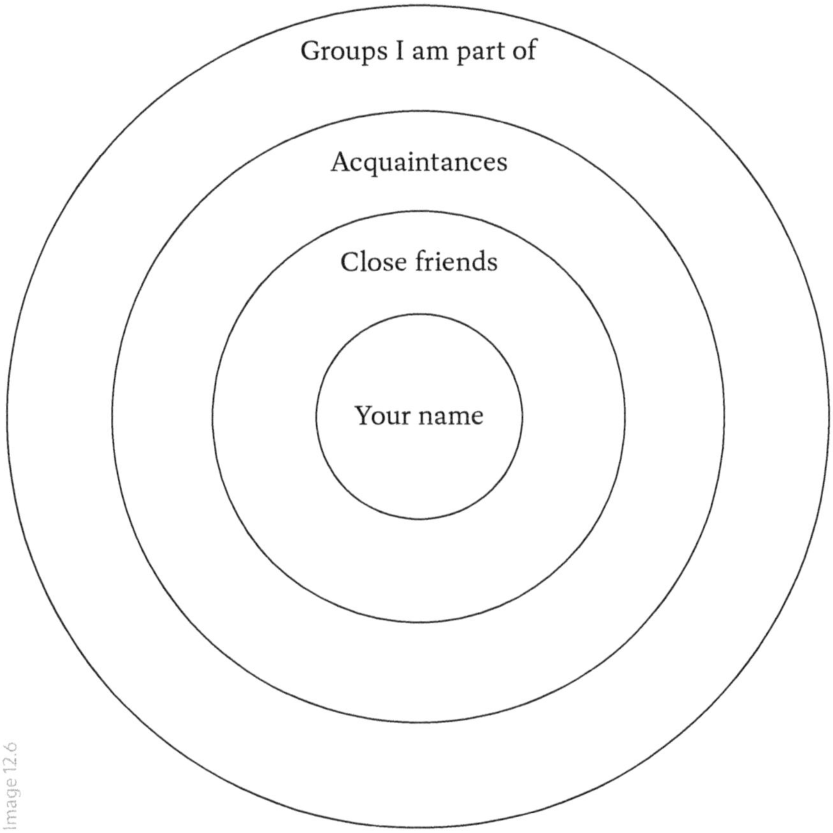

Image 12.6

What do you notice when you look at your map?

Session 5: Learning From a Bad Decision

Objectives:

1. Students will explore the emotions they feel when they make a bad decision.
2. Students will learn steps to take when they make a bad decision.
3. Students will discuss ways to avoid making a bad decision.

Materials needed:

"Recovering From a Bad Decision Road Map" worksheet

Pens/pencils/crayons/markers

Duration: 35 minutes

Instructions:

1. Welcome group members and revisit group ground rules. Remind them that next week is our final group meeting.
2. Discuss today's topic: handling what happens when you make a bad decision.
3. Ask students to share how they feel when they have made a bad decision that got them in trouble at home or at school. Ask what they did next.
4. Role-play in dyads: One of you just got in trouble and sent to the principal's office. The other is a friend trying to cheer them up. Then switch roles.
5. Discuss how they felt playing each role.
6. Introduce the "Road Map" worksheet. Ask students to fill out the bottom section about a bad decision they made and how they handled it.

Road Map to Follow After Making a Bad Decision

Name: ______________________________ Date: ______________

When you make a bad decision remember to:

1. Forgive yourself.
2. Think about what happened.
3. Ask, was it in my control?
4. Determine what you need to do next time.
5. Share what happened with a friend or caring adult.

Share a time you made a bad decision and what you did afterwards:

____

____

____

____

____

Image 12.7

Session 6: Wrapping Up

Objectives:

1. Synthesize learning about decision-making.
2. Set goals for making better decisions moving forward.

Materials needed:

Progress monitoring sheet

Rank order worksheet

Plain paper

Pen/pencil

Duration: 35 minutes

Instructions:

1. Welcome students and remind them it is their final meeting.
2. Review their completed progress monitoring sheets. What do they notice?
3. Review activities that we took part in together.
4. Ask students to rank the activities on their worksheet.
5. Ask students to share why they ranked them that way.
6. Ask students to write themselves a letter encouraging themselves to use at least three strategies we utilized for making decisions.
7. Let students know you will be checking in on them to see how they are doing in coming weeks.

Decision-Making Group Activities

Name: ______________________________ Date: ______________

Activity	What I Learned	Rank Order 1–7
My Magical Choices Decision-Making Cards activity		
Playing Pick Up Sticks		
What makes you a good decision-maker?		
Buddy bench skits		
Reading and discussing *What if Everyone Did That?*		
Making your social map		
Learning from bad decisions role-play		

Post-Intervention Communication to Parent/Guardian

English Version

Dear Parents/Guardians,

Today we finished up our small group counseling sessions designed to practice key decision-making skills. Each week we discussed a different topic and filled out a progress monitoring sheet to track if they were using their new decision-making strategies at recess, in the classroom, and out in the community. Make sure to ask your students to share the tracking sheets and what strategies are working best for them. In a month's time we will meet to have a quick booster check-in meeting to see how things are going. As always, do not hesitate to reach out to let us know if you have any questions, comments, or suggestions. You are an essential partner in cultivating your student's decision-making skills!

Sincerely,

Student Support Team Member

Spanish Version

Queridos padres/guardianes,

Hoy terminamos nuestras sesiones de asesoramiento en grupos pequeños diseñadas para practicar habilidades clave para la toma de decisiones. Cada semana discutimos un tema diferente y completamos una hoja de seguimiento del progreso para rastrear si estaban usando sus nuevas estrategias de toma de decisiones en el recreo, en el aula y en la comunidad. Asegúrese de pedirles a sus alumnos que compartan las hojas de seguimiento y qué estrategias funcionan mejor para ellos. Dentro de un mes nos reuniremos para tener una reunión rápida de control de refuerzo para ver cómo van las cosas. Como siempre, no dude en comunicarse con nosotros para informarnos si tiene alguna pregunta, comentario o sugerencia. ¡Usted es un socio esencial para cultivar las habilidades de toma de decisiones de su estudiante!

Atentamente,

Miembro del equipo de apoyo al estudiante

Plan for Implementation Fidelity

Group leaders will adhere to the six lessons and reflect on students' level of engagement throughout. Student, teacher, and caregiver surveys will be distributed to measure the effectiveness of the group and to share suggestions for improving the experience for future students.

Small Group Process Notes

Decision-Making Skills for Middle and High School Students

Curtis Darragh, IV and Kara Clement

Description of Skill

As students journey from their first, tentative drop-off at their kindergarten classroom to that momentous day they cross the stage for their high school graduation, their decisions become increasingly more important and impactful. Once students begin middle school, they are prompted both in and out of school about the person they are going to become and their plans for high school. Whether it's a traditional high school setting, technical high school, or AG-STEM, students across the nation are looking into high school choices that are best suited for them. They must make decisions about how to spend their time, who to forge friendships with, and whether to engage in risky behaviors. According to CASEL (2020), responsible decision-making is defined as "the abilit[y] to make caring and constructive choices about personal behavior and social interactions across diverse situations" (para. 7).

Of course, to make good decisions about ourselves, we need to develop our self-awareness and self-management. A student might ask themselves, "Should I try out for the basketball team or try out for a part in the musical? How will I compare to the other students who are trying out?" The decision to "put myself out there" is weighty and requires reflection. In matters of right and wrong, a student must take into account ethical standards and safety concerns. Likewise, when selecting between two options (French or Spanish, cross country or soccer), students need to weigh the potential benefits and consequences. The discrete skills of decision-making are addressed in this Tier 2 kit:

- demonstrating curiosity and open-mindedness and surrounding yourself with a healthy environment
- creating solutions for personal and social problems
- learning to make a reasoned judgment after analyzing information, data, and facts (e.g., definition differences in friendships and social media)
- anticipating and evaluating the consequences of one's actions, such as creating a pro/con list
- recognizing how critical thinking skills are useful both inside and outside of school, such as setting boundaries
- reflecting on one's role to promote personal, family, and community well-being

Pre-Intervention Communication With Parents/Guardians/Teachers in Languages Represented in the School

English Version

Dear Parents/Guardians,

Your (sixth, seventh, or eighth) grader has been selected to take part in a small group focused on responsible decision-making skills. This 11-week group will take place [indicate when] and will not interfere with their academic classes. The goal of this group is to delve into what goes into making good decisions that impact their life at school, friendships, well-being, and postsecondary plans. We will discuss our current strategies for problem solving and decision-making while learning new approaches. This will involve reflection, sharing experiences, case studies, and role-playing. Each student will complete a pretest prior to the group and a posttest as we finish up.

In this Tier 2 kit of middle school decision-making, our lessons will include the variety of topics:

- Seven decision-making steps
- Making a pro and con list
- Healthy relationships
- Friends versus frenemy
- Making responsible decisions about social media
- Using "I" statements
- Self-control
- Making a plan

Our goals are to explore and master how to do the following:

- Identify the nature of the decision to be made.
- Clarify all the viable options.
- Weigh the pros and cons of the most likely options.
- Gather all necessary information to make the best decision.
- Use reasoning to identify the best option.
- Select the option that makes sense, feels right, and brings us closer to our goals.
- Follow through on our decisions.

If you have any questions about this intervention group or would like to discuss your student's participation in the group, please do not hesitate to reach out to me.

Sincerely,

Student Support Team Interventionist

Spanish Version

Queridos padres/guardianes,

Su hijo (de 6.º, 7.º u 8.º) grado ha sido seleccionado para participar en un grupo pequeño centrado en habilidades de toma de decisiones responsables. Este grupo de 11 semanas se llevará a cabo [indicar cuándo] y no interferirá con sus clases académicas. El objetivo de este grupo es profundizar en lo que implica tomar buenas decisiones que impactan su vida en la escuela, las amistades, el bienestar y los planes postsecundarios. Discutiremos nuestras estrategias actuales para la resolución de problemas y la toma de decisiones mientras aprendemos nuevos enfoques. Esto implicará reflexión, intercambio de experiencias, estudios de casos y juegos de roles. Cada estudiante completará una prueba previa al grupo y una prueba posterior cuando terminemos.

En este kit de nivel 2 sobre toma de decisiones en la escuela secundaria: nuestras lecciones incluirán una variedad de temas como:

- Siete pasos para la toma de decisiones
- Hacer una lista de pros y contras
- Relaciones de salud
- Amigos contra enemigos
- Tomar decisiones responsables sobre las redes sociales
- Usar declaraciones en primera persona
- Autocontrol
- Hacer un plan

Nuestros objetivos son explorar y dominar cómo:

- Identificar la naturaleza de la decisión a tomar.
- Aclarar todas las opciones viables
- Sopese los pros y los contras de las opciones más probables
- Reúne toda la información necesaria para tomar la mejor decisión.
- Utilice el razonamiento para identificar la mejor opción.
- Seleccionar la opción que tenga sentido, que nos parezca adecuada y que nos acerque a nuestros objetivos.
- Cumplir con nuestras decisiones.

Si tiene alguna pregunta sobre este grupo de intervención o le gustaría hablar sobre la participación de su estudiante en el grupo, no dude en comunicarse conmigo.

Atentamente,

Intervencionista del equipo de apoyo al estudiante

Permission Slip

After reading the description of this Tier 2 small group, I, _______________________, give permission for my student _______________________ to take part in the group which will meet on _______________________ from [date] to [date]. I understand that this group is confidential and that I will be made aware if my student is making good use of this group experience. Should I need to be contacted, the best number to reach me at is _______________________.

Hoja de permiso

Después de leer la descripción de este grupo pequeño de Nivel 2, yo, _______________________, doy permiso para que mi estudiante _______________________ participe en el grupo que se reunirá el _______________________ de [fecha] a [fecha]. Entiendo que este grupo es confidencial y que se me informará si mi estudiante está haciendo un buen uso de esta experiencia grupal. Si necesito que me contacten, el mejor número para comunicarse conmigo es _______________________.

Goals of Intervention

- Identify the nature of the decision to be made.
- Clarify all the viable options.
- Weigh the pros and cons of the most likely options.
- Gather all necessary information to make the best decision.
- Use reasoning to identify the best option.
- Select the option that makes sense, feels right, and brings us closer to our goals.
- Follow through on our decisions.

CASEL Standards Addressed

- Responsible decision-making: The ability to make caring and constructive choices about personal behavior and social interactions across diverse situations.

ASCA Mind-Sets and Behaviors

B-LS 1. Critical thinking skills to make informed decisions

B-LS 9. Decision-making informed by gathering evidence, getting others' perspectives and recognizing personal bias

B-SMS 9. Personal safety skills

B-SS 5. Ethical decision-making and social responsibility

B-SS 9. Social maturity and behaviors appropriate to the situation and environment

Materials Needed

Lesson plans

Hand-outs

Blank paper

Student journals

Pens, markers, tape

Google Chromebook

Access to Google Classroom/Schoology or online educational platform

Pre-/Post-Assessment

Statements to Answer

1. I look at the risks associated with each option before making a decision.	Not at all	Rarely	Sometimes	Often	Very often
2. After I make a decision, it's final because I know my process is strong.	Not at all	Rarely	Sometimes	Often	Very often
3. I try to determine the real issue before starting a decision-making process.	Not at all	Rarely	Sometimes	Often	Very often
4. I rely on my own personal experience to find an answer to my problem.	Not at all	Rarely	Sometimes	Often	Very often
5. I tend to have a strong gut instinct, and I rely on it in decision-making.	Not at all	Rarely	Sometimes	Often	Very often

6. I am sometimes surprised by the actual consequences of my decisions.	Not at all	Rarely	Sometimes	Often	Very often
7. I think before I act.	Not at all	Rarely	Sometimes	Often	Very often
8. I prefer to come up with solutions alone rather than in a group.	Not at all	Rarely	Sometimes	Often	Very often
9. If I don't know how I feel about my decision, I go back and recheck my process.	Not at all	Rarely	Sometimes	Often	Very often
10. I consider a variety of potential answers before I make my final decision.	Not at all	Rarely	Sometimes	Often	Very often
11. In a group decision-making process, I tend to support my friends' ideas and try to find ways to make them work.	Not at all	Rarely	Sometimes	Often	Very often
12. When communicating my decision, I include my reasoning.	Not at all	Rarely	Sometimes	Often	Very often
13. I prefer to make decisions on my own and then let other people know what I've decided.	Not at all	Rarely	Sometimes	Often	Very often

14. I often make decisions without thinking about consequences.	Not at all	Rarely	Sometimes	Often	Very often
15. I avoid making decisions.	Not at all	Rarely	Sometimes	Often	Very often
16. I feel like I am responsible when I make most decisions.	Not at all	Rarely	Sometimes	Often	Very often

Source: "How Good Is Your Decision-Making?" by Mind Tools Content Team, https://www.mindtools.com/a0psx3v/how-good-is-your-decision-making.

Sessions 1–10

These sessions are designed to teach and reinforce skills. Make note of which sessions students respond well to and which they are less responsive to. Make additions or improvements to maximize student engagement and optimize desired outcomes. Ask students for specific feedback at the end of sessions.

Session 1: Our Decision-Making Style

Objectives:

1. Students will understand their decision-making style.
2. Students will understand steps to making good decisions.

Materials:

KWL chart

Goal-setting sheet

Duration: 40 minutes

Instructions:

1. Welcome and introduction; ask each student to share their favorite after-school snack when they introduce themselves.
2. Set ground rules, and ask for students' input. Record rules on a poster board; ask all group members to sign it.
3. Explain the purpose of the group: We are here to talk about how we go about making decisions. Our ability to think for ourselves and make choices that put us on the path to becoming the best versions of ourselves is an essential part of healthy development. Making decisions can be difficult, and we need strategies much like someone climbing a steep rockface might need in order to reach the summit.
4. What do you already know about making decisions?
5. Fill out a KWL chart with the students.

KWL Making Decisions

K: What do you know about making good decisions?

W: What do you want to know about decision-making?

L (fill out later): What did you learn about making good decisions?

Know	Want to Know	Learned

1. Reflection prompts:
    - How do you know when you have made a good decision?
    - Describe a time when you made a good decision but the outcome was not what you expected.
    - Describe a time when you made a bad decision but the outcome was good. Were you aware in either case that the decision was separate from the outcome?
    - When have you used a process to make a decision? Was the process helpful?
    - Describe a time you wish you had help in making a difficult decision. What do you wish you had to make the decision process more effective?
2. Set goals for the 6-week group.

Name: ______________________ Date: ____________

My goals for this group:

Goal 1:	I will reach this goal by:
Goal 2:	I will reach this goal by:
Goal 3:	I will reach this goal by:

Session 2: Making Decisions for Ourselves

Objectives:

1. Students will recognize good decision-making skills.
2. Students will learn how to utilize a pros and cons list.

Materials:

Case study

Pros and cons chart

Duration: 30–40 minutes

Instructions:

1. Welcome group members back. Remind them of ground rules agreed to week 1.
2. Ask students to share about a good decision they made this week.
3. Review case study "Carl" and ask discussion questions.

Case Study: Carl

Carl wanted to join the Air Force when he graduated high school. He had always wanted to serve his country and knew he could gain real-world experience and receive tuition assistance for college. He did a lot of research, spoke to several people serving in the Air Force, and arrived at his decision only after careful consideration and many discussions with his school counselor, the Air Force recruiter, and his parents. Carl had the support of the adults he trusted. He believed he had made a good decision. After several months of being in the Air Force though, Carl realized he was unhappy. He began feeling anxious and had trouble making friends. He felt challenged, but it was not what he had expected.

- Did Carl make a good or bad decision? How would he know?
- What can Carl do now if he believes he made a good decision but his outcome is less than desirable?

Turn the Tables: Journal Reflections

1. What important decision(s) are you trying to make right now?
2. Who do you turn to when making decisions?
3. What is your process for making an impactful decision like what to do after high school?
4. Teach students how and why to use a pros and cons chart. Making a pro/con list can be a helpful visual tool when it comes to decision-making.

Using a Pros and Cons Chart

Name: ______________________________ Date: ____________________

Decision 1:

Pro	Con

Decision 2: Choosing between two options

Choice 1	
Pro	**Con**

Choice 2	
Pro	**Con**

1. Reflection prompts:
    - Looking at your pro/con list, does one side have more reasons than the other?
    - Based on this observation, can you clearly come to a final decision because either pro or con has more reasons than the other?
    - Describe how you felt before making your pro/con list versus how you feel about your pro/con list now.

Session 3: Types of Decisions

Objectives:

1. Students will be able to distinguish between three types of decisions (life-shaping, significant, and in-the-moment decisions).
2. Students will practice making different types of decisions.

Materials:

Types of decisions index cards

Journals

Pens/pencils

Duration: 40 minutes

Instructions:

1. Welcome group members back. Check in.
2. Introduce topic for today: different types of decisions.
    a. Life-shaping decisions
    b. Significant decisions
    c. In-the-moment decisions that require an immediate response

Different decisions require different processes, so it is important to be clear about what kind of decision one is making. Asking oneself probing questions, seeking help from others, and practicing good decision habits all help young people become more adept at identifying the correct type of decision and the appropriate process for handling it. Here are some points to remember when thinking about types of decisions:

- Decisions come in all shapes and sizes, but one can generally think about three levels of decisions (big, significant, and in the moment).
- Determining the type of decision will direct the type and intensity (time, amount of deliberation, involvement of others) of the process one uses to reach the decision.
- Asking probing questions is helpful.
- Seeking guidance from others to help size up the decision type is also useful.
- Practicing good decision behavior until it becomes a habit allows one to more easily identify and categorize decisions one faces.

    d. Provide small index cards with the following decisions and ask students to categorize.

Big, Life-Shaping Decisions	Significant Decisions	In-the-Moment Decisions
Should I go to college or take a gap year?	Should I stay in this relationship with my boy/girlfriend?	Should I go to the party with my friends even though I know the parents will not be there?
Which parent should I live with after a divorce?	Should I go out for the soccer team or focus more on my grades?	Should I join everyone who is skipping school today?
Should I take the job instead of going to college?	Should I let go of a friendship that has lasted many years?	Should I tell the teacher I saw someone cheating on the test?
Should I join the armed forces?	Should I run for student government?	Should I ask my boss for the day off to go to my sister's recital?
Should I stay close to home or go to college far away?	Should I take AP classes?	Should I try [drugs, alcohol, vaping, smoking, etc.]

Source: Adopted from "Decision Concepts," by The Decision Education Foundation, 2009, https://global-uploads.webflow.com/61f9dd1631151d61d2f5d51a/622298b9f83d055756a5a557_Advisory_Part_II_Decision_Concepts.pdf.

Journal Reflections

- Share an experience when you had to make a decision that could not be reversed.
- How long did it take you to make that decision?
- Discuss a time you decided not to stop and think before making a decision. What prompted you to be impulsive?
- Do you sometimes get stuck when trying to make a decision?
- Have you ever put off making an important decision. Why? Why not?
- Who do you turn to when making decisions?
- How much time do you typically spend making decisions?

Session 4: Thinking for Myself

Objectives:

1. Students will understand the importance of thinking for themselves when making a decision.

Duration: 40 minutes

Instructions:

1. Welcome students and check in.
2. Ask students how they did with making decisions this week.
3. Ask students about a time when someone was influencing an important decision they were trying to make.
4. Introduce today's topic: thinking for ourselves when we make decisions.
5. Divide the small group into dyads.
6. Ask them to consider a time when they were attempting to make a decision and someone important in their life was trying to sway their decision.
7. Invite them to role-play a typical conversation between the two parties (the decider and the persuader).
8. Ask others to observe and make note of the things both the decision maker did to "stand their ground" and what the other person did to persuade them.
9. After each dyad:
    a. Decision-maker: How did it feel to have the other person attempt to sway your decision? Is there anything you wish they had said or done differently?
    b. Persuader: How did it feel when the decision-maker resisted your line of thinking? Do you think taking a stance on this person's decision was in their best interest?
10. For discussion:
    a. When is it okay to be part of someone's decision-making process (when you are invited into their process, if you are responsible for this person, etc.)?
    b. How can you ask others to give you space to make your own decision maturely?

Journal Reflections

- When am I comfortable asking others to weigh in on my decisions?
- When am I uncomfortable asking others to weigh in on my decisions?
- What can I do to hear my own voice better when I am making an important decision?

Session 5: Seven Steps to Good Decision-Making

Objectives:

1. Students will learn the seven steps to effective decision-making.
2. Students will use the seven steps to make a decision for themselves.

Materials:

"Seven Steps to Effective Decision-Making" worksheet

Pens/pencils

Duration: 40 minutes

Instructions:

1. Welcome students back. Check in.
2. Ask students how they go about choosing what to eat when they order take out or eat in a restaurant. What goes into their decision?
3. Read "7 Steps to Effective Decision Making" (https://www.umassd.edu/media/umass-dartmouth/fycm/decision_making_process.pdf).
4. Ask group members to identify a difficult decision a high school student might have to make.
5. Discuss each step of the decision-making process.
6. Ask students to work through a decision using the seven-step process handout.

Seven Steps to Good Decision-Making

1. Identify the decision: You realize that you need to make a decision. Try to clearly define the nature of the decision you must make. This first step is very important.
2. Gather information: Collect some pertinent information before you make your decision: what information is needed, the best sources of information, and how to get it. This step involves both internal and external work. Some information is internal: You'll seek it through a process of self-assessment. Other information is external: You'll find it online, in books, from other people, and from other sources.
3. Identify alternatives: As you collect information, you will probably identify several possible paths of action, or alternatives. You can also use your imagination and additional information to construct new alternatives. In this step, you will list all possible and desirable alternatives.
4. Weigh the evidence: Draw on your information and emotions to imagine what it would be like if you carried out each of the alternatives to the end. Evaluate whether the need identified in step 1 would be met or resolved through the use of each alternative. As you go through this difficult internal process, you'll begin to favor certain alternatives—those that seem to have a higher potential for reaching your goal. Finally, place the alternatives in a priority order, based upon your own value system.
5. Choose among the alternatives: Once you have weighed all the evidence, you are ready to select the alternative that seems to be the best one for you. You may even choose a combination of alternatives. Your choice in step 5 may very likely be the same or similar to the alternative you placed at the top of your list at the end of step 4.
6. Take action: You're now ready to take some positive action by beginning to implement the alternative you chose in step 5.
7. Review your decision: In this final step, consider the results of your decision and evaluate whether it has resolved the need you identified in step 1. If the decision has not met the identified need, you may want to repeat certain steps of the process to make a new decision. For example, you might want to gather more detailed or somewhat different information or explore additional alternatives.

Image 12.8

Source: University of Massachusetts: Dartmouth, "7 Steps to Effective Decision Making," https://www.umassd.edu/fycm/decision-making/process/.

Using the Seven Steps to Decision-Making

Name: ______________________________ Date: ______________

Using the seven steps to effective decision-making, work through a decision related to school that you are currently trying to make.

1. Identify the decision.	
2. Gather information.	
3. Identify alternatives.	
4. Weigh the evidence.	
5. Choose among the alternatives.	
6. Take action.	
7. Review your decision.	

For homework, interview an adult you admire. Ask them to discuss a difficult decision they had to make and how they went about choosing the option or course of action that was best for them. Be prepared to share what you learned with the group.

Session 6: Social Media and Responsible Decision-Making

Objective:

1. Students will understand how to make effective and responsible decisions using social media technology.

Duration: 1 hour

Instructions:

1. Welcome students back. Check in.
2. Ask each person to share about their interview with an adult about their decision-making process.
3. Introduce today's topic: social media and responsible decision-making.
4. Content: Think before you post anything online. Don't say anything online that you wouldn't say in real life. Don't post anything that would be hurtful to someone. Remember to treat others the way you would want to be treated. Don't post pictures or videos that may be embarrassing for yourself or others.
5. Ask the group, "What is social media? Which, if any, social media sites are you currently active on?"
6. Split groups into dyads. Ask them to brainstorm and record their answers:
   a. Why is it important to make effective and responsible decisions when using social media? What kinds of decisions do you need to make?
   b. Share handout: What to Consider When Using or Posting on Social Media.

What to Consider When Using or Posting on Social Media

Use your head and your heart when using social media.

Head – What are the outcomes that can happen based on what I post or what I view on social media? Is it appropriate? Am I making the right choice in what I am posting, watching, or listening?

Heart – This is the empathy component. How does what I post, view, or listen to affect others? Can what I hurt someone else or can it make them feel better?

Image 12.9

1. Ask students to think about the last time they posted on social media. Fill out a new seven-step decision-making worksheet to detail how they decided to publish their post.
2. Consider two scenarios:

Scenario 1:

Juan made a funny video with his friend Daniel. They had fun doing it, and Juan wanted to post it on a social media site for all to see. Dan asked Juan not to post it because it did not include one of their friends, Bill. He worried that Bill might feel bad that he was not involved in the video since the friends were like the "three musketeers." They did everything together. Juan did not think Bill would mind and wanted to post it anyway.

What do you think? Think about how you would use your head and your heart to make this decision.

Scenario 2:

Shamelle had a birthday party and invited some of her closest friends. Her parents gave her a limit of how many friends she could invite. This was difficult because she had a lot of friends. Shamelle's sister took some great pictures of her party and wanted to post them on Instagram and Facebook. Shamelle asked her sister not to post them because some of her friends who weren't invited to the party may see them, especially if the post is tagged.

Do you think Shamelle is making a responsible decision? Think about how you would use your head and your heart to make this decision.

Session 7: Friend or Frenemy?

Objective:

1. Students will be able to define what makes a person a true friend.

Materials:

Paper

Pens/pencils

Duration: 40 minutes

Instructions:

1. Welcome students to the group. Ask them to check in about their week.
2. Introduce today's topic: What makes someone a true friend? What does it mean when someone is a "frenemy"? What would you choose to do if you found out someone was a frenemy to you?
3. Divide students into groups of three.
4. Ask them to think of a scenario when someone was being a frenemy and their so-called friend decided to confront them.
5. Write a brief skit giving a role to each member of the group.
6. Perform the skits for the larger group.
7. Ask these reflection questions:

   Define a friend versus a frenemy.

   Given the skits and the lesson taught today, can you identify some friends and frenemies in your life currently? How do you feel about this realization or were you aware before?

   Why is it important to know who is a true friend when it comes to responsible decision-making?

Session 8: Self Control: Communicating Effectively—I Statements

Objectives:

1. Students will learn about the importance of using an I statement when communicating their thoughts, feelings, and opinions.
2. Students will practice developing and sharing I statements.

Duration: 40 minutes

Instructions:

1. Welcome the group back. Check in about the last week.
2. Introduce content: One way to come to a decision about taking accountability for our actions is to realize how we communicate with others using I statements. These kinds of statements will communicate how you feel instead of putting the blame on others.
3. Say, "To write an I statement effectively, please identify the following:
    a. how you feel [specific emotion]
    b. when you feel it (not putting the hurt or the blame on anyone else)
    c. why you feel this way
    d. what you wish for the future of this relationship"

    I feel ___ [emotion] ___ when ___ [when it happens] ___ because ___ [why it happens] .

    Next time, _________ [what you'd like to happen] _________.

I statement examples:

- I feel angry when you ask for my answers to the worksheet because every time you do this, you threaten my friendship with you, and next time you do this, I want you to put yourself in my shoes and realize that this isn't fair. I want to be friends with you, but my friendship with you cannot be threatened by this unfairness.
- I feel frustrated when you do not complete your part of the group project because you want to talk to other kids in the class or play games on your device. Next time, please consider the group and our need to split the work evenly to get a good grade we all deserve.

Let's Practice I Statements!

Name: ______________________________ Date: ____________

Read each scenario and come up with an I statement.

Problem	I Statement
Kara gets angry when she isn't first in line for the bus.	
Curtis gets emotionally unstable when other kids are whispering about him and starting rumors.	
Carrie gets upset when she finds out there were pictures taken of her without her consent.	

Session 9: Making A Plan to Get an Assignment Done

Objectives:

1. Students will learn about the importance of deciding to plan ahead in order to complete a long-term project.
2. Students will practice using a planner to complete a long-term assignment.

Materials:

Planning worksheet

Pens/pencils

Duration: 30–40 minutes

Instructions:

1. Welcome students back and check in.
2. Ask students to pair share about their last long-term assignment. What was it about? How did they go about completing it? Did they get it in on time? Were they happy with their grade on it?
3. Introduce today's lesson: deciding to plan ahead to get a long-term project done.
4. Content: "Before a middle schooler can start homework, planning and time management plays a key role in decision-making. When making plans and decisions, you are training your brain for what is to come. Once the decision is final, it will be easier to start right away rather than putting things on the waitlist. Plan for what, when, where, how, and why. To get started, you have to plan out what your day or week will look like. For example, you are creating a project about how water has an impact on society and the environment:
    a. What: How does water impact the environment?
    b. When: Due in 2 weeks!
    c. Where: At my desk in my bedroom
    d. How: Create a slideshow presentation with videos and pictures that demonstrate the impact of water on the environment
    e. Why: To have a higher GPA, so I can reach honor roll status by the end of the trimester
5. Ask students to complete the following chart to plan for their next long-term assignment. Now the task initiation is a lot easier for you!

Planning a Long Term Assignment

Name: ______________________ Date: ____________

Make a plan by answering the questions by picking a task you have to do today or this week.

What?	
When? Include mini due dates along the way	
Where?	
How?	
Why?	

Now you have a better understanding of what your plan looks like going forward! Hopefully getting started will be a lot easier for you.

Session 10: Taking Stock of Learning and Wrapping Up

Objectives:

1. Students will synthesize their learning about decision-making.
2. Students will be able to articulate what they learned in the group and apply it to their day-to-day life.
3. Students will be able to identify ways they have changed their behavior as a result of this group.

Materials:

KWL charts

Goal sheets

Posttest

Pens/pencils

Duration: 30–40 minutes

Instructions:

1. Welcome students and remind them that this is the final group. Remind students that you (and other student support team members) are always available if they would like to discuss an important decision they are trying to make.
2. Ask each group member to share what they learned from their interview. Ask a student to record the "lessons learned" on a piece of chart paper.
3. Return to their individual KWL handout. Ask students to record what they feel like they learned during the 11-week group. Invite students to share with the group.
4. Return to the goal setting sheet. Ask students to work in groups of three to discuss whether they achieved their goals for the group.
5. Take posttest.
6. Closure activity: Write a letter to yourself about making good decisions. The group leader will send these to the students in 6 weeks' time as a reminder to the group members.

Post-Intervention Communication to Parent/Guardian

English Version

Dear Parents/Guardians,

As you know, your student, [Name], took part in a 6-week group that focused on responsible decision-making. We encourage you to ask [Name] to share what they learned about their decision-making style, the challenges they encounter, and the seven steps to decision-making:

1. Identify the decision.
2. Gather information.
3. Identify alternatives.
4. Weigh the evidence.
5. Choose among the alternatives.
6. Take action.
7. Review your decision.

Since the decisions our students make as they prepare for life after high school are of great importance, it's helpful to spend time meeting in small groups to discuss strategies for making decisions that are best for our well-being and safety.

If you have any questions, please do not hesitate to contact us.

Sincerely,

Student Support Team Interventionist

Spanish Version

Estimados padres/tutores,

Como sabe, su estudiante, [nombre], participó en un grupo de 6 semanas que se centró en la toma de decisiones responsable. Lo alentamos a que le pida a [nombre] que comparta lo que aprendió sobre su estilo de toma de decisiones, los desafíos que enfrenta y los 7 pasos para la toma de decisiones, que incluyen:

1. Identificar la decisión
2. Recopilar información
3. Identificar alternativas
4. Ponderar la evidencia
5. Elige entre las alternativas
6. Tomar acción
7. Revise su decisión

Dado que las decisiones que toman nuestros estudiantes mientras se preparan para la vida después de la escuela secundaria son de gran importancia, es útil dedicar tiempo a reunirse en grupos pequeños para discutir estrategias para tomar decisiones que sean mejores para nuestro bienestar y seguridad.

Si tiene alguna pregunta, no dude en ponerse en contacto con nosotros.

Atentamente,

Intervencionista del Equipo de Apoyo Estudiantil

Plan for Implementation Fidelity

To achieve the intended outcomes of this intervention, it is helpful to colead the small group with a colleague, reflect on student responses to the activities, and seek support to keep engagement in the group high. Tier 2 small group facilitators should seek peer coaching and ask for feedback to make sure the intervention is implemented with fidelity.

Small Group Process Notes

Credits

IMG 12.1: Copyright © 2018 Depositphotos/Warmworld.
IMG 12.2: Source: Adapted from https://authorbcummings.com/freebiess/.
IMG 12.3: Source: Adapted from https://authorbcummings.com/freebiess/.
IMG 12.4a: Copyright © by Microsoft. Reprinted with permission.
IMG 12.5: Copyright © 2021 Depositphotos/IrynaTolm.

■ CHAPTER 13

Tier 2 Intervention Kits for Academic Success

Social and Academic Success for Elementary School Students

Karina Nguyen

Image 13.1

Description of Skill

For kindergarten students who are entering education for the first time or students who have not been to school, the rules of school and expectations of social interactions are brand new. Most students will pick up on routines while others will be slower to adjust. Upon coming to school, it may be the first time that students are introduced to unfamiliar adults, and students and may face social blunders. Students may exhibit behaviors such as leaving their seat or calling out in class, hitting or kicking during play or recess, and having difficulty following other expected behaviors appropriate for school. The inability to self-regulate and make good choices can negatively affect students' ability to socialize and impact their self-esteem and academic success. The purpose of this Tier 2 kit is to teach elementary students the social skills needed to be successful in school and to be able to reach their academic and social goals. Students can either be recommended by their academic teachers, counselor, parent or guardian or via self-advocacy for intervention.

Pre-Intervention Communication With Parents/Guardians/Teachers in Languages Represented in the School

English Version

Dear Parent/Guardian,

Your child has been presented with an exciting opportunity! Through teacher, parent or counselor recommendation, or self-volunteer, your child, ______________________________, has been recommended for a social skills group starting on _____________. In this social skills group, we will be exploring topics such as school expectations, friendships, conflict resolution, and more over the course of 5 weeks. Each week for 30 minutes your child will meet with me along with a group of their peers to play a game, listen to a story, talk, or do other fun things to learn about ways they can be successful in school. If you would like for your child to participate, please sign the form provided. If you have any questions, please contact me at [phone] or [email].

Warm Regards,

Your School Counselor

Spanish Version

Estimado padre/Guardianes,

¡A su hijo se le ha presentado una oportunidad emocionante! Por recomendación de un maestro, padre o consejero, o por iniciativa propia, su hijo, ______________________________ , ha sido recomendado para un grupo de habilidades sociales que comienza el _____________ . En este grupo de habilidades sociales, exploraremos temas como expectativas escolares, amistades, resolución de conflictos y más en el transcurso de 5 semanas. Cada semana, durante 30 minutos, su hijo se reunirá conmigo junto con un grupo de compañeros para jugar, escuchar un cuento, hablar o hacer otras cosas divertidas para aprender cómo pueden tener éxito en la escuela. Si desea que su hijo participe, firme a continuación. Si tiene alguna pregunta, comuníquese conmigo al (teléfono) o (correo electrónico).

Un cordial saludo,

Tu consejero escolar

Permission Slip (If Applicable)

I, ____________________[parent or guardian], give my permission for ____________________ [child's name] to participate in the student success skills group starting on ____________________ .

Spanish Version

Yo, ____________________ (padre o tutor), doy mi permiso para que ______________ (nombre del niño) participe en el grupo de habilidades para el éxito estudiantil a partir del ____________________ .

Goals of Intervention

- Teach and reinforce the social skills needed to be successful in school and to be able to reach their academic and social goals.
- Assist students in successfully navigating forming new relationships with peers and adults.
- Help students to form positive habits as they begin their school journey.

CASEL Standards Addressed

- Taking others' perspectives
- Demonstrating empathy and compassion
- Developing on positive relationships
- Reflecting on one's role to promote personal, family, and community well-being
- Having a growth mind-set

ASCA Mind-Sets and Behaviors

M 1. Belief in development of whole self, including a healthy balance of mental, social/emotional and physical well-being

M 2. Sense of acceptance, respect, support, and inclusion for self and others in the school environment

M 3. Positive attitude toward work and learning

B-SMS 1. Responsibility for self and actions

B-SMS 2. Self-discipline and self-control

B-SMS 7. Effective coping skills

Materials Needed

Crayons or colored pencils

The Little Book of Friendship by Zack Bush and Laurie Friedman

I'm Sorry by Sam McBratney

Gizmo's Pawsome Guide to Mental Health (https://www.gizmo4mentalhealth.org/wp-content/uploads/2017/09/GizmoPawesome.pdf; you can find more Gizmo curriculum resources at https://www.gizmo4mentalhealth.org/)

Coloring pages

Pre-/Post-Assessment: Social and Academic Skills

Name: ______________________________ Date: ______________

Please read the following questions and circle one of the following:

1 = Strongly disagree 2 = Disagree 3 = Neutral 4 = Agree 5 = Strongly agree

1. I feel good about what I can accomplish in school.	1	2	3	4	5
2. I know how to meet new people and make friends.	1	2	3	4	5
3. Sometimes, I am not sure what I am supposed to be doing with my hands and feet.	1	2	3	4	5
4. Not knowing what to do ruins my day.	1	2	3	4	5
5. I know how to be safe in the school and on school grounds.	1	2	3	4	5
6. I use kind words with my peers and adults in my school.	1	2	3	4	5
7. I know what to do when I feel upset.	1	2	3	4	5
8. I know how to resolve problems with my peers.	1	2	3	4	5
9. I know how to make good choices.	1	2	3	4	5

Weekly Tracking Form

Student Name: ______________________________ Date: ______________

Instructions:	
1. The student carries this form each day and is required to fill in weekdays. 2. Additional student comments may be made on the back of this form. 3. The student reviews this form each Friday with ______________ who initials the bottom row of this form.	1 = Poor 2 = Fair 3 = Average 4 = Very good 5 = Outstanding My goal is 80% points for the week

Check target behavior:

_______ Student is able to stay in their designated area.

_______ Student is able to keep hands and feet to self.

_______ Student raises hand to speak.

_______ Student completes classwork/stays on task.

_______ Student is respectful to peers and adults.

	Date:	Comments
Monday	TB 1: 1 2 3 4 5 TB 2: 1 2 3 4 5	
Tuesday	TB 1: 1 2 3 4 5 TB 2: 1 2 3 4 5	
Wednesday	TB 1: 1 2 3 4 5 TB 2: 1 2 3 4 5	
Thursday	TB 1: 1 2 3 4 5 TB 2: 1 2 3 4 5	
Friday	TB 1: 1 2 3 4 5 TB 2: 1 2 3 4 5	
Reviewed by:	_____/ 50 = ______ %	

Met goal: ☐ Yes ☐ No

Signatures: ______________________________ ______________________________

Student Teacher

Sessions 1–5

Session 1: Welcome to School!

Objective:

1. Students will identify the expectations of school and why it is important for them to follow them.

Materials:

School Expectation Worksheet

crayons

Duration: 30 Minutes

Instructions:

1. The counselor will introduce themselves and the topic of the group.
2. The counselor will ask students to help make a list of ground rules for the group and write them on a poster board. Students will sign them to indicate they will follow the ground rules.
3. The counselor will start the group with an icebreaker and have each student share their name and their favorite food with their peers.
4. The counselor will establish the rules of the group with the students.
    a. Everything that is said in group stays in the group.
    b. When someone is speaking, we are listening.
    c. In group, we are to sit and stay at our table unless we ask permission to leave.
    d. Show respect.
    e. Be kind.
5. The counselor will start the group with a story about school rules and will explain why it is important that we follow them.
6. The counselor will talk about following school rules as being a good choice because it allows us to learn and the other friends in our class to learn too.
7. Students will receive a worksheet about good choices and bad choices. Students will be able to match the pictures to the correct column.
8. The counselor will close groups by reviewing the good choices. Optional: The weekly behavior chart can be introduced as a reinforcer.

School Expectations

Name: ______________________________

1. Put a big "X" on the bad choices.
2. Color in the good choices we can make at school.

Image 13.2

Quiet mouth

Image 13.3

Running

Image 13.4

Raising your hand and staying in your seat

Image 13.5

Looking at the teacher

Image 13.6

Listening

Image 13.7

Ignoring people

Now that you have identified some of the rules in school, your homework is to try your best to follow them. Good luck!

Session 2: Let's Be Friends

Objective:

1. Students will learn what a friend is and how to maintain friendships.

Materials:

Smartboard

The Little Book of Friendship by Zack Bush and Laurie Friedman

Duration: 30 minutes

Instructions:

1. The counselor will welcome the students back to the group and start with an icebreaker question.
2. The counselor will review the rules of the group with the students and ask students how their week went in regard to their behavior charts.
    a. What went well?
    b. What could be better?
    c. How can we change our behavior this week to make it better?
3. The counselor will acknowledge the effort the students have put in and the good work that they have done.
4. The counselor will then introduce the topic of friendship by asking students what qualities they look for when making or looking for a new friend.
5. The counselor will write on the smartboard the qualities that students tell them.
6. Students will listen to a story about friendship and identify the qualities that they want in a friend from the story.
7. The counselor will read *The Little Book of Friendship*.
8. The counselor will review the day's lesson with the students by asking students questions. Is a good friend someone who
    a. shares their crayons with you?
    b. cuts you in the lunch line?
    c. teases you about being scared of something?
    d. helps you when you are confused about a math problem?
    e. calls you names you don't like?
    f. shares your secrets with other people?
    g. pushes you at recess?
    h. cares about you and helps you when you are hurt?
9. The counselor will close the group by reminding students that the qualities we look for in a friend are what people expect from us as a friend.

Session 3: How to Fix an Oopsies

Objective:

1. Students understand that conflicts are normal and that we can solve them if we use our words.

Materials:

I'm Sorry by Sam McBratney

Coloring page

Crayons

Duration: 30 minutes

Instructions:

1. The counselor will remind the student about the rules of the group.
2. The counselor will open the group by asking the group if there was ever a time they had a problem with a friend. What happened? What were they feeling? Why did it happen? How was it solved so that they felt better?
3. The counselor will explain that sometimes we might have an issue with someone and not get along with them. We might feel sad or mad. And sometimes, the other person feels sad, mad, or disappointed, too. We know that it doesn't feel good to feel sad or mad.
4. The counselor will introduce and read *I'm Sorry* by Sam McBratney.
5. The counselor will review the story by asking the group these questions:

    a. Who was the story about?
    b. Were the kids friends?
    c. What kind of things did they do as friends?
    d. Did the friends have a problem?
    e. What do you think they were feeling when they were no longer friends?
    f. How did they fix their friendship?

6. The counselor will talk to the students about feelings and let students know that everyone has them: "We all feel happy, excited, loved, mad, sad, scared, or other feelings. We know it doesn't feel good to be mad or sad. So, if we have done something that has made someone feel sad or mad, it is important that we stop and say sorry to them. If you do not know why someone is upset with you, you need to ask them so that you know what you need to stop doing. And if someone is making you feel sad or mad, you need to let them know this. Because they might not know that they are making us feel sad or mad and they need to know so that they can stop. At the end of this, it is always important to say that we are sorry if we have hurt someone. If you are having trouble with doing this, always ask for help from an adult. We are always here to help you!"
7. The counselor will hand out paper and crayons to students. Encourage them to make a card for someone they need to say sorry to. Ask them to share their cards if they feel comfortable.

Session 4: Take a Break

Objective:

1. Students will learn relaxation techniques and strategies for when they are feeling sad, mad, or worried.

Materials:

Gizmo's Pawesome Guide to Mental Health

Smartboard

Duration: 30 minutes

Instructions:

1. The counselor will remind the student about the rules of the group.
2. The counselor will open the group by asking the group if there was ever a time they felt sad, mad, or worried about something. What happened? What did they do to feel better?
3. The counselor will explain that we all have mental health, which is our feelings, thoughts, and actions: "Sometimes we have big feelings that can change how we usually feel, think, or act. Sometimes when we are mad or frustrated, we might feel like all of our muscles are really tight, or our face can feel really hot, or we can get really sweaty. When we are worried about something, we might feel our hearts beating fast, we have trouble breathing, and we might get sweaty. These are some signs our mental health needs attention. There are things we can do every day to help ourselves when we are feeling sad, mad, or worried."
4. The counselor will read to students *Gizmo's Pawesome Guide to Mental Health* (https://www.gizmo4mentalhealth.org/wp-content/uploads/2017/09/GizmoPawesome.pdf).
5. The counselor will ask students to identify things that they can do on their own to take care of their mental health when they are feeling sad, mad, or worried and write them on the smartboard.
6. The counselor will then ask students what some of the things they wrote down that they can do in school and follow school rules at the same time and circle the answers.
7. Counselor will pick three healthy coping strategies and spend 2 minutes practicing each one with the group.
8. The counselor will review the coping strategies that students identified to use when they are in school to help them relax.

**Gizmo's Pawesome Guide to Mental Health* (Copyright © 2017 All rights reserved) is a free resource developed under the Connecticut Networks of Care for Suicide Prevention (NCSP) Initiative and is currently maintained by United Way of Connecticut. The free Gizmo book and materials are accessible through the Gizmo website at www.Gizmo4mentalhealth.org. Additionally, the Guides accompanying curriculum for elementary youth in third and fourth grade, *Gizmo's Pawesome Guide to Mental Health Elementary Curriculum* (2020) is available on the website for purchase.

Session 5: I Can Do It!

Objective:

1. Students will be able to identify strengths.

Materials:

"This is Me" Worksheet

Certificates of completion

Duration: 30 minutes

Instructions:

1. The counselor will welcome everyone to the last group session.
2. The counselor will pass out the coloring page to each student.
3. The student will first complete the sentences by reflecting on what they have learned from the group or what they have accomplished because of the group. (Counselor may need to assist students with spelling.)
4. The counselor will ask each student to draw a picture of themselves. They can draw and color themselves exactly how they are today (shirt, pants, dress, skirt, short, hair, etc.) or however they want to look.
5. When the students are done, the counselor will have the student flip their paper over and write their name on the blank back. They will pass it to the person on their right.
6. The counselor will instruct the students to give a compliment to their group member by picking from a bank of adjectives. Once the student has written a compliment, they will pass it to the person on their right until their paper comes back to them.
7. The counselor will then present each picture with their sentences and the compliments their group mates wrote about them. The counselor will also add in their own compliments for the students of what they have improved or achieved in the group based on teacher observation or weekly tracker.
8. The counselor will present each student with a certificate and remind them that they can always ask for help if they need it.

This Is Me

Name: ______________________

I am proud of ______________________.

I will succeed at ______________________.

Draw a picture of yourself.

Adjective bank:

Kind

Smart

Caring

Amazing

Polite

Good listener

Cute

Friendly

Joyful

Nice

Funny

Cool

Creative

Happy

Fabulous

Fun

Helpful

Leader

Sweet

Trusting

Unique

Post-Intervention Communication to Parent/Guardian

English Version

Dear Parent/Guardian,

We just wrapped up our small group designed to foster social and academic skills. Your child made the most of this opportunity! We explored topics such as school expectations, friendships, conflict resolution, and more over the course of 5 weeks. Please ask your child about the activities they enjoyed most. During the group we played games to encourage turn taking, listened to stories about friendship, and did several activities to inspire them to be successful in school. I will be reaching out with a brief survey in the next few days to ask you about your child's experience in the group. If you have any questions, please contact me at [phone] or [email].

Warm Regards,

Your School Counselor

Spanish Version

Estimado padre/Guardianes,

Acabamos de concluir nuestro pequeño grupo diseñado para fomentar habilidades sociales y académicas. ¡Su hijo aprovechó al máximo esta oportunidad! Exploramos temas como expectativas escolares, amistades, resolución de conflictos y más en el transcurso de 5 semanas. Por favor pregúntele a su hijo sobre las actividades que más le gustaron. Durante el grupo jugamos juegos para alentarlos a tomar turnos, escuchamos historias sobre la amistad e hicimos varias actividades para inspirarlos a tener éxito en la escuela. Me comunicaré con ellos con una breve encuesta en los próximos días para preguntarles sobre la experiencia de su hijo en el grupo. Si tiene alguna pregunta, comuníquese conmigo al (teléfono) o (correo electrónico).

Un cordial saludo,

Tu consejero escolar

Plan for Implementation Fidelity

Interventionists will follow plans for sessions in suggested sequence, making note of which activities and questions sparked engagement and which did not. Reviews of pre- and posttests will reveal what students learned during the group. Adjustments will be made if less than 80% of the learning goals were obtained for this group. Surveys to teachers and caregivers will give the interventionist important information about students' ability to generalize the content from the group to their everyday life in school.

Small Group Process Notes

Middle School Executive Functioning

Dr. Peg Donohue

Description of Skill

Executive functioning comprises many skills. It is most often defined as the mental processes and skills that help us plan, organize, sustain attention, and persist in order to complete a task or solve a problem. By middle school, most students should be able to demonstrate the following consistently:

- planning and prioritizing
- time management
- emotional control
- organization
- working memory
- sustained attention
- task initiation
- metacognition
- response inhibition

Given the challenges of changing classes and interacting with multiple adults each day, middle schoolers can struggle to develop the skills, abilities, and knowledge they need to maximize their potential as students. This Tier 2 kit should be used with students who continue to struggle after these skills are taught in Tier 1 lessons.

Pre-Intervention Communication With Parents/Guardians/Teachers in Languages Represented in the School

English Version

Dear Parents/Guardians,

As you know, we are committed to providing small group interventions for students who can benefit from reteaching core skills. Your child has been recommended for our current group in executive functioning. Executive functioning skills help us to initiate and complete tasks, stay tuned into learning, and achieve goals. We will spend 6 weeks meeting to work on key skills such as time management, organization, limiting distractions, and improving working memory. Your child will have homework to attempt the strategies we are learning each week as they complete their homework. Make sure to ask them what strategies they are working on this week so you can reinforce them. Should you have any questions or concerns, please contact us.

Sincerely,

Student Support Team Members

Spanish Version

Estimados padres/Guardians,

Como usted sabe, estamos comprometidos a brindar intervenciones en grupos pequeños para estudiantes que puedan beneficiarse al volver a enseñar habilidades básicas. Su hijo ha sido recomendado para nuestro grupo actual en Funcionamiento Ejecutivo. Las habilidades del funcionamiento ejecutivo nos ayudan a iniciar y completar tareas, estar atentos al aprendizaje y alcanzar metas. Pasaremos 6 semanas reuniéndonos para trabajar en habilidades clave como gestión del tiempo, organización, limitación de distracciones y mejora de la memoria de trabajo. Su hijo tendrá "tarea" para intentar las estrategias que estamos aprendiendo cada semana a medida que completa su tarea. Asegúrate de preguntarles en qué estrategias están trabajando esta semana para que puedas reforzarlas. Si tiene alguna pregunta o inquietud, comuníquese con nosotros.

Atentamente,

Miembros del equipo de apoyo estudiantil

Permission Slip (If Applicable)

My child, ________________, has my permission to take part in the 6-week small group focused on improving their executive functioning skills. If you need to contact me [Caregiver's Name], I ________________ can be reached at (phone #) ________________.

Signature: ________________

Hoja de permiso

Mi hijo ________________tiene mi permiso para participar en el grupo pequeño de 6 semanas enfocado en mejorar sus habilidades de funcionamiento ejecutivo. Si necesita comunicarse conmigo (nombre del cuidador), ________________ puede comunicarse con mí al (número de teléfono) ________________.

Firmado (firma del cuidador)________________

Goals of Intervention

- Improve academic performance by developing new executive functioning skills.
- Improve time management skills.
- Improve organizational skills.
- Enhance ability to limit external and internal distractions.
- Improve working memory.
- Increase homework completion rates.

CASEL Standards Addressed

- Demonstrating curiosity and open mindedness
- Identifying solutions for personal and social problems
- Anticipating and evaluating the consequences of one's actions
- Recognizing how critical thinking skills are useful both inside and outside of school
- Reflecting on one's role to promote personal, family, and community well-being
- Evaluating personal, interpersonal, community, and institutional impacts

ASCA Mind-Sets and Behaviors

M 3. Positive attitude toward work and learning

M 4. Self-confidence in ability to succeed

M 5. Belief in using abilities to their fullest to achieve high-quality results and outcomes

B-LS 3. Time-management, organizational and study skills

B-LS 4. Self-motivation and self-direction for learning

B-LS 7. Long- and short-term academic, career and social/emotional goals

B-SMS 2. Self-discipline and self-control

B-SMS 3. Independent work

B-SMS 5. Perseverance to achieve long and short-term goals

B-SMS 10. Ability to manage transitions and adapt to change

Materials Needed

Handouts

Writing instruments

Sticky notes

Items for memory game

Pre-/Post-Assessment: Executive Functioning for Middle Schoolers

Source: Adapted from Lifeskillsadvocate.com.

Review each statement. Circle the number for the response that most accurately describes you in the past month.

Planning Tasks						
Statement	**Never**	**Rarely**	**Sometimes**	**Often**	**Always**	**Comments**
When I start homework, I finish it in one sitting.	1	2	3	4	5	
I use a calendar to remind me of events.	1	2	3	4	5	
I like to have a plan so that I don't feel overwhelmed.	1	2	3	4	5	
I know which task to start first when I begin a project.	1	2	3	4	5	
I know how to put steps in order to complete a long-term project.	1	2	3	4	5	
Time Management Tasks						
Statement	**Never**	**Rarely**	**Sometimes**	**Often**	**Always**	**Comments**
I am on time for appointments, class, and events.	1	2	3	4	5	
I can accurately estimate how long it will take me to complete a task.	1	2	3	4	5	
I don't put off tasks or procrastinate.	1	2	3	4	5	
I make a list of what I need to do each day.	1	2	3	4	5	
I can prioritize what tasks to do first.	1	2	3	4	5	
Task Initiation Skills						
Statement	**Never**	**Rarely**	**Sometimes**	**Often**	**Always**	**Comments**
I know how to get started with most tasks.	1	2	3	4	5	
I can set aside a fun activity when I have something important to do.	1	2	3	4	5	
I easily finish tasks I don't like to do.	1	2	3	4	5	

(*Continued*)

(*Continued*)

I complete tasks without reminders.	1	2	3	4	5	
Procrastination is not usually a problem for me.	1	2	3	4	5	
Organizational Skills						
Statement	**Never**	**Rarely**	**Sometimes**	**Often**	**Always**	**Comments**
I like my spaces to be neat and tidy.	1	2	3	4	5	
I feel better when my space is organized.	1	2	3	4	5	
People who know me say I am organized.	1	2	3	4	5	
I try to have a place for everything.	1	2	3	4	5	
I have a system for organizing my schoolwork.	1	2	3	4	5	
Problem-Solving Skills						
Statement	**Never**	**Rarely**	**Sometimes**	**Often**	**Always**	**Comments**
I can easily identify problems when they start.	1	2	3	4	5	
I can easily identify facts and gather information.	1	2	3	4	5	
I can get to the bottom of why problems start.	1	2	3	4	5	
Most times I evaluate pros and cons before I take the next step.	1	2	3	4	5	
When I select a solution, I know how to implement it.	1	2	3	4	5	
Flexibility Skills						
Statement	**Never**	**Rarely**	**Sometimes**	**Often**	**Always**	**Comments**
I recognize problems and make changes to address them.	1	2	3	4	5	
I am okay if there is an unexpected change.	1	2	3	4	5	
Switching tasks is easy for me.	1	2	3	4	5	

I can adjust to different teachers' styles.	1	2	3	4	5	
I don't mind if things go wrong or if I have to try a new solution.	1	2	3	4	5	
Working Memory Skills						
Statement	**Never**	**Rarely**	**Sometimes**	**Often**	**Always**	**Comments**
I pay close attention to avoid mistakes.	1	2	3	4	5	
I can remember multiple instructions from the teacher.	1	2	3	4	5	
Others say I have a good attention span.	1	2	3	4	5	
I finish chores/homework I start.	1	2	3	4	5	
I can keep track of lots of facts and share them with others.	1	2	3	4	5	
Emotional Control Skills						
Statement	**Never**	**Rarely**	**Sometimes**	**Often**	**Always**	**Comments**
When bad things happen, I bounce back quickly.	1	2	3	4	5	
I control my big emotions.	1	2	3	4	5	
I know how to handle frustration in a healthy way.	1	2	3	4	5	
Others say I am patient.	1	2	3	4	5	
I can handle frustration and work through difficult emotions.	1	2	3	4	5	
Impulse Control Skills						
Statement	**Never**	**Rarely**	**Sometimes**	**Often**	**Always**	**Comments**
I read and follow directions carefully.	1	2	3	4	5	
I think about decisions beforehand.	1	2	3	4	5	
I am okay with waiting for something or someone.	1	2	3	4	5	
I like to think before I speak.	1	2	3	4	5	

(*Continued*)

(*Continued*)

Others describe me as consistent and reliable.	1	2	3	4	5	
Sustaining Attention Skills						
Statement	**Never**	**Rarely**	**Sometimes**	**Often**	**Always**	**Comments**
I can complete tasks that have a lot of steps.	1	2	3	4	5	
I can complete tasks even when they are boring.	1	2	3	4	5	
I can focus on homework without getting distracted.	1	2	3	4	5	
If I get interrupted in the middle of something, I can easily go back to it.	1	2	3	4	5	
I can focus on my work even when people are talking near me.	1	2	3	4	5	
Self-Monitoring Skills						
Statement	**Never**	**Rarely**	**Sometimes**	**Often**	**Always**	**Comments**
I try to get better at things over time.	1	2	3	4	5	
I can read situations and adjust my behavior.	1	2	3	4	5	
I can see problems from others' points of view.	1	2	3	4	5	
I can evaluate my own progress toward a goal.	1	2	3	4	5	
I am open to feedback so I can do a better job next time.	1	2	3	4	5	

Is there anything else you would like us to know about you before our group begins?

Is there anything else you would like us to know about you now that the group is over?

Sessions 1–6

These sessions are designed to teach and reinforce skills. Make note of which sessions students respond well to and which they are less responsive to. Make additions or improvements to maximize student engagement and optimize desired outcomes. Ask students for specific feedback at the end of sessions.

Session 1: Planning

Objective:

1. Students will understand the importance of planning ahead to improve school performance.

Duration: 40 minutes

Instructions:

1. The counselor will introduce themselves and the topic of the group.
2. The counselor will ask students to help make a list of ground rules for the group and write them on a poster board. Students will sign them to indicate they will follow the ground rules.
3. Invite students to introduce themselves by sharing their favorite time of day or activity at school. Ask how they go about planning for things (school projects, parties, getting together with friends, etc.). Make a list on the board.
4. Discuss obstacles to planning. Make a list on the board.
5. Establish ground rules for the group and write them on chart paper. Ask students to give their input. Ask all students to sign the list of rules.
6. Encourage students to try out the strategy of creating a study plan for the upcoming week.

Weekly Study Plan

Time	Monday	Tuesday	Wednesday	Thursday	Friday
3:00–3:30					
3:30–4:00					
4:00–4:30					
4:30–5:00					
5:00–5:30					
5:30–6:00					
6:00–6:30					
6:30–7:00					
7:00–7:30					
7:30–8:00					
8:00–8:30					
8:30–9:00					
9:00–9:30					

Saturday	Sunday
Activities:	Activities:
Homework:	Homework:

Stay Organized – Create a Handy Homework Box

Creating a homework box encourages students to put everything they need to complete their assignments in a central location. This minimizes time spent searching for items (i.e., erasers, tape, etc.). Ask students to assemble the necessary items at home or school.

Materials (some can be brought in from home):

Shoe box or small plastic bin for each student

Scissors

Stapler/staples

Hole puncher

Markers

Colored pencils

Pens/pencils/erasers

Calculator

Ruler

Index cards/sticky notes

Kitchen timer

1. Ask students to assemble all items in the box. Label it "Homework Box." This box travels with them wherever they are going to do homework (bedroom, kitchen, library, etc.) so that they have whatever they need and do not get distracted looking for items.
2. Inform students that they will be reporting about how it went to use the weekly study planner and homework box in the next meeting.

Session 2: Time Management

Objective:

1. Students will learn about the benefits of using a weekly study planner to manage time.

Materials:

Progress monitoring sheet

Electronic or paper calendar

Duration: 40 minutes

Instructions:

1. Welcome students.
   a. Check in. Remind them of group ground rules.
   b. Check in with students about their use of the weekly study planner and homework box over the past week.
2. Discuss barriers and workarounds that came up while using the strategies. Introduce progress monitoring sheet.
   a. Using monthly paper calendars and electronic calendars with reminders.
   b. Share an example of an electronic calendar. Demonstrate how to set reminders.
   c. Explain benefits. Note: Not all students may have access to an electronic calendar or cell phone.
3. Create a monthly calendar (on paper).
   a. Encourage students to add key dates that are coming up (tests, long-term assignments), sporting events, community events, and so on.
4. Tracking time.
   a. Ask students to estimate the time it takes for them to write a letter to a friend describing what they did yesterday (from waking up to going to sleep) in paragraph form.
   b. Caution: Do not use this activity with students who struggle with writing; select a different activity.
   c. Collect student's predictions. Encourage them not to rush the letter and to do it well.
   d. Put the start time on the board.
   e. Give students time to complete the letter.
   f. If you are under time constraints for the group, stop all students after 10–15 minutes and ask students how far they got in their day (i.e., dinner time) and ask them to estimate how much time they think they will need to complete the letter.
   g. Debrief by discussing how students managed their time.

5. Working in "bursts."
    a. Acknowledge that most people have limited attention spans. Introduce the use of a timer to work in bursts.
    b. They can set the timer for 5 minutes to complete some part of another task (writing about what you plan to do tomorrow) and then take a break.
    c. Each time they use the timer, expand by 5 minutes.
    d. The goal is to work up to 20 minutes of sustained attention.
    e. Encourage students to schedule working periods or bursts followed by breaks.
    f. Discuss positive things to do during brief (5–10 minute) breaks (e.g., walk up and down the stairs, get fresh air, clean up an area of their room).
    g. Encourage students to set a timer for breaks as well. Over time, if this is a useful strategy for students, they will internalize this process.
    h. Add "working in bursts" to the progress monitoring sheet.

Progress Monitoring to Improve My Executive Functioning Skills

Circle one for each week. Add new strategies as they are introduced in the group.

Strategy	Week 2	Week 3	Week 4	Week 5	Week 6	Booster Session
Weekly study planner	Did not use Used sometimes Used daily	Did not use Used sometimes Used daily	Did not use Used sometimes Used daily	Did not use Used sometimes Used daily	Did not use Used sometimes Used daily	Did not use Used sometimes Used daily
Homework box	Did not use Used sometimes Used daily	Did not use Used sometimes Used daily	Did not use Used sometimes Used daily	Did not use Used sometimes Used daily	Did not use Used sometimes Used daily	Did not use Used sometimes Used daily
	Did not use Used sometimes Used daily	Did not use Used sometimes Used daily	Did not use Used sometimes Used daily	Did not use Used sometimes Used daily	Did not use Used sometimes Used daily	Did not use Used sometimes Used daily
	Did not use Used sometimes Used daily	Did not use Used sometimes Used daily	Did not use Used sometimes Used daily	Did not use Used sometimes Used daily	Did not use Used sometimes Used daily	Did not use Used sometimes Used daily
	Did not use Used sometimes Used daily	Did not use Used sometimes Used daily	Did not use Used sometimes Used daily	Did not use Used sometimes Used daily	Did not use Used sometimes Used daily	Did not use Used sometimes Used daily
	Did not use Used sometimes Used daily	Did not use Used sometimes Used daily	Did not use Used sometimes Used daily	Did not use Used sometimes Used daily	Did not use Used sometimes Used daily	Did not use Used sometimes Used daily

Monthly Calendar

Sunday	Monday	Tuesday	Wednesday	Thursday	Friday	Saturday

Add use of electronic calendar with reminders (if applicable) and monthly calendar to list of strategies on progress monitoring sheet.

Session 3: Limiting Distractions in Your Homework Space

Objectives:

1. Students will identify distractions that impair their efforts to complete homework.
2. Students will learn how to eliminate or reduce distractions.

Materials:

Blank paper

Pens/pencils/markers

Handout

Sticky notes

Duration: 45 minutes

Instructions:

1. Welcome students and check in. Remind them of group rules.
2. Introduce topic. Ask what is the most distracting thing when they are at home trying to do homework.

Activity 1: Picturing Your Workspace

3. Ask students to draw a picture of the place where they do their homework. Ask them to include as many details as possible (e.g., windows, televisions, computer game consoles, etc.).
4. When they are done, ask them to share their picture and explain why they choose to do their homework in this location (be sensitive; some students may not have any choice about where they do homework).
5. Ask them to include themselves in the drawing. Are they wearing headphones and listening to music? Is their phone next to them? Is anyone else in the room with them?
6. Next, invite students to circle things in their picture that are potential distractions. Share with the group. Together strategize ways to limit each distraction. For example, if a student does their homework in their room and their cell phone is a distraction, encourage the student to charge it in the kitchen while they are doing homework.
7. Add strategies to the progress monitoring sheet.

Activity 2: Organizing Materials

1. Now that you have a sense of where your students are completing homework most of the time, share this strategy for organizing hardcopies of materials.
2. Give each student three different colored sticky notes. Ask them to write "Get Ready" on one for materials they have to prepare to complete (e.g., worksheets, books, etc.). Place it on the upper left of their workspace. Write "Do" on one that is directly in front of them. This will become where they put their work in process. If they are interrupted,

they will be able to get back to the task more easily. On the final sticky note write "Done." All completed assignments go here. It might be helpful to create a homework folder to place in the done area. That way assignments will be returned to school and handed in.

3. Add organizing your workspace to the progress monitoring sheet.

Suggestion: Organize your workspace like this:

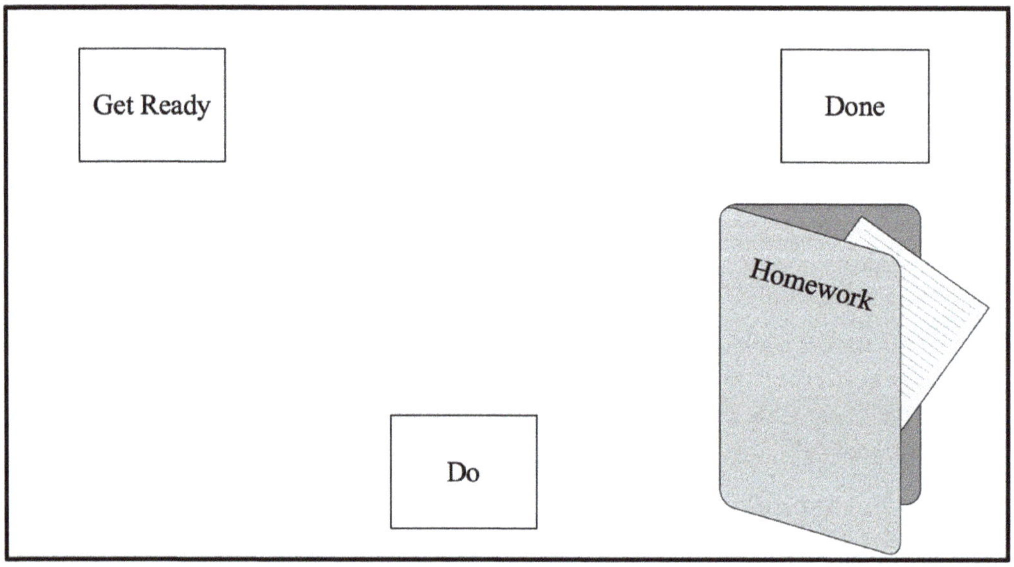

Image 13.8

Activity 3: Packing Your Backpack Before Bed

1. Encourage students to put all completed materials and supplies needed for the next day of school prior to going to bed. The backpack should be placed in a convenient location by the door. Note: Make sure to email parents and caregivers about the strategies you are introducing so that they can reinforce them at home.
2. Update the progress monitoring sheet before closing.

Session 4: Working Memory

Objective:

1. Students will understand the importance of improving working memory.

Materials:

Tray filled with 10–15 everyday items (e.g., pencil, marker, eraser, playing card, etc.)

Towel to cover items

Pen and paper for each participant

Duration: 30 minutes

Instructions:

1. Welcome students and ask them to check in by sharing what they had for breakfast 2 days ago.
2. Introduce topic: working memory. Make the connection between increasing one's working memory and improving executive functioning.
3. Tell them you are going to play a memory game.
4. Bring out tray with items covered with a towel. Give them each paper and pencil and explain that the are first going to look at all of the items on the tray without talking. They will have 2 minutes to look at the tray.
5. Then give them 5–6 minutes to list as many items as possible, keeping their eyes on their own paper.
6. Show items and have students identify items that they forgot.
7. Next give each student a paper plate full of six to 10 items. Give them a few minutes to arrange the items in a way that makes sense for them. They can talk out loud during this activity. They can section off the plate to categorize their items using a pencil and labeling each section if they wish.
8. Cover their individual plates. Then ask them to repeat the activity with their own items.
9. Discuss what was similar and what was different.
10. Update the progress monitoring sheet before closing.

Session 5: Sustained Attention

Objective:

1. Students will understand the importance of sustaining their attention to complete homework and class work.

Materials:

Distractions worksheet

Duration: 30 minutes

Instructions:

1. Welcome students back. Check in on how things have gone for the past week. Remind them of group ground rules.
2. Remind students that in session 3 we discussed limiting distractions in their workspace. Check in with them about how their strategies are working by reviewing their progress monitoring sheets.
3. Discuss the fact that they have been limiting external distractions by doing things like charging their cell phone in another room while they are doing homework. Explain what an internal distraction might consist of (e.g., daydreaming, thinking about an upcoming event, etc.).
4. Have students complete the worksheet.

Managing My Key Distractions

Name: ______________________ Date: ____________

External Distractions	My Plans for Limiting External Distractions

Internal Distractions	My Plans for Limiting Internal Distractions

Session 6: Summing Up Our Learning

Objectives:

1. Students will synthesize their learning about executive functioning.
2. Students will articulate ways they have improved during the group.
3. Students will set goals to continue developing their executive functioning skills.

Materials:

Completed progress monitoring sheets

Pens/pencils/markers

Duration: 30 minutes

Instructions:

1. Welcome students. Remind them this is the final group. Ask them to check in by sharing what their favorite group activity has been or a strategy we learned that they are using regularly.
2. Review completed progress monitoring sheets. All strategies should be listed on the sheet.
3. Ask students to circle strategies they used consistently and plan to continue to utilize to improve their school performance.
4. Ask students what they have noticed about their grades and overall effort in school since they started the group.
5. Celebrate the gains that students have made.
6. Let them know you will convene a booster session in 1 month's time to check in to see how they are doing
7. Administer posttest.

Post-Intervention Communication to Parent/Guardian

English Version

Dear Parents/Caregivers,

Congratulations! Your child has successfully completed a 6-week Tier 2 group focused on improving executive functioning skills, including time management, organization, and minimizing distractions. Please make time to review their progress monitoring sheet and their plans for maintaining these strategies. We will be meeting in 1 month's time on ________________ for a booster session to check in and see how well they are utilizing these skills. In the meantime, please make sure to reach out to me if you have any questions or concerns. I will be in touch with your child's teachers to see how well they are utilizing their executive functioning strategies.

Thank you for the opportunity to get to know your child better by encouraging their participation in this small group.

Sincerely,

Student Support Team Members

Spanish Version

Estimados Padres/Cuidadores,

¡Felicidades! Su hijo ha completado con éxito un grupo de Nivel 2 de 6 semanas centrado en mejorar las habilidades del funcionamiento ejecutivo, incluida la gestión del tiempo, la organización y la minimización de distracciones. Tómese el tiempo para revisar su hoja de seguimiento del progreso y sus planes futuros para mantener estas estrategias. Nos reuniremos dentro de un mes el ________________ para una sesión de refuerzo para verificar y ver qué tan bien están utilizando estas habilidades. Mientras tanto, asegúrese de comunicarse conmigo si tiene alguna pregunta o inquietud. Me pondré en contacto con los maestros de su hijo para ver qué tan bien están utilizando sus estrategias de funcionamiento ejecutivo.

Gracias por la oportunidad de conocer mejor a su hijo fomentando su participación en este grupo pequeño.

Atentamente,

Miembros del equipo de apoyo estudiantil

Plan for Implementation Fidelity

All materials for this Tier 2 kit will be available each time a new session is initiated. Pre- and posttest scores and copies of progress monitoring sheets will be reviewed by the intervention team to see if adjustments need to be made to the intervention.

Small Group Process Notes

Time Management and Organizational Skills for High School Students

Ashley Moutinho and Stephanie Williams

Description of Skill

Two of the most essential skills for high school students are the ability to effectively manage their time and get organized. **Time management** is the process of organizing and planning how to divide one's time between different activities. If high school students can get it right, they can work smarter, not harder, and get more done in less time—even when time is tight and pressures are high. We know that the highest achieving high schoolers manage their time exceptionally well. **Organizational skills** make it possible for the student to use both their time and resources efficiently and effectively. Well-organized students are able to manage their time, energy, and physical workspace(s) so they can accomplish tasks successfully. Today's high school students experience significant challenges when managing their time and getting organized to learn. The increase in availability of smartphones, proliferation of social media use, and the significant mental health challenges are just a few of the barriers today's teens must navigate to be successful at school. This Tier 2 kit helps them to improve their time management and organizational skills to maximize their learning in high school

Pre-Intervention Communication With Parents/Guardians/Teachers in Languages Represented in the School

English Version

Dear Parents/Guardians,

Your [ninth, 10th, 11th or 12th] grader has been selected to take part in a small group focused on improving their time management and organizational skills. This 6-week group will take place [indicate when] and will not interfere with their academic classes. The goal of this group is to discover new ways to manage their school assignments and materials to maximize their learning. This small group opportunity will involve reflection, sharing experiences, goal setting, and experimenting with new strategies. Each student will complete a pretest prior to the group and a posttest as we finish up.

Our goals are to do the following:

- Manage time effectively (i.e., meet assignment deadlines).
- Identify places and times of day they work best.
- Identify activities that they engage it that are "time wasters."
- Learn how to break down a long-term assignment into smaller sections with separate deadlines.
- Learn how to prioritize tasks.
- Explore using a paper or electronic calendar.

- Organize learning tools (binders, notebooks, tablets).
- Organize backpacks.
- Organize locker and study space.
- Discover strategies for coming to class well prepared.

If you have any questions about this intervention group or would like to discuss your student's participation in the group, please do not hesitate to reach out to me.

Sincerely,

Student Support Team Interventionist

Spanish Version

Queridos padres/guardianes,

Su alumno de [9.º, 10.º, 11.º o 12.º] ha sido seleccionado para participar en un grupo pequeño centrado en mejorar su gestión del tiempo y sus habilidades organizativas. Este grupo de 6 semanas se llevará a cabo [indicar cuándo] y no interferirá con sus clases académicas. El objetivo de este grupo es descubrir nuevas formas de gestionar sus tareas y materiales escolares para maximizar su aprendizaje. Esta oportunidad de grupo pequeño implicará reflexión, compartir experiencias, establecer objetivos y experimentar con nuevas estrategias. Cada estudiante completará una prueba previa al grupo y una prueba posterior cuando terminemos.

Nuestros objetivos son:

- Administrar el tiempo de manera efectiva (es decir, cumplir con los plazos de las tareas)
- Identifique los lugares y horas del día en los que funcionan mejor.
- Identificar las actividades en las que participan y que son una "pérdida de tiempo"
- Aprenda cómo dividir una tarea a largo plazo en secciones más pequeñas con fechas límite separadas
- Aprenda a priorizar las tareas
- Explora usando un calendario en papel o electrónico
- Organizar herramientas de aprendizaje (carpetas, cuadernos, tabletas)
- Organizar la mochila
- Organizar el casillero y el espacio de estudio.
- Descubre estrategias para venir a clase bien preparado

Si tiene alguna pregunta sobre este grupo de intervención o desea hablar sobre la participación de su estudiante en el grupo, no dude en comunicarse conmigo.

Atentamente,

Intervencionista del equipo de apoyo al estudiante

Permission Slip

After reading the description of this Tier 2 small group, I, ______________, give permission for my student ______________ to take part in the group which will meet on ______________ from [date] to [date]. I understand that this group is confidential and that I will be made aware if my student is making good use of this group experience. Should I need to be contacted, the best number to reach me at is ______________.

Hoja de permiso

Después de leer la descripción de este grupo pequeño de Nivel 2, yo, ______________, doy permiso para que mi estudiante ______________ participe en el grupo que se reunirá el ______________ de [fecha] a [fecha]. Entiendo que este grupo es confidencial y que se me informará si mi estudiante está haciendo un buen uso de esta experiencia grupal. Si necesito que me contacten, el mejor número para comunicarse conmigo es ______________.

Goals of Intervention

- Manage time effectively (i.e., meet assignment deadlines).
- Identify places and times of day they work best.
- Identify activities that they engage it that are "time wasters."
- Learn how to break down a long-term assignment into smaller sections with separate deadlines.
- Learn how to prioritize tasks.
- Explore using a paper or electronic calendar.
- Organize learning tools (binders, notebooks, tablets).
- Organize backpacks.
- Organize locker and study space.
- Discover strategies for coming to class well prepared.

CASEL Standards Addressed

- Motivating oneself to set and achieve goals
- Behaving responsibly in personal, professional, and community contexts
- Making constructive and respectful choices that consider the well-being of self and others

ASCA Mind-Sets and Behaviors

M 3. Positive attitude toward work and learning

M 4. Self-confidence in ability to succeed

M 5. Belief in using abilities to their fullest to achieve high-quality results and outcomes

B-LS 3. Time-management, organizational and study skills

B-LS 4. Self-motivation and self- direction for learning

B-LS 7. Long- and short-term academic, career, and social/emotional goals

B-LS 8. Engagement in challenging coursework

B-SMS 3. Independent work

B-SMS 4. Delayed gratification for long-term rewards

B-SMS 5. Perseverance to achieve long and short-term goals

B-SMS 7. Effective coping skill

Pre-/Post-Assessment

Name: ______________________________ Date: ______________

Please read the following questions and circle Yes or No.

1. I notice that my time management and organization negatively impact my grades.

   Yes / No

2. I think I have the tools to manage my time wisely.

   Yes / No

3. When I am studying, I can find my notes in my locker easily.

   Yes / No

4. When I am starting my homework, I can find it in my binder easily.

   Yes / No

5. I understand the role that time management and organization will play in my academic life now and in the future.

   Yes / No

Sessions 1–6

Session 1: How Do I Work Best?

Objective:

1. Students will explore different situations and figure out in which they produce their best work.

Materials:

Time management quiz

Scenario strips

Duration: 30 minutes

Instructions:

1. Welcome students and explain the purpose of the group.
2. Invite group members to provide input on group ground rules. Record them on poster paper and ask students to sign the poster paper.
3. Students will take a time management quiz to bring awareness to how well they manage their time.

Activity 1:

1. Pass out time management quiz and give students a few minutes to complete. You should go around and share answers (raise hands or have volunteers). The key idea is that there is a "good" time to get work done and that time should be found and happen every day! The students have full control over this.

Activity 2:

1. Pass out scenario cards. Each student should have at least one. Each student should read it to themselves and answer the questions: Do you think this is the best situation for quality work? What could be done differently? Each student should go around and share the scenario and answers. Discussion should be around identifying the best environments to work in and how to achieve this.

Activity 3:

1. Pass out "When I Do My Best Work . . ." worksheet. Have students take a few moments to brainstorm how they best work. Cluttered desk? Sitting on their bed? With a video game playing in the background? Students should hand in the card at the end of the group. Ask students to think about this in the week between meetings: Are they in the best environment to get their work done?

Name: ________________

1.	On weekdays, do you do your homework at about the same time?	Yes	No
2.	Do you start studying before 8:00 p.m. each night?	Yes	No
3.	Do you study each night during the week?	Yes	No
4.	How many hours do you spend studying during the week?	____________	
5.	Do you go to bed about the same time each night?	Yes	No
6.	How much sleep do you usually get each night?	____________	
7.	How much time per week do you spend watching TV and movies or playing videogames or working?	____________	

How I Work Best Scenarios

Johnny's older brother has two friends over playing video games and listening to music in the living room. Johnny takes his homework to the living room so he can be a part of his brother's crew.

Sammy has a 10-page paper due on Thursday. Tuesday she has still not started it. She decides to start it Wednesday night because she works better under pressure. She starts at 8:30 p.m. after being up since 7:00 a.m.

Joe sits on his bed when he is reading his textbook. He usually has his TV on his favorite show. He likes to have his music playing too.

Tina does her homework at the dining room table when she gets home from school. She makes sure she has a snack and a clean workspace. She leaves her cell phone in her room.

Bobby waits until 8:00 p.m. to open his backpack. He likes to play videogames right when he gets home from school. Tonight, he forgot he had to take a shower, so he does that before starting his homework.

Lisa does her homework at her desk in her room. She has papers and books all over it. She keeps her cell phone right next to her so she can check her Snapchat. She usually does one page of homework and then takes a break.

How Do I Work Best?

Write down some thoughts you had after going over the scenario cards together. How do you usually work? Do you think that is the best idea? Why? If not, what may be a better idea?

____

____

____

____

____

____

"The Golden Study Rules"

Rule 1

Set a regular time to study each weekday and on the weekend and stick to it. Don't make it late at night or you'll be too tired to work well.

Rule 2

Study every night even if you don't have assigned homework. You can read books or magazines, review and practice subjects in which your skills are weak, or study ahead.

Rule 3

Get enough sleep. Students your age should sleep 8–10 hours each night.

Rule 4

Cut down on the number of hours you watch TV and movies or play videogames. Ten hours a week should be the most time you spend on these.

Source: by Louisiana Teachers As Educational Advisors and Mentors, http://home.insightbb.com/~D-VW-G306/mts/9th/Handouts/Lesson_03_Handout_1.pdf

Session 2: Scheduling and Time Management

Objectives:

1. Students will learn to map out their day and find structured time to get work done.
2. Students will identify "time wasters."

Materials:

"Tracking Time" worksheet

"How to Study: Manage Your Time" worksheet

"Top Time Wasters" worksheet

Duration: 30 minutes

Instructions:

1. Welcome students. Remind them of ground rules. Ask them to introduce themselves by indicating what is their most common form of procrastination.

Activity 1: Tracking Time

2. Students will be handed out a Tracking Time worksheet. They will be asked to try and track how they have used the past 24 hours starting with yesterday afternoon. Students will tally up their time spent on certain events (sleeping, studying, on the phone, with friends, with family, in class, working, other). Students will be asked to answer the questions at the bottom regarding what they feel they did not accomplish and how they feel about it.
3. Students will come up with a list of the top time wasters and discuss how to get around them in their daily activities. Schedule time to put down your phone! (see https://self-controlapp.com).

Activity 2: Daily Schedule (precursor to looking at school agenda)

1. Students will be asked to fill out a weekly assignment chart for the upcoming week. Students will fill out academic assignments/homework as well as "to do/errands."
2. Assessment/evaluation:
3. Students will hand in their daily schedule assignment chart at the end of the week and reflect on how it helped them accomplish their goals.
4. *Adapted from Upper Iowa University Time Tracker Resources https://uiu.edu/wp-content/uploads/Time-Management-Worksheet.pdf*

Tracking Time

Use the chart to track how you've spent the past 24 hours or so. Start with yesterday afternoon.

1:00 p.m.		1:00 a.m.	
2:00 p.m.		2:00 a.m.	
3:00 p.m.		3:00 a.m.	
4:00 p.m.		4:00 a.m.	
5:00 p.m.		5:00 a.m.	
6:00 p.m.		6:00 a.m.	
7:00 p.m.		7:00 a.m.	
8:00 p.m.		8:00 a.m.	
9:00 p.m.		9:00 a.m.	
10:00 p.m.		10:00 a.m.	
11:00 p.m.		11:00 a.m.	
Midnight		Noon	

Tally: Calculate the time you spent doing the following activities:

Sleeping ______________ Studying ______________ In class ______________

On the phone ______________ With friends ______________ With family ______________

Working ______________ Other ______________

Is there anything you needed to accomplish yesterday that you didn't quite get around to doing? How did it make you feel?

How can you change your schedule for the next 24 hours in order to accomplish what you need to get done?

Daily Schedule

Daily Schedule Assignments Due	Date: Schedule
	5:00 a.m.
	6:00 a.m.
	7:00 a.m.
	8:00 a.m.
	9:00 a.m.
To Do/Errands:	10:00 a.m.
	11:00 a.m.
	12:00 p.m.
	1:00 p.m.
	2:00 p.m.
	3:00 p.m.
	4:00 p.m.
	5:00 p.m.
Homework:	6:00 p.m.
	7:00 p.m.
	8:00 p.m.
	9:00 p.m.
	10:00 p.m.
	11:00 p.m.
	12:00 a.m.

**Reflecting on this activity the following group meeting may be beneficial for progress monitoring points (e.g., How many assignments did I miss? What was late?)

Session 3: Tackling Long-Term Assignments

Objective:

1. Students will use what they have learned about time management to find structured time to work on long-term assignments.

Materials:

"The Four Quadrants of Prioritizing" worksheet

Blank calendar

"Procrastination Manager" worksheet

Duration: 30 minutes

Instructions:

1. Welcome students. Check in on their week.

Activity 1:

1. Pass out The Four Quadrants of Prioritizing worksheet. Each quadrant should be explained. The students should brainstorm things that would make them fall under each category. For example, "The Procrastinator" quadrant could have exam tomorrow, 10-page paper due tomorrow. Students should take a guess at which quadrant they fall in and where they would like to be.

Activity 2:

1. Pass out blank calendar. Students should bring up any long-term assignments they have and mark the due date on the calendar. Referring to the quadrants, the instructor should ask, "When would the procrastinator start this project? The prioritizer? The yes man? The slacker?" The students should think about setting smaller due date for themselves. The first step is to break down the project into different parts. Because this may be specific to each different student, the general template should be handed out too. Students should work for a few minutes on this. They should mark these new due dates on their calendar (keeping in mind when they work best!).

Activity 3:

1. Pass out the Procrastination Management worksheet. Each student should practice going over it. The instructor can make this more fun by adding silly distractors. For example, "Are you working on it?" No! "What are you doing instead?" Playing videogames, duh! "How are you justifying not getting to work?" I have my highest score in Call of Duty and can't lose it." The reality of using this chart is that it can be a very helpful reminder to get "the slacker" back onto "the prioritizer" path to success!

The Four Quadrants of Prioritizing

	URGENT	NOT URGENT
IMPORTANT	The Procrastinator	The Prioritizer
NOT IMPORTANT	The Yes man	The Slacker

Image 13.9

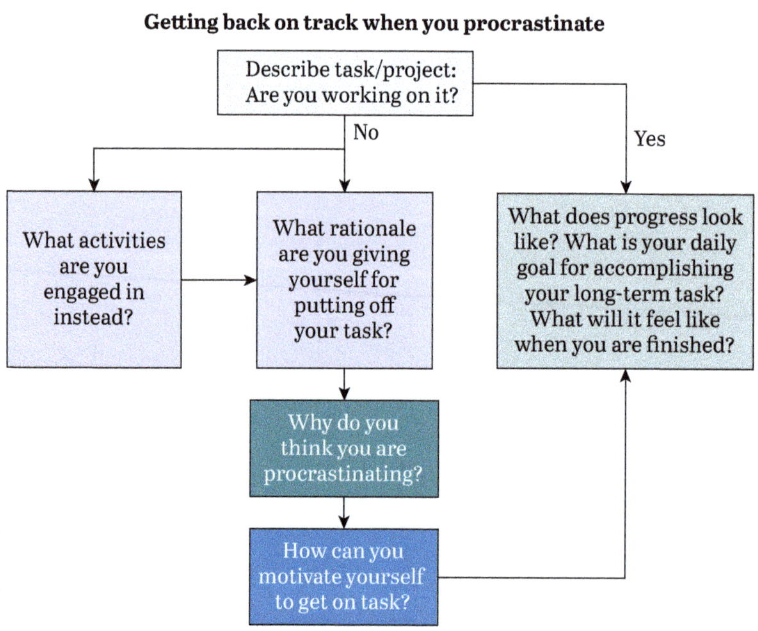

Image 13.10

Session 4: Organizing Your Assignments

Objective:

1. Students will learn how to organize binders, notebooks, and folders to keep assignments neat.

Materials:

"Organizing Your Assignments" worksheet

Example of an organized binder

Example of notebook and folder

Binders

Tabbed dividers

Notebooks

Folders

Duration: 20 minutes

Instructions:

1. Welcome students. Check in.
2. Introduce topic: organizing school materials.
3. Content: "To make sure that you are prepared for each class, you will need to make sure you have your notes and assignments organized. We have come up with a few organization tips to help you keep everything neat and organized. This will help you, your parents, and your teachers know where everything is. First up is your binders and notebooks."
4. The counselor will pass out the Organizing Your Assignments worksheet to each student.
5. The counselor will go over each step and use the example binder to model what an organized binder should look like.
6. Students will use either their own binders or be provided a binder, notebook, and folder to use for one subject. They will follow along and set up each as modeled by the counselor.

Organizing Your Assignments

Image 13.11

Binders are a very important part of staying organized. They may seem bulky, but they will allow you to keep everything for your specific classes in one location.

1. Keep one 1" binder for each subject you have.
2. Divide each binder into sections using dividers; Examples: Make one divider for class-work, one for completed homework, and one for completed tests. You can add more depending on the subject.
3. Have a different colored binder for each subject and make sure they have plastic pockets on the front cover. You can slide a piece of paper with the class name and your name on it. This will allow you to easily distinguish between subjects. Also, insert the subject on the binding so that you can see it from the side.

Folders and **notebooks** are also important when trying to stay organized. They allow you to keep your homework, classwork, and tests neat.

1. You should have one notebook and one folder for each subject that is the same color as each of your binders (e.g., green binder, notebook, and folder for biology).
2. Always title and write the date at the top of the page when you take notes in class. This will help you to separate different days and make it easier for you to study.
3. Use both sides of your folder. Use one side to hold assignments or things that need to go home. Use the other side to hold completed assignments that you still need to hand it. Once you get them back, use a hole punch and insert them in your binder.

Session 5: Organizing Your Backpack

Objective:

1. Students will learn how to organize backpacks to keep assignments, books, and personal items safe.

Materials:

"Organizing Your Backpack" worksheet

Waste basket

Pencil cases

Duration: 20 minutes

Instructions:

1. Welcome students. Remind them that next week is the final group meeting.
2. Introduce topic: organizing your materials in a backpack.
3. Content: "Once you have your notes and binders organized, you are going to need to organize your backpack. This will allow you to transport your books and assignments to and from school easily and help to make sure you have everything you need. I am going to go step by step with you on how to organize the backpack you already have."
4. Have the students grab their backpacks and put them on the desk or table. If possible, keep some distance between students so that their things to do get mixed together.
5. Pass out the Organizing Your Backpack worksheet to each student. The counselor will go through the steps listed on the handout, being sure to give time between steps for students to follow.
6. Before reading step 3, pass out pencil cases to each student.
7. Oversee as the students repack their backpacks.
8. Clarify that each student is welcome to check back in every Monday morning to show the progress of their organization.

Organizing Your Backpack

Image 13.12

Backpacks allow you to transport your books and assignments to and from school easily and help to make sure you have everything you need. Keeping it organized will be a big help in keep you prepared.

1. Empty out your backpack. This means flip it over and dump everything out of it. Make sure that you keep it all together in front of you. Don't let anything roll away. Examine your backpack to make sure nothing is left—no scraps of paper, no pencils. Even your keys and cell phones need to be out. Conduct a close inspection to make sure you got everything out.
2. Organize the huge pile of objects found in your backpack. Put all of your textbooks, papers, binders, and folders into separate piles—one for each subject. Anything extra—pens, calculators, cell phones—should be put in a separate "other" pile. Do not throw anything out yet.
3. Put away all of your writing utensils. You are each getting a pencil case. All of your writing utensils (pencils, pens, highlighters, etc.) should all go in the case. Put this in a smaller pocket so that they are easy to get to.
4. Textbooks go in first. Place them in the part of your backpack that will hit your back. The largest one should be against your back; it will give you more room and it will be more comfortable for you.
5. Binders and notebooks go in next. Take each pile and place it in your backpack. Organize them in the order you have them. For example, your last class of the day should be against your textbooks. This will help you to easily grab what you need when it is time to do your homework.

Session 6: Organizing Your Locker

Objective:

1. Students will learn how to organize lockers to keep assignments, books, and personal items safe.

Materials:

"Organizing Your Locker" worksheet

Magnets

White sheets of paper

Clear plastic sleeves

Hooks

Dry-erase markers

Duration: 20 minutes

Instructions:

1. Welcome students. Remind them this is the final group. Ask them to check in by sharing a strategy we have learned that has been helpful to them.
2. Introduce today's topic: organizing your locker.
3. Content: The last place we are going to organize is your locker. Lockers can easily become messy and cluttered. You only have a few minutes to get from class to class, and oftentimes you may just throw your books and notebooks into your locker. This also means that it may be more likely that you forget something. Keeping your locker organized will make it easier to swap out your books between classes.
4. Pass out the Organizing Your Locker worksheet and go through each step with students.
5. Show examples of magnets and hooks that can be used to organize student lockers.
6. Pass out a single sheet of paper and a clear plastic sleeve to each student, along with a dry-erase marker.
7. The students will create their own dry-erase boards for their lockers.

Organizing Your Locker

Image 13.13

Lockers can easily become messy and cluttered. You only have a few minutes to get from class to class, and oftentimes you may just throw your books and notebooks into your locker. This also means that it may be more likely that you forget something. Keeping your locker organized will make it easier to swap out your books between classes.

1. Use the shelf at the top of your locker to organize your supplies. Keep your binders and notebooks at the top of your locker. Keep them upright and you can easily swap them out between classes. Use the bottom of your locker for your textbooks, since the weight of your books may weaken or break the shelf.
2. Use magnets to hang notes and reminders on your locker door. Keep a little magnetic note pad or Post-It notes in your locker. This way you can write little reminders about tests and assignments. Since you go to your locker pretty often throughout the day, this will help you to remember important things.
3. Keep a whiteboard on your locker door. Jot down quick notes or reminders to yourself on a whiteboard if it is easier for you. If you don't have one, you can make one pretty easily. Just get a white piece of paper and a clear plastic sleeve. If you write on the sleeve with a dry erase marker; you will be able to erase it easily.
4. Keep backup supplies in your locker. Keep a small container of backup pens, pencils, erasers, and highlighters in your locker. This way, if you lose or drop one in the hallway, you'll have extras in your locker. Just be sure to replace them if you notice your supply is getting low.
5. If your locker doesn't already have one, attach a hook or two on the inside to give you a place to hang your coat, lunchbox, or backpack so that it is not on the floor or covering your books.

Student Time Management and Organization: Teacher Survey

1. The student comes to class on time.

   Always Usually Occasionally Never

2. The student comes to class prepared.

   Always Usually Occasionally Never

3. The student hands assignments in on time.

   Always Usually Occasionally Never

4. The assignments handed in were not ripped or stained.

   Always Usually Occasionally Never

5. The student asks to retrieve something from locker.

   Always Usually Occasionally Never

Progress Monitoring

Name: ______________________________ Week of: ______________

0 = Disorganized 1 = Semi-organized 2 = Organized		Monday	Tuesday	Wednesday	Thursday	Friday
Morning	Backpack					
	Locker					
Afternoon	Planner					
	Binder and Notebook					

Additional data points to consider for progress monitoring:

- assignment tracking forms from activities (e.g., how many assignments missed)
- homework completion percentage/grades per teacher report
- tracking of trips to locker (increase/decrease) per class

Post-Intervention Communication to Parent/Guardian

English Version

Dear Parents/Guardians,

Your student, ______________, took part in a 6-week small group focused on improving academic success. They were invited into the group because they were struggling in one or more classes. I am pleased to share that your student was an active participant in this small group and has several new strategies for managing their time, keeping track of their materials, and managing their stress related to their academic day. Please take some time to speak with your student about the things we discussed in the group. Not all students will utilize all of the strategies we covered, but, hopefully, they will utilize those that seemed most helpful to them. We reminded the students that any new habit takes roughly 6 weeks to become a regular part of their routine. We will continue to check in with your student to see how they are doing academically and in regard to integrating these strategies into their school week.

If you have any questions or would like to discuss your student's progress, please do not hesitate to contact us.

Sincerely,

Student Support Team Member(s)

Spanish Version

Queridos padres/guardianes,

Sus estudiantes ______________ participaron en un grupo pequeño de 6 semanas enfocado en mejorar el éxito académico. Fueron invitados al grupo porque tenían dificultades en una o más clases. Me complace compartir que su estudiante participó activamente en este grupo pequeño y tiene varias estrategias nuevas para administrar su tiempo, realizar un seguimiento de sus materiales y controlar el estrés relacionado con su día académico. Tómese un tiempo para hablar con su estudiante sobre las cosas que discutimos en el grupo. No todos los estudiantes utilizarán todas las estrategias que cubrimos pero, con suerte, utilizarán aquellas que les parecieron más útiles. Recordamos a los estudiantes que cualquier hábito nuevo tarda aproximadamente 6 semanas en convertirse en una parte habitual de su rutina. Continuaremos comunicándonos con su estudiante para ver cómo le está yendo académicamente y con respecto a la integración de estas estrategias en su semana escolar.

Si tiene alguna pregunta o desea hablar sobre el progreso de su estudiante, no dude en contactarnos.

Atentamente,

Miembro(s) del equipo de apoyo estudiantil

Plan for Implementation Fidelity

To achieve the intended outcomes of this intervention, it is helpful to colead the small group with a colleague, reflect on student responses to the activities, and seek support to keep engagement in the group high. Tier 2 small group facilitators should seek peer coaching and ask for feedback to make sure the intervention is implemented with fidelity.

Small Group Process Notes

Credits

Index

N

O

P

R

S

About the Author

Dr. Peg Donohue is an Associate Professor and School Counseling Program Coordinator at Central Connecticut State University in the Department of Counselor Education and Family Therapy. Prior to becoming a counselor educator, Dr. Donohue spent 16 years working as a teacher and school counselor in both Connecticut and California. She is a graduate of Georgetown University (BA), the Harvard Graduate School of Education (EdM), San Francisco State University (School Counseling Credential), and the University of Connecticut (PhD). She derives her most significant professional satisfaction from supporting her students as they grow personally and professionally as they pursue their degree in school counseling. She helped found the CCSU Center for Excellence in Social and Emotional Learning. Dr. Donohue's primary research interests include aligning school counselor programs and preparation with multiple tiered systems of support (MTSS), fostering social and emotional learning, school counselor ratio, operationalizing culturally affirming Tier 2 interventions, and universal screening for mental health concerns in schools. She is a co-author of *The School Counselor's Guide to MTSS* (Routledge, 2023) and *Making MTSS Work* (ASCA, 2020). She has published in *Professional School Counseling*, *The Professional Counselor*, and *The Journal of School Counseling*. She has presented at state, regional, and national conferences and has co-founded a consulting collaborative *School Counselors for MTSS*. In her free time, Dr. Donohue enjoys spending time with her family and friends on the Connecticut shore, playing pickleball, and skiing and hiking in Vermont.

About the Contributors

Jenna Angello graduated from the school counseling program at Central Connecticut State University in 2016. She currently works as a licensed professional counselor (LPC) at West Hartford Holistic Counseling in West Hartford. She enjoys working individually with her counseling clients. In her free time, she enjoys any outside activity in the summer, especially being on the water.

Stephanie Barbagallo graduated from the school counseling program at Central Connecticut State University in 2021. She is currently a school counselor at Plainville High School in Plainville. She likes to run groups focused on informing students about college scholarships. In her free time she enjoys reading and taking walks.

Kara Clement graduated from the school counseling program at Western Connecticut State University in 2023. She is currently a teacher at Westside Middle School in Danbury. She enjoys running decision-making groups.

Erica Mastronardi Cumpstone graduated from Central Connecticut State University in 2016. She is currently an independent educational consultant.

Isabella Donohue graduated from the University of Vermont in 2023 with a degree in Community and International Development and Applied Economics with a minor in Spanish. She assisted with Spanish translations in this book. She's currently a Case Worker for the Champlain Valley Office of Economic Opportunity where she assists individuals to locate affordable housing and other essential services. In her free time she likes to listen to live music, appreciate the outdoors with friends and family, and travel.

Curtis Darragh, IV graduated from the University of Connecticut in 2015. He is currently a school counselor serving Danbury Public Schools. He was the 2021 Connecticut School Counselor of the Year. He enjoys using CICO as a Tier 2 intervention. In his free time he enjoys traveling the world as a guide for student trips and long summer beach days along the Atlantic.

Nicole Ferreria is a former school counseling student at Central Connecticut State University. She now works as a regulatory state filings specialist. In her free time, she enjoys hiking and snowboarding.

Gaby Granitto graduated from the school counseling program at Central Connecticut State University in 2023. She currently works as a school counselor at Booth Free in Roxbury and Burnham Elementary School in Bridgewater. She enjoys running girls' groups for her fourth graders. In her free time, she enjoys making improvements on her new home and planning vacations.

Lucia Greene graduated from Central Connecticut State University in 2022. She currently works at Roberto Clemente International Dual Language School in Waterbury. She enjoys running her Peacekeepers Group, a conflict-resolution group in which students build and maintain their school garden. In her free time, she loves to participate in community theater performance and practices yoga.

Karyn L. Hester graduated from the School Psychology Program at Southern Connecticut State University in 2018. She is currently a school psychologist at Old Saybrook High School in Connecticut. She enjoys running dialectical behavior therapy groups for students with emotional disabilities. When she isn't at the high school, she enjoys gardening in her backyard and taking yoga classes.

Katherine Molinari graduated from Central Connecticut State University in 2024. She is currently working as a school counseling intern. She enjoys running small groups to teach students how to use mindfulness. In her free time, she enjoys reading and hiking.

Ashley Moutinho graduated from Central Connecticut State University in 2018. She is currently a school counselor at Kennedy High School in Waterbury. She enjoys running small groups to address organization and time management. In her free time, she enjoys reading and practicing yoga.

Karina Nguyen graduated from Central Connecticut State University in 2021. She is currently a school counselor at Washington Elementary School in Waterbury. She loves running social skills groups to support her students. In her free time, she enjoys being a new mom and spending time with her family.

Jaclyn Pierce graduated from Central Connecticut State University in 2023. She is currently an elementary school counselor at Elmwood Park Memorial High School in New Jersey. She enjoys running groups to foster self-management skills development, which includes organizational skills, task lists, and time management tracking, and develop self-regulation. Her Take a Break groups aims to mitigate disruptive behaviors occurring in class. In her free time, she enjoys going for walks and spending time with her dogs.

Vareesha Rahman graduated from Central Connecticut State University in 2021. She is currently a school counselor at Driggs Elementary School in Waterbury. She likes running social skills groups for her students. In her free time, she enjoys baking and pursing her interest in photography and film.

Vanessa Rodriguez is a 2020 graduate from the CCSU School Counseling Program. She now serves a dual role as a High School Counselor/Student Support Center Staff at Manchester High School in Manchester, CT. She enjoys running her New Student Mentor Group at the high school for students transitioning from one high school to another and a Girls Group focused on building skills in healthy relationships, healthy images, conflict resolution skills, effective communication, and empowerment. In her free time, she enjoys spending quality time with her daughter, usually going out for lunch or dinner, bowling, and axe throwing.

Emma Bee Schwarz graduated from Central Connecticut State University in 2023. She is currently an elementary school counselor at Washington Primary School and Shepaug Valley

School in northwestern Connecticut. She enjoys running girls' friendship groups. In her free time she enjoys hiking and drawing.

Kayla Snyder graduated from Central Connecticut State University in 2024. She is currently working as a school counseling intern at Prudence Crandall Elementary School in Enfield. She enjoys running small groups to address stress management. In her free time, she enjoys playing tennis and spending time with loved ones.

Breanna Soto graduated from Central Connecticut State University in 2023. She is currently a freshman academy school counselor for Hartford Public Schools. She enjoys engaging her ninth graders in small groups. In her free time, she enjoys reading and walking her dog.

Jennifer Estrella Vanterpool graduated from the school counseling program at Central Connecticut State University in 2020. She currently works as a school counselor at F.J. Kingsbury Elementary School in Waterbury. She enjoys helping her students develop their social skills through lunch bunches. As a mom of two, her favorite hobbies are napping and just relaxing on the couch in her free time.

Stephanie Williams graduated from Central Connecticut State University in 2018. She is currently a school counselor at Nashoba Regional School District and a doctoral student. She enjoys running groups for students with anxiety using TRAILs and for students who need support improving their executive functioning skills. In her free time, she enjoys hiking and reading.

www.ingramcontent.com/pod-product-compliance
Ingram Content Group UK Ltd.
Pitfield, Milton Keynes, MK11 3LW, UK
UKHW052006041026
15590UKWH00008B/2191

9 798823 314268